# THE FEARLESS TREASURE

*A story of England*
*from then to now*

*The*

# FEARLESS

# TREASURE

*a story of*

*England*

*from then*

*to now*

*by*

NOEL STREATFEILD

ILLUSTRATED BY DOROTHEA BRABY

*London*

MICHAEL JOSEPH

*First published in Great Britain by*
MICHAEL JOSEPH LTD
*52 Bedford Square*
*London, W.C.1*
SEPTEMBER 1953
SECOND IMPRESSION OCTOBER 1954
THIRD IMPRESSION DECEMBER 1956
FOURTH IMPRESSION APRIL 1963
FIFTH IMPRESSION NOVEMBER 1970



7181 0134 0

*Printed lithographically in Great Britain by Hollen Street Press Ltd at Slough and bound by James Burn at Esher, Surrey*

# *All That's Past*

WALTER DE LA MARE

Very old are the woods;
  And the buds that break
Out of the brier's boughs,
  When March winds wake,
So old with their beauty are—
  Oh, no man knows
Through what wild centuries
  Roves back the rose.

Very old are the brooks;
  And the rills that rise
Where snow sleeps cold beneath
  The azure skies
Sing such a history
  Of come and gone,
Their every drop is as wise
  As Solomon.

Very old are we men;
  Our dreams are tales
Told in dim Eden
  By Eve's nightingales;
We wake and whisper awhile,
  But, the day gone by,
Silence and sleep like fields
  Of amaranth lie.

(Reproduced by kind permission of the author and
Messrs. Faber and Faber)

# CONTENTS

CHAPTER ONE
*The Six*
9

CHAPTER TWO
*Mr. Fosse*
25

CHAPTER THREE
*Bath*
31

CHAPTER FOUR
*Being Britons*
49

CHAPTER FIVE
*Romans*
59

CHAPTER SIX
*In the Air*
82

CHAPTER SEVEN
*Whitby*
90

CHAPTER EIGHT
*Normans*
119

CHAPTER NINE
*The Knight's House*
145

CHAPTER TEN
*The Years Between*
159

CHAPTER ELEVEN
*The Fair at Norwich*
168

CHAPTER TWELVE
*The Wedding*
190

CHAPTER THIRTEEN
*London Town*
219

CHAPTER FOURTEEN
*The Mill*
247

CHAPTER FIFTEEN
*The Prize*
265

CHAPTER ONE

# *The Six*

IT was the end of the summer term. In six schools in different parts of England three boys and three girls were sent for by their headmasters or their headmistresses.

William Beaumont was twelve, his hair was mouse-coloured, and however much he tried to smooth it down a piece always stood up at the back. He was short-sighted and his grey eyes peered out from behind extraordinarily dirty tortoiseshell-rimmed spectacles. William was the only boy in the middle of a family of three. Mr Beaumont, William's father, was a parson, so William and his sisters lived in a vicarage in a little village in the Sussex Downs of which his father was vicar. Mr Beaumont was poor, so the vicarage was shabby, but full of lovely old things that had been handed down to Mr Beaumont from his ancestors. There was a large garden, but it was not tidy because the Beaumonts could not afford a gardener, but parts of it were full of glorious flowers because William's mother loved flowers and gardening. Being poor did not matter to the Beaumonts; all their family were poor so they were used to it, and, as Mr Beaumont said, 'If you had to be poor, one of the best places to be poor in was a village in the Sussex Downs.' The Downs were so old and unchanging and kind, as well as full of excitement: old paths to follow, strange flowers to find, and odd things to pick up.

Every day William went by bus to the nearby town to school. It was really a boarding-school, but William and one or two other boys whose fathers could not afford the fees for boarding were allowed to attend as day boys. William did not think much of this arrangement; he would rather have gone to a school where all the boys were day boys, but he did not worry about it, for he was the sort who took things as they came along without fuss.

It was in the week before the end of the summer term that William, on his way out from prayers, was stopped by his headmaster, Mr Tomlinson.

'Pop along to my study, William, I want a word with you.'

Mr Tomlinson's study was a large, dusty, barracky room full of books. William wandered round for a bit wondering what Mr Tomlinson wanted to see him about. He was not clever, but he had worked hard and kept his place in the form, so it wasn't that. He hadn't exactly shone at the end of term examinations but he hadn't done badly, so it wasn't that. He hadn't got his colours for the first cricket eleven, but Mr Tomlinson hadn't expected him to, and he'd done all right in the second eleven, so it wasn't that. There had been no row about anything that he could remember, so it wasn't that. Sensibly he decided that probably it was nothing to do with him, more likely a message for his father, so he wasted no more time guessing, but took a copy of *David Copperfield* out of a shelf and read it until Mr Tomlinson arrived.

Mr Tomlinson was not a wasting-time sort of man; he rushed into the room and, as he did so, sat down at his desk.

'I've got a bit of interesting news for you, come here.' Mr Tomlinson opened a drawer and took out a blue cardboard folder tied with a tape bow. Stuck to the outside of the folder was a white label with WILLIAM BEAUMONT typed on it. 'Sit down. You, together with two other boys and three girls, have been chosen from all the children of England to go on a journey.'

William could not have been more surprised.

'Me, sir! Why, sir?'

'Can't imagine; that's

what I've been asking myself ever since I heard the news. "Why William Beaumont?" I said. "Nice boy and all that, but if you're only picking six . . ." Neither, if it comes to that, can I imagine why your host chose this school; still, he did, and that's all that matters to us. Now listen carefully, because I don't want to waste my time repeating anything twice. Your parents know what I'm going to tell you, and they know my instructions were that I was to give you this folder and break the news to you that you'd been picked.' Mr Tomlinson tapped the folder. 'Inside here are the instructions for the first step of your journey.'

'Where's the journey to, sir?'

'I don't know. I only know the start.' Mr Tomlinson untied the folder and took out a railway ticket. 'Here is a return ticket to London.' He held up an envelope. 'In here is a pound note for expenses in getting to your first destination.' He picked up a piece of cardboard and tossed it across to William. 'That shows you where you've got to get to.'

The piece of cardboard was rather larger than a postcard. On the top of it was written WILLIAM BEAUMONT, and underneath somebody had drawn a map. The map showed a square marked 'Victoria Station,' and the roads by which you could get from the station to Dover Street. In Dover Street there was another square marked 'Brown's Hotel.' Inside the square marked Victoria Station there were three arrows, painted in red, green and black. The black arrow was marked 'taxi,' the red arrow 'omnibus,' and the green one 'underground.' Like all hand-drawn maps William's had an exciting look; he had been to London and, studying it, he could see in a minute the sensible way to get to Dover Street. He considered for a second the grandeur of travelling by himself in a taxi, and the pleasures of travelling by Underground, but neither made sense.

'I'll go by bus, sir.'

'Go which way you like; your host says if you prefer to save money by travelling in a cheap way, you will have more over for other things. Any change from that pound when you arrive is yours.'

William was still studying the map.

'I'd rather go by Underground, but it says here that I'd have to get out at Green Park Station, and that's on the Piccadilly line, you can't get there from Victoria without changing.'

Mr Tomlinson threw a piece of paper across to William.

'Here are your instructions, the clothes you will need, who you're to ask for at Brown's Hotel, and so on. At the bottom you will read you're to take no money with you except that pound; don't suppose you'll find that last difficult, but some of your companions may have plenty of money and I expect your host wants you to start square. Any questions?'

William was bursting with questions, it was just the matter of which bubbled to the top first.

'Who's inviting me, sir?'

Mr Tomlinson leant back in his chair.

'I was expecting that. Somebody I've never met, very famous fellow in his way, but I'm not to tell you his name, and I don't suppose you'd know it, you ignoramus you, if I did. To you six he is taking on this journey he is to be known as Mr Fosse.'

William was looking at the instructions.

'It says here that when I get to Brown's Hotel I'm to ask for Mr Mummery. Who's he, sir?'

'Chauffeur, I believe; he's picking up you six and taking you where you're going next.'

'How long am I going to be away, sir?'

'I've no idea. Mr Fosse told me to tell your parents you would be with him as long as it took to complete the journey.' Mr Tomlinson got up and walked to the window. 'I have an idea you've struck a bit of luck, young William. I think you'll have a good time; but as well, unless I'm much mistaken, you'll pick up a lot of useful information on the way.' He swung round. 'I'm glad you've got this chance; I don't mind telling you I'd give the ears off my head to be you at this moment.' He nodded at the folder. 'Pack that stuff back and put it somewhere safe or you're sure to lose it. Now pop back to your class. I shall look forward to seeing you at the beginning of next term and hearing all about it.'

* * *

Grace Thwaite lived in Barnsley. She had never been out of Yorkshire, and never supposed she would go out of Yorkshire. Grace's father was a miner, and earned good money, but he was not very strong and frequently out of work, and, though holidays were often planned and dreamed of, when it came to the point there just was not the money, so the six Thwaite children were used to making their fun at home. Grace never thought about going away, for she knew plenty of things she wanted to do in and around Barnsley, and looked forward to the summer holidays just as much as those children did who were going to grand places such as Blackpool or Colwyn Bay.

It was dinner-time, and Grace was just running out of the school door when a shout from another girl told her the head teacher, Miss Gristhorpe, wanted her. Grace stood for a moment, trying to remember if she had done anything lately which was likely to get her into trouble, but there was nothing. It was her last term; she had become that odd age eleven plus in February, and had sat for the examination you had to take at that age in March, and had gained a place in the Girls' High School, and was going there next term. On the whole, mostly because of the scholarship and not because of behaviour, Miss Gristhorpe was pleased with her. Grace pushed back her red hair, for Miss Gristhorpe did not like hair hanging over your face, smoothed her much-too-short shabby cotton frock, pulled up her socks, and ran back into the school and up to Miss Gristhorpe's room.

Miss Gristhorpe was sitting behind her desk with a blue folder in front of her. She smiled at Grace, a smile which showed that whatever she might be going to say it had nothing to do with trouble.

'Your father and mother already know what I am going to tell you. . . .'

Grace listened to what Miss Gristhorpe told her, with an expressionless face, but an inside that felt as if it was being stirred by a ladle. At the end a question burst from her.

'Will I be goin' to Lunnon?'

Miss Gristhorpe explained about the railway ticket, and gave Grace her map and her sheet of instructions, then, just in the way Mr Tomlinson had asked William, she asked if there were any questions. Grace looked at the cardboard folder, with its white label with GRACE THWAITE written on it. She thought of the railway ticket inside, and of getting across London to Brown's Hotel by herself. It was in her mind to ask if she must travel alone; wasn't there somebody else going the same way? But pride held her back. Her father and mother knew that she was going away and why, and there was plenty of time to talk when she got home. There were five others going with her, and she doubted if they would be so gormless as to ask a lot of daft questions when they could find out the answers for themselves. She got up, and holding the folder tight against her, unable to speak for the turmoil inside her, shook her head, hurried out of the room, and, as if she were competing in a race, ran all the way home.

* * *

Robert Ackroyd in his three terms at his public school, except for saying 'Good morning, sir' or 'Good evening, sir,' had never spoken to his headmaster. He was in his first year and as such the lowest form of life in the school. There was only one specimen who was lower than he was, a boy called Jones who, owing to illness, had arrived half-way through his first term. The highest contact with authority Robert had so far reached, was speaking to his housemaster. He never expected to speak to the headmaster, and never wished to. When Jones, breathless with running, brought him a message from a prefect to say that the Head wished to see him immediately, the room spun round and he saw as many fireworks as if it were the 5th November.

It had taken Robert all his first term to understand the school rules and the school language. After much tribulation he had learnt to keep his feet at the 'ready,' so that he should run fast enough to beat Jones whenever a prefect should shout. In his second term he had a serious set-back for he had spent six weeks having measles. This term, his first summer term, he had lived in a continual muddle about junior cricket, and about clothes. Every other boy in his house seemed to grasp which list they should read to find where they were supposed to be playing cricket and when, but not Robert, who was constantly late and therefore constantly in trouble. Other people seemed able to hear when it was announced what was to be worn for different occasions, but somehow Robert not only did not hear, but, not having heard, faced the appalling shame of being the only boy in the wrong clothes. On receiving his summons to see the Head he knew at once what it was about. The school could no longer tolerate such a failure, he was to be expelled. He looked at Jones for comfort, but there was none to be had there; Jones had an expressive face and at that moment it was saying as clearly as if he were speaking, 'The firing party is waiting outside.'

Robert succeeded in losing his way to the Head's study; only too well he knew where it was, he had spent much of his first term learning that sort of information, but in the agony of the moment he forgot and set off at a smart canter in the wrong direction, and when he realized his mistake, to make up for lost time, restarted in the right direction at a sprint which brought him breathless and trembling to the Head's door. Outside the door, as he was struggling to get back some breath, he tried to remember the way he had been taught he should address the Head if ever he met him, but before he could recall the proper formula there was a shout of 'Come in' in answer to his feeble knock, and he found himself on the other side of the door stammering 'Sir?'

The Head was standing by his window studying his rose garden; he turned and looked at Robert's pale face, his green, anxious eyes peering out from under his sandy-coloured hair.

'Come here, Ackroyd.'

Robert was so overcome that the Head knew him by sight that his legs almost refused to move, but somehow he reached the window and then, of all extraordinary things, the Head put a hand on his shoulder then pushed him into a chair, settled himself in his own chair at his desk, and held up a blue folder.

'Your father and mother know what I'm going to tell you, but it is part of the instructions that I should inform you. You are going on a journey. . . .'

Robert was an only child; every day, in fact almost every minute of the holidays, he heard his father lament that this was so, and that his only son should be a fool, but whether he was a fool or not some day, Robert was reminded, he would become the sixth baron and have to take his father's place as chairman of the various family textile businesses. To Robert travelling was no novelty; he had two homes: an expensive unfriendly flat in London and an ugly, stately home in Lancashire. He had travelled ever since he was a baby, but none of his travels had been much fun, because he had visited places only because his father and mother were going there, and it was not convenient to leave him at home. The idea of travelling with five other children would have pleased him, but even while the Head was explaining the details of his journey to him, just as Mr Tomlinson had explained them to William and Miss Gristhorpe to Grace, he was wondering, in fact feeling increasingly certain, that there must be some mistake. There was not another Ackroyd in the school, but perhaps there was a name rather like it and that was the boy the Head thought he was talking to. When he asked if there were any questions he would like answered, he said, after three stammering attempts at getting out the words:

'Are . . . I mean are you sure it's me, sir?'

The Head laughed.

'Of course I'm sure. You find it difficult here, don't you Ackroyd, but you'll settle down, you know. I know your father expects great things of you, but I wouldn't worry if I were you; doing the best you can is quicker in the end. This adventure is just the thing for you; your five companions come from different schools from this, and from different backgrounds. I'm pleased that one boy should have been chosen from here, and I feel confident I can trust you to account for yourself in a way which won't disgrace us.'

Robert could hardly believe his ears.

'Me, sir! Why have I been chosen, sir?'

The Head said nothing for a moment; when he spoke again there was excitement in his eyes, it was almost as if he were going on the journey himself.

'I haven't a clue. Mr Fosse, as you are to call him, is a man who knows what he is about, and is unlikely to have made a mistake in his choice of guests. I'll tell you one thing, I'd give up the best holiday I've ever had, and I've had some splendid ones, to be the guest of Mr Fosse and to go on the journey that I suspect he's taking you. You're at the beginning of a great adventure. When you come back next term I shall want to see you and hear all about it.' He passed Robert the folder. 'Good luck, old man.'

* * *

Elizabeth Hamblett was thirteen. She lived in Pimlico in London. Her home was one floor of a large shabby house that had once housed a whole family. Her father had a clerical job. He was not a clever or an ambitious man, and he had chosen his job because, without being either clever or ambitious, he could rise slowly, year by year, to a slightly better position, and, provided that he did nothing outside the law, his job was safe. Her mother was the feckless sort, trying ineffectually to bring her family up to be a little better than their neighbours. Because of this Elizabeth and her two brothers, who were both younger than herself, were not allowed to go to State schools, but instead were sent to small private ones. Elizabeth's school was called, very grandly, 'Herriot House.' At Herriot House Elizabeth and thirty other girls whose parents thought they were better than their neighbours, received for a small fee a very indifferent education.

Elizabeth was a pretty girl with blue eyes and fair hair, and a spirit that rose above Herriot House and her home. Inside her she knew that some day the world would hear of Elizabeth

Hamblett; she was not sure how, but she was convinced her future was not going to be a bit like her family's. She was not going to be contented with a job because it was safe; she was going to do something exciting, and make her mark in the world. It was not easy to see how she was going to do this, for at Herriot House, though she learned a lot of subjects, including dancing and to play the piano, nothing was well-taught, so she was full of little bits of knowledge but knew nothing well.

Elizabeth was not at all surprised when she heard that the elder of the two Miss Browns, who owned Herriot House, wanted to see her, for the elder of the two Miss Browns was always wanting to see her. The two Miss Browns prided themselves on the fact that, whatever they did not give the girls entrusted to them, they did see that they turned out little ladies. Elizabeth was a disappointment; she dashed along the roads with her coat swinging open, and her hat in her hand. She had no shame; if the elastic broke in her knickers she thought nothing of pulling up her frock in the road to tie it together. She asked aggravating questions; she was not contented to accept facts out of geography or history books as they were told to her. When the younger Miss Brown, who taught geography, read out information about mountains and isthmuses, Elizabeth would ask: 'Does anyone live there?' 'What sort of people are they? I mean, what do they look like? What do they do?' The younger Miss Brown, who only knew what the book said, found these questions very depressing indeed. At history, which was taught by the elder Miss Brown, Elizabeth would not be contented with a nice straight fact such as that Henry VIII had six wives, but would ask: 'If they were all here now, which would be the nicest to know, do you think?' The elder Miss Brown, when talking to Elizabeth, frequently found herself falling back on the phrase: 'That has not been revealed to us, dear.'

The elder Miss Brown looked at Elizabeth's rather dirty cotton frock and Elizabeth's eager face with disapproval. She and her sister considered it extraordinarily trying that out of their thirty pupils, the unsatisfactory Elizabeth Hamblett should have been selected for what appeared to be an honour. Why Elizabeth, they asked each other? If this Mr Fosse, as he called himself, had asked their advice, they could have sent him so much more satisfactory a visitor. Only six children chosen out of the whole of England and he had to pick on Elizabeth. It was, of course, an honour that a child should be chosen at all from Herriot House, but would it prove an honour in the long run? Elizabeth was very unlikely to prove an acceptable guest, she was almost certain to say and do the wrong thing, and quite possibly would be returned to her home in disgrace before the journey was half completed. To the elder Miss Brown there was something very peculiar about the instructions they had received, something a little unnatural, so much mystery. If the host's real name had not been so august that even she had heard of it, she would have advised Mr and Mrs Hamblett against Elizabeth being allowed to accept the invitation. She drew the blue folder towards her and, making its exciting contents sound as dull as if she were reading out an arithmetic problem, repeated what she had been asked to say.

'Elizabeth, you are going on a journey. . . .'

* * *

John Fish lived in Norwich. John's father was in the fruit and vegetable business, he had a shop in Norwich and as well a fruit stall in Yarmouth for the summer visitors. John was the eldest of a family of six. He was thirteen and was attending a secondary modern school, but in the autumn he was going to Norwich Technical School. It had been a great pride to his father when the headmaster of the secondary modern school told him that he should apply for John to be admitted to the technical school, for, although he worked in the fruit and vegetable business, he had skilful hands, as had all his family. It was the pride of the Fish family that they never called workmen into their homes or businesses, for anything that wanted making or mending they could do themselves. It was fine that John had inherited this gift and was

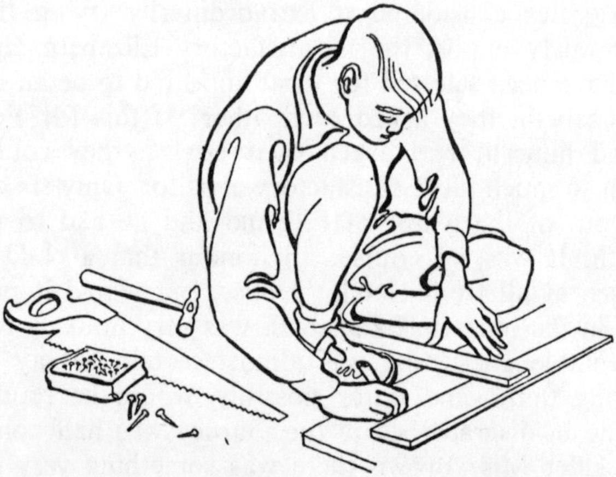

to be trained for a craft. John was quite happy at his present school, but he was full of excitement at the thought of the autumn term. Already, hanging in his cupboard, was the new school uniform; a cap and blazer, grey flannel trousers and a school tie. There were, too, special clothes for gymnasium, and overalls for the workshops. He was thinking of these things and how near it was to the end of the term when his headmaster, Mr Phillipson, called:

'John Fish, come in my study a moment, I want a word with you.'

All the Fish family had tow-coloured hair, grey-blue eyes and rather square faces with high cheekbones. John liked Mr Phillipson, whose interest in him had got him the place in the technical school. He looked at him with an easy, trusting expression. Mr Phillipson told him to shut the door, and when he had done so pointed to a chair, and told him to sit.

Mr Phillipson thought that what he had to say to John was the nicest bit of news he had given a boy since he had become a schoolmaster. He knew all about Mr Fosse; he could not imagine how he had landed on young Fish, but he thought he was an admirable choice; he had a fine, hard-working father, a thrifty, careful mother, and the boy himself was the sort to get the best out of an adventure such as the one before him. There was no need to say much to John Fish; his parents would see that he had the clothes he was ordered to take, that they were clean and in good condition; there was no need to tell John how to behave or that he ought to be a credit to the school, the Fishes brought their children up strictly and well, with plenty of washing, as good food as could be managed, and chapel twice on Sundays. It was a big moment for Mr Phillipson as he untied the blue folder.

'You've come into a bit of luck, young Fish. You're going on a journey. . . .'

* * *

The girls at Borthwick knew that they attended the finest girls' school in the country. Fifty years before a Miss Borthwick, who had modern ideas on education, had started her school with twenty girls, drawn from the best families. She had wanted girls to have the same sort of education as their brothers received: plenty of games and a prefect system which would lead to character training. At the same time she wished them to grow up fitted to take their place in the society to which they belonged. This meant that although they were at a school they must learn to dress for dinner. For the evenings the original Miss Borthwick had designed a strange garment of plum colour, with the arms of the school embroidered in front, and fifty years later the girls still wore the same strange garment after six o'clock.

Selina Edgecombe had been three terms at Borthwick. She was thirteen but small for her age, with brown hair and brown eyes. Her home was in Devonshire. Up till 1939 the

Edgecombes had been very rich indeed, and Selina and her two small brothers had been brought up never knowing what it was to want for anything. Since the Second World War, the family had been a little less well-off, but there was still plenty of money about, for Mr Edgecombe had interests in many businesses. Selina did not know that she was fortunate; there had always been cars, always horses in the stables, always a staff of servants, and she had always had more clothes than she really needed. She was not exactly arrogant, but accepted that because she was born an Edgecombe it was her right to have everything that she wanted. Even at Borthwick, where many of the girls were well-off, she was better off than most. Her home was a lovely, mellowed, rambling old house in the Exe valley. In so far as she liked being at school at all, Selina liked being at Borthwick. She would have preferred to stay at home where she could ride every day, but she accepted that a girl in her position must mix with other girls; besides, as her father sometimes laughingly said, with things going the way they were there was no saying what might happen, she might even have to earn her own living some day, so a good education was an investment.

It was not usual for girls in the junior house to see Miss Marion, the present head of Borthwick; seeing her and getting to know her was a privilege that she liked her girls to work towards. She did not teach herself, she influenced. She liked to feel that from her pretty, chintz-hung drawing-room a spirit, a kind of essence of Borthwick, flowed out over the school. It was her pride that at no time of the day or night did anyone—teachers, staff or pupils—find her out of character, as it were. She loved blue and mauve, and had dresses of dignity and charm designed for her in these colours, and every day a hairdresser from a nearby town came to her bedroom to pile her grey hair into the pretty waves and curls which were a feature of her. When Miss Marion sent for a girl to see her she made a little ceremony of it. The visit was a memory to be treasured, and there should be some visible memento of the occasion. In her neat, scholarly handwriting, she wrote a note: 'I would like to see you at . . .' and underneath, spaced well away from the letter, so that the girl could, if she wished, cut out the signature for her autograph album, she signed her name. Then she rang her bell and gave the note to Graves, her old butler, to deliver.

Selina was lolling at her desk, thinking about the summer holidays, when Graves delivered Miss Marion's note. The note caused a sensation; there was no mistaking where it came from, Miss Marion's grey envelopes were well known, and no one else sent notes by Graves. All over the class girls raised questioning eyebrows, and the girls on either side of her nudged Selina. 'An invitation from the Duchess to play croquet?' 'What's the royal command about?'

Selina stood up. At Borthwick you always stood up to attract the attention of a mistress. The mistress was as interested in the grey envelope as the girls. She smiled fondly at the child who had received this benison.

'Yes, dear?'

'Might I be excused, Miss Marion wants to see me?'

Miss Marion was graciousness itself to Selina. If she was puzzled why, in a school so bristling with the daughters of the exalted, Selina had been selected, there was nothing in her manner to show it. It was, of course, no surprise to her that a girl from Borthwick was to be one of the party, her only surprise was that if three girls were invited, they were not all from Borthwick. She held the blue folder as if it were some beautifully illuminated missal. She pointed to a stool.

'Bring that over here, dear. Close beside me. You and I have got something very exciting to talk about.'

CHAPTER TWO

# *Mr Fosse*

THE library was a big room, it stretched the length of the house. It had many windows looking out across the garden to woods and beyond that to hills. Between the windows there were bookcases filled with books in lovely bindings. Under a window Mr Fosse was working. All round him lay books that he had used for reference, and in front of him were sheafs of notes written in so fine a handwriting it was as if a spider had dipped a leg in the ink and written the words. Mr Fosse matched his handwriting, he was little, thin, and had a transparent air, as if one breath of wind would blow him away. His hair was white and his face lined, but no one could say 'there is a very old man,' for Mr Fosse did not seem old, for he had interested sparkling eyes, and moved as nimbly as a cat. Because he had lived in his beautiful house in a fold of the Somerset hills for so long that no one could remember his not being there, he had an air of belonging, in the way old trees belong to places.

The door opened and Alfred Mummery came in. Alfred and his wife had looked after Mr Fosse ever since they were married, over forty years ago. Mrs Mummery was the housekeeper and Alfred what Mr Fosse called his right hand, which meant that Alfred remembered everything that Mr Fosse forgot, and did all the tiresome things Mr Fosse would have done if Alfred were not about to do them for him. Alfred came over to the desk.

'They've finished their supper, sir. Will I bring them in?'

Mr Fosse laid down his pen.

'Did everything go off all right? Have they settled down?'

Alfred was a man who thought before he spoke.

'Not to say settled, you couldn't expect it, but everything went off as you'd planned it would. They all arrived different times just as you said they would, and they all asked for me.

As instructed I sent the girls up to Mrs Mummery and I took the boys in hand. By the time we had them changed into the clothes you ordered, they might, save for their voices, be all one family. There's no saying now by the look of them who comes from where.'

Mr Fosse got up, or rather sprang up, for he never moved slowly.

'Capital. Bring them in. I shall guess which is which.' Alfred turned to go, Mr Fosse stopped him. 'Did they object to changing their clothes?'

'Not to say object. One of the girls, so Mrs Mummery says, told her if she'd known what was expected she'd have had the dress made, she didn't quite care for the fit I understand, but Mrs Mummery soon put that right. She had her needle ready and there was plenty of time. I'll fetch them now, sir.'

A few minutes later the library door opened again and Elizabeth, William, John, Selina, Grace, and Robert came in. The boys were wearing blue shirts and grey shorts, and the girls frocks of the same shade of blue as the boys' shirts, they all had bare legs and wore sandals. Mr Fosse came down the room to meet them.

'Now do not tell me who you are, I am going to guess.' He looked from one to the other, then he pointed at Grace. 'You are Grace Thwaite from Yorkshire.'

In the train from London the children had learnt a little about each other. Elizabeth said:

'I bet you guessed that because you knew she had red hair.'

Mr Fosse lifted his head as if listening. Then he smiled in a pleased way.

'That voice belongs to London. You are Elizabeth Hamblett.' He turned to William. 'What sort of a journey did you have?'

'Very nice, thank you, sir.'

Mr Fosse shook his head.

'I am not sure about you.' He looked at John. 'Was your journey comfortable?'

John was feeling a little awkward in so big a house. A part of him would have been glad to be back at home.

'It was all right, sir.'

Mr Fosse seemed to guess how John would be feeling.

'You are John Fish from Norfolk. Bit strange to-night? You will feel settled to-morrow.' He looked from Robert to William. 'I have got to guess which is which.' He nodded at Robert. 'Tell me young man, how did you get from the station to the hotel?'

Robert blushed. He had supposed there were but two ways of travelling from stations to hotels, one was in a private car

and the other was by taxi. But during the railway journey he had talked to John and William, and discovered that while they had almost the whole of their pound left, he had used up seven shillings of his on porters and taxis. He did wish Mr Fosse had not picked on him to answer that question.

'By taxi, sir.'

There was a rather shocked 'Oh' from everybody but Selina. Mr Fosse held up a finger for silence.

'Everybody had a right to travel as they liked. I remember spending money that I certainly could not afford on riding in a hansom cab when I was a boy. I believe now I have guessed. You are Robert Ackroyd.' He turned to William, 'So you must be William Beaumont.' Then he smiled at Selina, 'and you must be Selina Edgecombe. Now will you all come over here, I have something I wish to show you.'

There was a table in the corner, and on it was a map of England, and on the map there were scarlet circles, and lines.

'We are going on a journey you know.' He looked at the map

and smiled. 'I always think a map is such an exciting thing. You look at that now.' With his finger Mr Fosse traced a line. 'That is the railway you travelled on to-day, and here,' he pointed to a red cross, 'is my house where we are now. This,' he pointed to a scarlet ring, 'is our first move.'

The children leant forward to look.

'Bath,' said Selina.

'Which of you have been to Bath?' Mr Fosse asked.

'I have,' said Selina, 'but I don't remember it very well, I went after measles.'

'I—I think I went there once,' said Robert shyly, 'but I'm afraid I've forgotten it rather, I was very young at the time.'

Mr Fosse stroked the map as if it were a cat.

'It does not matter whether you have been there before or not, for the Bath we shall visit is not there any more. Bath has a long history, you know. Now, suppose you sit down while I tell you a little of what I have planned we shall do, but first I shall ring for my man, Mummery. I always think it is so much easier to talk over plans with a glass in one hand and something to eat in the other. I know you have just had supper, but I hope you can manage what they call a snack. I can generally find room for a snack, and so I expect you can.'

The snacks which Alfred brought in on large silver dishes were tiny iced cakes, crystallized fruits, and sweets of all kinds. The drink was one the children had never tasted before, it was poured out with an air of respect by Alfred from glass decanters. It was amber coloured. Mr Fosse held his glass to the light and looked at it with affection.

'We make this from honey from our own bees. It is quite harmless. I call it nectar, we only drink it on great occasions, is that not so, Mummery? This is a very great occasion. Later we shall drink a toast to it.'

Mr Fosse was quite right. It was much easier to talk and to listen with a glass of nectar in one hand and one of the glorious snacks in the other. Mr Fosse spoke of the journeys they would take. Some lasting two days, some more. The whole journey would finish, as it began, in his house.

William was the first to ask a question.

'You said we were going to see a Bath which isn't there any more. How can we see it if it isn't there?'

Mr Fosse sipped his nectar. He leant back in his chair, and looked thoughtfully at the ceiling.

'I think we can leave that until the time comes. It has been quite an experience you have had to-day, so I do not think we want to begin our journeyings to-night.' He looked at Grace. 'I expect you are tired, you had to start very early, I am afraid.'

Grace could scarcely keep her eyes open, for apart from the journey being long, she had been too excited to relax for a second, but she was not going to let the others think she was a weakling.

'I'm not complainin' th' knows.'

'I know you are not, but Mrs Mummery will be scolding me if I keep you up late.'

Selina felt that it was time Mr Fosse noticed her. She did not feel neglected exactly, but she was rather different from the other two girls, and she thought he ought to realize it.

'Before we go to bed could you tell us why you chose us?'

Mr Fosse was out of his chair in a moment, and before the children knew he had moved, he was half-way down the library and half-way back again.

'No, no, no, Selina Edgecombe. That is the fun of the thing. You will see why presently, for each of you has a special place on our journey.'

'Well, couldn't you give us a hint?' Selina pressed. She looked a little superciliously round at the others. 'I mean why us? Only six of us and we come from all over the country.'

Mr Fosse was off again, right over to the door this time.

'Of course you come from all over the country. You had to. No, not one word. You wait and find out for yourself.'

'When shall we find out?' William asked. 'To-morrow?'

Mr Fosse was back to his chair. In passing he gave Robert's head an affectionate pat, which made Robert tremble like a frightened horse.

'No, William, not to-morrow. To-morrow is too soon, to-morrow is the beginning.'

'The beginning of what?' said Elizabeth.

Mr Fosse raised his glass. The amber-coloured nectar glowed as if it were alight.

'Of our adventure. Of the things we find out. Now stand up

all of you, and we will drink our toast, and then off you go to bed.' He waited until the children were on their feet, then he said solemnly, 'Let us drink to adventure. To that something which you share, that has brought you together. Let us drink to the hope, which I hold in my heart, that at our journey's end we may find a treasure many have lost, and through the finding of it, be granted understanding of our past, courage in our present, and faith in our future.'

## CHAPTER THREE

# *Bath*

THEY travelled to Bath in a shooting-brake. Mr Fosse in his quick, cat-like way jumped up in front to sit beside Alfred, who was driving. Mrs Mummery, an enormous picnic basket, several rugs, and the children, travelled in the back. It was the first chance that had come to the children to get to know Mrs Mummery properly, and very nice they found she was. She was fat, in fact almost round, with a warm, cosy laugh that matched her shape, and seemed a very unfussy sort of person, her favourite remark being: 'It'll all come out in the wash, me dears.'

The journey finished on a hill which looked from the east down on to the city of Bath. It was a glorious day, perfect for a picnic, and the place where Alfred had stopped the brake seemed just right for exploring. Below them sloped a bumpy, coarse grass field which finished up in a tangle of blackberry bushes and scrubby beech trees, behind which seemed to be a sheer drop to the outskirts of Bath.

'My word,' said Elizabeth, 'if we had tea trays we couldn't half toboggan here.'

Mr Fosse, who had been standing staring down at Bath, gave a little spring in the air, sat down, and patted the grass beside him.

'Sit, all of you, we are going quite a distance, but not on toboggans. You will learn on that journey why I chose you six to make it. At the end there will be a prize.'

Elizabeth tingled all over at the word 'prize.' If there was a prize going she must win it. Winning a prize from a person like Mr Fosse was the sort of thing she had always known she was meant to do.

'Is the prize just for right answers, or for neatness, spelling, and all that?'

Mr Fosse turned to look at Elizabeth. Having all Mr Fosse's attention, Elizabeth found, made her feel peculiar, it gave her the sort of sucked-away feeling she had when she had been too long in the sun. After a moment, in which he seemed to be seeing right through her, he said:

'For a right answer, if there is a right answer.'

William's grey eyes peered in a puzzled way at Mr Fosse through his dirty tortoiseshell-rimmed spectacles.

'If there are lots of right answers, how will you decide who wins?'

Selina was not enjoying herself. It was nothing to her to ride in a shooting-brake, nor to stay in a house such as Mr Fosse's, and all the time the thought nagged at her that she ought to assert herself, that the others, except Robert, should feel she was different from themselves. Because of this she spoke rather as if she were Miss Marion trying to get a new girl to understand Borthwick standards.

'Mr Fosse will know who wins, of course. After all, he sets the competition, so he must know the answer he wants.'

Mr Fosse turned to Robert.

'What are you seeing?'

Robert had been gazing in dreamy contentment at Bath. How easy everything was; he seemed only to have one type of clothes so it was impossible to make a mistake in what to wear. Everything was arranged, all he had to do was to follow the others. In spite of being picked by Mr Fosse for this journey nothing special seemed to be expected of him. It gave him a gorgeous, sleepy feeling to be a boy of whom nothing was expected. Mr Fosse's question made him jump; he had no idea what he had asked, he only knew that he had been spoken to and that the others were looking at him waiting for his answer. He flushed and stammered:

'Y—yes, sir? Please, sir?'

Mr Fosse smiled.

'You were looking at Bath. Isn't she lovely? I think, as you have been studying Bath, Robert, you should find it easy to tell me what I want to know.' He raised his arms and swept them in front of him as if to encircle Bath. 'What can you all see? That train, for instance, puffing away on our left. I do not want each building separately, but types of buildings, the churches, for example, but as well the Abbey. Give them paper and pencils, Mummery.'

For a long time there was silence except for the songs of birds, the sound of an aeroplane, the distant hum of lorries and cars, the chug of a train, and the scratch of pencils. When they had all written down as many things as they thought they could see, Mr Fosse told John to read out his list, and the rest of them could compare their lists with his, and add to them if they had missed anything out.

On the children's combined lists were field, stone wall, blackberries, beech trees, railway, railway arches, trains, terraces of houses, ordinary houses, council houses, small farms, factory, hotel, churches, abbey, cars, bicycles, buses, aeroplane, gasworks, birds, greenhouses, school, barbed wire fence, lightning conductor, television aerials, telegraph posts, sports' ground. They might have added other things, but Mr Fosse interrupted their looking.

'Add the Roman baths, they lie down there beside the Abbey, a hospital, a post office, a telephone kiosk, shops, especially a chemist's shop, waterworks, the River Avon, which lies behind those willows at the end of the sports' ground, a police station, a library, and printing works.' He waited until the children had finished writing, then he jumped up and clapped his hands. 'Mummery! Mrs Mummery! We are ready for the magic handkerchiefs.'

There were six silk handkerchiefs in the luncheon basket. Mrs Mummery unpacked them, and she, Alfred and Mr Fosse blindfolded the children with them. They were ordinary silk handkerchiefs; Elizabeth, noticing this, decided that if Mr Fosse thought he could fool the other five she would show him he could not fool her.

'There's nothing magic about these handkerchiefs, they're just ordinary, look at the laundry marks.'

Mr Fosse blindfolded her.

'Magic, Elizabeth Hamblett, can be found in anything: a brick, a piece of flint, an iron nail, or in the laundry mark on a silk handkerchief. Perhaps this handkerchief which I have just tied round your eyes holds the rarest form of magic. It is possible that you who think now, in your sharp cockney way, that no one shall make a fool of you, will become a diviner of magic. Maybe the best diviner of us all.'

To be suddenly shut from the sun on a bright summer's day is the strangest sensation. Darkness did not come at once, before the children's eyes were whirling red balls, rings of green and violet, and flashing stars. Then, as Mr Fosse began to speak, the world seemed to slow down and grow quiet, almost as if it were listening to his voice, which had a singing note like a small wind among water reeds. The red balls, rings of green and violet, and flashing stars faded, and what Mr Fosse could see the children began to see.

Mr Fosse rubbed the city of Bath away as though it had been drawn in pencil, and he held a giant piece of india-rubber. He rubbed away too, many everyday sounds. There were no aeroplanes, no rumbling of distant lorries, no cars, no trains. Cutting out the sounds of transport left the children's ears free for other sounds. They heard more and different kinds of birds, a dog barking, sheep bleating, a cow moo-ing, the cheep of a cricket, a rustle that might have been made by a field-mouse, the drone of bees, the whirr of a dragonfly, and countless little sounds from tiny moving creatures. Mr Fosse directed their ears to these sounds, and told them to keep listening to them, because they belonged where they were going. Then he turned their eyes to the country around them. He showed them that where Bath had been they were now looking down on a forest; they could see solidly massed the tops of oak and beech trees, and he told them that in the forest lived wolves, bears and wild boars. If they followed his eyes to the south-east they would see a rough track, which would lead them eventually to the Wiltshire Downs. He wanted them to keep an eye on that track, because presently along it would come someone who would be of great importance to them.

'You see, we have slipped back nearly two thousand years. It is still August, but the year is A.D. 43. There are many real sites where our forefathers lived we might have chosen to visit; we could have had a look at a lake village, or an important town like Maiden Castle, but I wanted to start our journey in an easy way, so I thought we would have a look at a few very simple people, who may well have lived on the hillside just above where we are sitting now. They are all related, a farming community, working under the leadership of the head of the family. Can any of you see them?'

A.D.43. The children racked their brains to remember what they knew about early Britons.

'Painted blue?' Grace suggested.

Selina had been going to say the same thing, and was annoyed that Grace had spoken first. She said, in a correcting sort of voice:

'It was called woad.'

Robert had been beginning to see people. This talk of their being painted blue bothered him.

'They . . . I mean they don't look blue to me.'

Mr Fosse was pleased.

'Blue, indeed! Oh, dear me, no. Our farming friends are not painted blue. Maybe at one time a few warriors used woad to give them a fierce look. You take a look at our farming friends, and remember these are very simple folk, but even so I think you will agree they are too advanced to run about naked painted blue.'

Selina was convinced she had been told at Borthwick that ancient Britons were painted blue. She was not going to accept easily that what Borthwick said was wrong and what Mr Fosse said was right.

'If they aren't painted blue, what are they wearing?'

Mr Fosse paused before he answered. In the little silence it seemed as if the bleating of sheep and lowing of cattle came nearer and there was the smell of a wood fire on the breeze.

'We have travelled back a long way, and so cannot see with certainty the materials, the colours, or the designs; but we can make a pretty good guess. Spinning and weaving has been going on all over the country for generations. Spinning is done by the girls. They tease the wool, that is to say they fluff it up, and then comb it ready for their spindles. When you three girls grow up, if before you marry you have to sign legal documents, you will have to state that by profession you are spinsters. Queer how these things stick. Weaving is one of the arts which has never changed much. Materials to-day are usually made on a machine in a factory, whereas the material worn by our friends here on the hillside is made on hand-looms at home, but their material, as ours, has a warp running through the whole length of it, and over and under the warp runs the cross-thread, or woof.'

'What colours?' asked Selina.

'Almost certainly a good dark red, from a dye made of a lichen growing on the trees, and I daresay for blue they use the woad you and Grace wished they painted themselves with. In design I see the women's and girls' clothes as simple and becoming, a long tunic drawn in at the waist, and cloaks for cold weather.'

Selina hugged her knees. In her imagination she took the sleeves out of her plum-coloured Borthwick dress for evenings, lengthened it to just above her ankles and drew it in at the waist. This made her think of the school coat-of-arms embroidered on the chest.

'They have jewellery, of course, haven't they, Mr Fosse?'

'They could have, there are fine pieces to be bought, but as I see them they have some simple bits, beads and a few ornaments, because unless they have come across fine pieces in the wares carried by visiting pedlars, they will not have seen the best and so will not have nagged their husbands and fathers to give them the like. Of course if someone, presumably the wife of the head of the family, has got hold of fine pieces, say a gold necklace, a bronze brooch with a coral stud, and a mirror to admire herself wearing the things, it is safe to guess that the rest of the women and girls have kept on at their menfolk to get similar gew-gaws for them. Women's insistence, and men's too, on having the same luxuries that their relatives and friends have, is worth remembering on our journey.'

Robert strained to catch a glimpse of the family on the hillside.

'What are the men and boys wearing?'

'Rather dashing colours I should say. Some of their garments I think are woven of what looks like a tartan. I see the men wearing tunics to their knees, and trousers tied in at the ankles, and the boys just the tunic. They have not got them on, as it is August, but both men and boys have cloaks for cold weather.'

William remembered a visit to the British Museum.

'Haven't they terrific great shields and helmets, and swords and things?'

Mr Fosse paused as if he were taking a look before answering William's question.

'There again, there is very fine workmanship about the country, beautiful chasing, and some nice enamel work, but such handsome weapons are I fancy used mostly by warriors. Our simple friends have to fight very little, except for stray bandits, so their weapons are mostly for hunting; sensible rather than ornamental, beaten out of bronze and iron, of course, but no fancy stuff. But again it depends what they have seen. If they have seen, and especially handled, a weapon, helmet or armlet, finely chased and ornamented, it is a safe bet the young men and boys have not rested till they have obtained shields, swords and what have you, ornamented in the same way. The aim, of course, being that what they own should be just a bit finer and more beautiful than that of the young man in the next hut.'

'Like boys wanting better bikes or television sets than the boy next door,' said Elizabeth.

John thought that a bit much.

'Or you girls wanting new dresses because some other girl's got one.'

Mr Fosse, though neither John nor Elizabeth could see it, was looking pleased with them both.

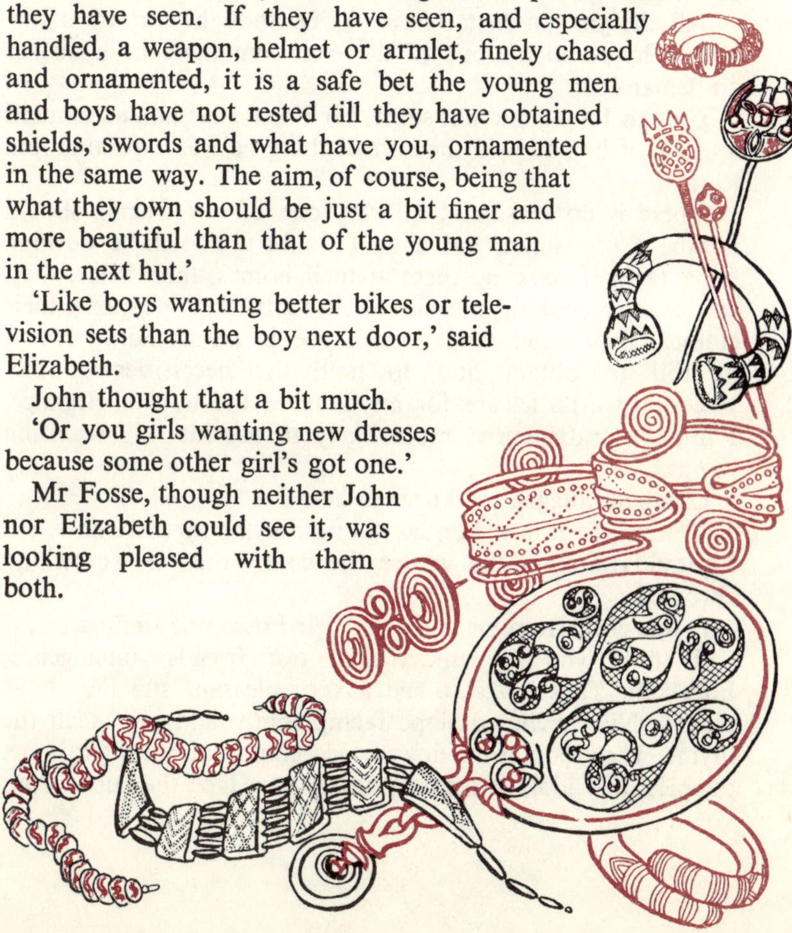

'Exactly like, and for the same reasons. That is one of nature's little dodges. She sees to it that young men and women have an urge to make the best of their looks and their talents. This makes them attract each other, which later leads to falling in love and marriage, and finally children. It is always babies that nature has her eye on.'

John was not interested in falling in love, marrying or babies, his interest was in what people made and used. He was sure, if only he could meet them, and talk to them, he would find that he liked this farming community. It must be nice to depend on yourself for everything, to have to make most of the things you needed. He thought it was rather snobbish of Mr Fosse to think that because they were simple farmers the people on the hill could not own as beautiful things as the next man, perhaps even make them.

'All designs on metal have to be thought out by someone. Why shouldn't one of the chaps up there be a master craftsman?'

Though John could not see it, Mr Fosse gave him an amused look, as if he had said the sort of thing he was expecting him to say.

'There is no reason at all why one of our friends should not be a craftsman, but if so I doubt if he will be working on a farm. I look up there at their homes, their fields, their cattle, their cooking utensils, their tools, their weapons, their clothes, their food, and what I see is an unending round of toil to obtain and to hold the necessities of life. I see very little leisure for anything in the way of elegance. I think a craftsman is more likely to use his skill repairing things.'

Elizabeth hugged her knees to her.

'Tell us about their houses. All right living up there now, but I should think in the winter the cold would be something chronic.'

It was clear from his voice that Mr Fosse was smiling.

'I think you are underrating our friends' intelligence, Elizabeth. That looks to me a very pleasant site they have picked. Nice sheltered slope facing south, and just smell the thyme. Then look at the flowers, scabious, mallow, nightshade, poppies, and look at the way those huts face the sun. Listen to that fellow up there, and all the other birds singing. I think as far as weather is concerned, winter or summer, they could not have chosen a better spot. Look, too, what a sensible place they have landed on. Remember what they grow, their animals, the things they have made and so on, are not only all they have in the world, their wealth in fact, but the difference between life and death. If you knew your cattle and your crops stood between you and starvation, where would you build? Somewhere with water, no doubt there is a spring; somewhere with a good view all round, so that you could see who was coming, and somewhere well away from too much undergrowth, to keep wild animals from sneaking up and killing your stock. You see, that is just what they have done, they have a wonderful view all round, and no forest nearer than what lies below us. I think from every angle they have a right to congratulate themselves on the site they have chosen.'

'But they don't depend only on the place where they live for protection, do they?' William asked. 'I mean, they've put up fences to keep robbers and animals out, haven't they?'

'Oh, dear me, yes. And not only a fence but a big ditch. Take a look, see first the ditch, and then a palisade of sharpened stakes, and over there another ditch and another palisade for the cattle at night.'

Grace, as if she were not blindfolded, turned to face the hill.

'Tell us about the houses, and the folk that live in 'em.'

'Not houses, huts made very much as we should build huts if our homes were suddenly destroyed. Of course, our friends are less finicky than we should be. They share their homes with many of their animals, though, mind you, there are plenty of spots in the world to-day where families are proud to have goats, pigs and chickens living under their roof.'

John liked to have a perfectly clear picture in his mind of anything which his hands might be called on to make.

'What are the huts supported by? Is it wood?'

'Yes, young trees with a good V-shaped fork, planted firmly, and in the forks crossway pieces of wood, on which they fix the roof of wattle and thatch. The walls are built of wattle and daub, which is a mixture of mud and tough bendable branches.'

'Mud! How dirty!' said Selina. 'I don't see how they can keep clean if the walls are of mud.'

Mr Fosse chuckled.

'Our friends' ideas about cleanliness are different from yours, Selina. If you ever saw a film in which our forbears ran around looking very much as you do, except in style of dress, forget it. You think to be clean you must use hot water and soap, but if you told your friends up there that, and could make yourself understood, which of course you could not, they would have no idea what you were talking about. There is no such thing as soap, and water is valuable, never wasted on washing, for on it depends life for themselves and their animals. There is a spring or they would not have chosen to live here, but springs have a way of drying up in hot weather, so with the utmost care and labour they have dug pits, and lined them with clay, in which to store water. They have as much rain and more than we do, so most years the spring serves and there is enough rainwater or accumulated dew for what they need, but sometimes water is a major problem, and they have to struggle down through that forest to the Avon, and carry water to the pits, no light job for their tracks through the forest are always getting overgrown. There is a strong probability they have discovered something unique to this neighbourhood. Without doubt our thrifty farmers drive their pigs down to the forest for beech nuts, and the pigs, sensible creatures, have long ago rooted out the fact that down there is mud, which is permanently hot, and therefore pleasant to wallow in. I would hazard a guess that our friends have learned to enjoy the hot mud as much as their pigs, and may have discovered healing properties in it. If they have they believe a goddess is responsible, probably the goddess Sul, and lying in her hot mud, thank her humbly for it, and ask her for good health.'

William was frowning.

'But if they live up there all alone, never seeing anyone, how do they know about their gods and goddesses?'

'They are not entirely isolated. There are good tracks, such as that one to the south-east, and pedlars not only from the island but from different parts of Europe probably visit them at intervals, and in that way news reaches them and some of the news almost certainly has to do with worship.'

William was not satisfied.

'They won't know much just hearing it that way.'

'They have probably other contacts, now and again they must take journeys to buy weapons, and so on, and there is no reason to think they would not undertake a journey for a religious purpose, even if such a journey was only undertaken once in a lifetime, it would be enough to keep knowledge going.'

William, brought up in a vicarage, thought this nonsense. Even with the church on your doorstep he knew from experience it was easy enough for people to forget what it was there for.

'I shouldn't have thought seeing how things were done just once would be much good.'

Elizabeth bounced with impatience.

'You are slow, William. Of course it would, you'd tell about it ever afterwards. I can see me after knowing about it once, telling and telling about it for ever and ever, and I suppose that's what they do.'

Selina was beginning to hate Elizabeth. She thought she was a pushing girl, and she loathed her cockney twang. She made a promise to herself that before this odd holiday with Mr Fosse was over she would squash her out of her bouncy ways.

'Of course you wouldn't know this, Elizabeth, always living in a town, but farmers don't talk much. I see quite a lot of them at home when I'm out hunting.'

William was a mild boy, not given to wanting to snub anyone, but there was something about Selina which infuriated him.

'Just riding to hunts you wouldn't know anything. You ought to hear the farmers at home when there's a market day, jabber, jabber, jabber.'

Mr Fosse's wind-in-the-reed voice broke in:

'I don't think we can compare our friends here with farmers to-day, a better comparison would be gipsies. You have seen them: a caravan parked just off the road, a horse tethered near, perhaps a dog, the woman stirring something in the pot, the man chipping away at clothes' pegs, the elder children busy, the younger ones sprawling about playing with each other like puppies, but if you come to think you do not hear them talking much. It would be my guess that though, of course, our people do not roam like gipsies, they too speak only when absolutely necessary. But one of the things they do talk about is worship. They are a superstitious lot fearing the elements, believing that bad weather and so on come as punishments, which means soothing down some deity, possibly a local one, or thanking them when things go right.'

William remembered barrows.

'Were graves to do with religion, Mr Fosse?'

'Partly, but the right way to bury your dead is also a social matter. If you don't do the thing properly and with sufficient style you are showing disrespect for the dead and are looked down upon by the neighbours. There was a fashion, as a matter of fact a revival of fashion, for cremating the dead, but I doubt if our friends here are quite so up-to-date as that. They may stick to the flat grave or barrow with the man or woman's possessions lying round them, and perhaps food and drink to help them on their journey. In every period you find old customs surviving, usually amongst country folk which have been out of fashion for years with townspeople, so it is very hard to be sure what our friends here think right and proper. But being simple folk we can safely hazard a guess that they carry on in more or less the way great-grandfather did, even if the custom was unpleasant, like throwing the dead bodies outside the palisade to be eaten by wild animals or, worse still, burying their children under the floor of their hut.'

'You're only guessing about lots of things, aren't you?' said Elizabeth. 'I mean, you don't know about Sul and all that?'

'It is a fairly safe bet, as you will see to-morrow.'

Selina could not get over the mud.

'Even if it does them good, I should think they'd hate lying in hot mud. Imagine it, with no water to wash it off!'

'There may be water to wash it off. After all, a hot stream rises down there, and there may be a place where they can lie in comparatively clean hot water.'

'Tha' makes too much fuss about water, Selina,' said Grace. 'If them folk know what's good for 'em, they leave muck on. Muck can be healthy, tha' knows. I've an auntie that says it's good for 'er asthma.'

Selina's tone showed what she thought of Grace's aunt.

'How funny! It must be very smelly inside their huts, isn't it, Mr Fosse?'

Mr Fosse evidently sat down again, for his voice came close to Selina's ear.

'It is. Without doubt everybody is verminous. Fleas hopping about on their bodies and lice crawling in their hair. But I do not believe it worries or inconveniences them in the least. I expect they accept such things, just as they accept that their sheep have ticks.'

None of the others shared Selina's absorption in washing. Fleas or no fleas, they wanted to get inside the huts and see how the people lived.

'Tell us about the inside of the huts, Mr Fosse,' said William. 'What are they like?'

There was quite a long silence before Mr Fosse answered; in the pause new sounds and smells came to the children. The sound of grinding, the crank of wooden wheels. The scent of wood-smoke grew stronger, and with it came a smell of cooking, a sort of Irish-stewish smell; as well as the bleating of the sheep, was the bleating of goats, the grunting of pigs, and the splish-splosh of cattle being driven across a farmyard.

'Come along, let us go inside the palisade.' In single file they seemed to follow Mr Fosse up the hill. Presently he stopped. 'First we cross this ditch, now we open the gate, a sliding hurdle you will notice. I think that means we can take it our friends have been fairly free from attack lately, or there would be a stronger gate, probably this same hurdle, but fortified by a sliding wooden bar fitted into a socket.'

There was no doubt that they were inside the palisade, the children heard the gate slide open, and all around them were the farm sounds. They picked their way up the hill towards a group of huts. When Mr Fosse spoke it was as if he was pointing out something they could actually see.

'The huts are very much alike, we will go into the biggest.' He lowered his voice as if they could be overheard. 'This is where the head of the family lives. You notice we walk straight in, that is because it is a fine day in summer; I imagine if we came back in the winter we would find skins hung across this entrance to keep the wet and the cold out.'

It felt as if they had stepped inside a small hut. The air was sour with the smell of unwashed bodies and animals, mixed with smoke and cooking. Mr Fosse seemed to like the smell of the food for he led them straight towards it.

'Nice stone hearth, you see, right in the middle of the hut. You may wonder why they keep this fire burning on a warm August day, instead of cooking outside; my guess is they always keep this fire going, saves trouble. See this boiling pot hanging over it? Put your noses to that; pleasant smell, is it not? Ought to whet your appetites for what we have in our picnic basket.'

The children sniffed. Mr Fosse was quite right, there was a gorgeous smell, coming from some sort of brown stew. William was fond of going out with a gun.

'Mostly wild game, isn't it?'

Mr Fosse took another sniff.

'That's right. Stag, deer, elk, bear, wild boar, plenty of food to be had for the taking.'

Grace took a deep sniff.

'There's a stink a' onions.'

Mr Fosse seemed to point upwards.

'And the vegetables in the pot are not the only ones. Look up there, see vegetables and herbs hanging from the beams?

They are being dried. They are using fresh stuff now, of course, those are for winter use.'

Elizabeth was not interested in cooking. In her home meals came mostly from tins. She had wandered off, and she almost saw something.

'Beds! Aren't those beds?'

Mr Fosse seemed to lead the other five across the hut to Elizabeth.

'And very comfortable too, skins laid on straw. If they had a good clean we could have a nice sleep.'

Miss Marion loved anything handwoven, so all Borthwick girls could weave. Selina turned to Mr Fosse.

'Where's the loom?'

'In the corner there is a frame, but it is not in use at the moment, for obviously the women and girls avoid working in a stuffy hut this weather. Here is something interesting. See this stone, slightly hollowed out in the middle, and this smaller rounded stone lying on it? Have a guess what they use this for.'

It seemed as if Mr Fosse was holding a flinty-looking stone with a hollow in it. Selina and William, because they were brought up in the country, guessed the answer.

'For grinding,' said William.

'Corn,' Selina added.

Mr Fosse seemed to put the grinding stones down again.

'These are rather out-of-date, a simpler method is in use, a millstone which turns by a handle, but I don't think our friends have got hold of it yet.'

Elizabeth knew no loaves except those sold in shops.

'You mean they have bread just like us?'

'No, coarse stuff more like a large flat biscuit, probably admirable for the inside, what doctors call roughage.'

'Lucky they've got some things to keep them well, poor things,' said Selina, 'otherwise having no doctors when they get ill they probably die.'

They all had something to say in answer to that.

'Of course they don't just die,' William burst out. 'I bet they know heaps of things about herbs we don't, you know, like putting dock leaves on a nettle sting, only more important.'

Elizabeth was a great film-goer.

'I suppose you never go to films, Selina, or you'd know about witch doctors.'

Grace leant towards Selina.

'My mother says tha's more good stuff growin' in't ground than comes out of doctors' bottles.'

'And they know what to do for accidents,' John pointed out. 'I mean, you don't need a doctor to tell you to press a cut together to stop it bleeding, they've got threads, so I wouldn't wonder if they knew how to sew a wound.'

'And you wouldn't need a doctor for breaks,' Robert put in. 'I mean, they've sticks, and stuff to cut into strips for bandages, so I bet they can set broken bones, can't they, Mr Fosse?'

'Grace's mother is right, there are plenty of medicines growing, if you know where to look for them, and how to use them. If those herbs we see drying are brewed right I expect they can cure most day-to-day illnesses. But looking round and admiring their possessions and ingenuity, we must not get carried away. These are very simple people, and in many ways, ignorant. Fear plays a large part in their lives. Not only fear of other men, or of animals, but of the unknown. I think it is easy for them to think an illness which they cannot understand has been laid upon the patient by a god or goddess, and they are not meant to interfere.'

Robert struggled to see the people more clearly.

'No schools or anything like that, of course.'

'Except their fathers and mothers showing them how to make and grow things,' said John.

Selina sounded pitying.

'No water for washing, no drains.'

'You and your washing,' said Elizabeth. 'It's having no shops I think I'd hate worst of all.'

'What tha's never had tha'll never miss,' Grace pointed out. 'And if there was shops, they'd have nowt for brass, would they, Mister?'

Mr Fosse laughed.

'Now you are going too far the other way. I daresay our people do not use money, though they may have some bronze and iron bars for trading put away, should a wandering merchant or pedlar turn up, but money is used. Heads of big clans have their own coins cast.'

'Where . . . what I mean is, where would traders come from?' Robert asked. 'I . . . I mean, for just a few people like this.'

'For centuries there have been rumours all over Europe of riches in Britain. There always have been men willing to go off the beaten track in search of wealth, but our friends are not off the beaten track, in fact they live on a track, as we can see for ourselves. In any case, they are just the types smart traders are on the look out for, they are simple, and will probably sell or barter what they have for a quarter of what the things are worth.'

They were outside the hut, the sun beat on their heads, the sounds of a busy farm were all around them. Wool was being spun, cloth woven, corn ground, wood chopped, meat cut up, and oxen watered. Baskets were being made; all the children had learnt basketwork, and they found out that the people of A.D. 43 made them in exactly the same way. They saw a pot made, not on a wheel but by hand, ring upon ring of clay dried in the sun and fired in a bonfire. A sheep-dog was lying in the sun, and sprawling over him was a baby. Babies seemed to be very unchanging; they could not see this one clearly, but they could hear gurgles and almost see a tiny hand clutching something carved out of a bone which might have been a boar.

'Come along, come along,' said Mr Fosse. 'We have a long journey in front of us, and little time left for this lot. But there is one thing you must see. You remember I told you to keep an eye on that track as someone would come along it who would be of importance to us. Now look where I look, and see what I see.'

There was a flurry of dust made by two heavy solid ponies galloping along drawing a chariot. In the chariot a man stood to drive. It was a fine sight, the horses' harness and the shield the man carried, and his horned helmet gleamed in the sunlight.

'He is causing a sensation,' Mr Fosse

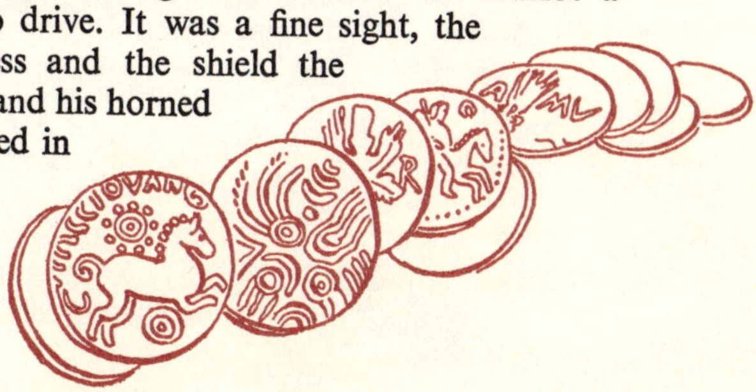

pointed out. 'Strangers are rare, all our friends are pointing at him; now this is a moment when they do talk. They are jabbering to each other.'

The children caught the excitement. They all asked questions at once. Who is he? What's he coming for? What's he going to tell them?

Mr Fosse stared at the man in the chariot.

'Though they do not know it, eventful news, even for our simple farmers. The Romans have landed in force this time. They have occupied parts of Kent.'

CHAPTER FOUR

# *Being Britons*

DRESSING up is always fun. There had been a lot of rushing in and out of rooms, and shouts of 'Look at me.' The boys were particularly pleased with themselves because they were wearing wigs, and wigs are a very quick way of making a person feel different all through. The wigs were shaggy affairs, the hair long enough to touch their shoulders. William and Robert wore short tunics with cloaks held in at the waist by leather belts into which were stuck daggers. John was the lucky one, he was dressed as a warrior. He had a horned helmet, a shield and a sword, all polished so that they glinted as if they were made of gold. Under his tunic he had trousers of a near tartan design, tied in at the ankles. The girls wore tunics too, but theirs were long: Selina's was red, Grace's was blue, and Elizabeth's grey. They too had cloaks. Selina's and Elizabeth's hair was in coarse nets, held in place with large bronze pins. Grace's hair was plaited, and she had a band matching her dress tied round her forehead. All six had jewellery of one kind or another, the girls coloured beads, and brooches made like safety-pins, set with coral or enamel. The boys had brooches too, and heavy armlets. John's jewellery was splendid, beautifully chased and worked in enamel, and set with coral and other stones. They all wore queer shoes made of hide, threaded through with thongs of leather which tied round their ankles. Mr Foss was delighted when he saw them.

'Capital! Not, of course, the real thing, but enough to give the idea. Now, let's take a look at your home.'

Their home was a hut almost exactly like the one they had visited on the hill above Bath, and it too was built on the slope of a field. It felt queer stepping over the ditch, opening the gate in the palisade, and going into the hut. It gave them a creepy feeling seeing something real which belonged to a dream. Inside the hut a real fire was burning, and a real pot on a tripod was hanging over it, and real herbs drying against the roof, and there were real beds made of skins, and even some real animals walking about: a nanny goat, who poked her face into the hut in an enquiring way, and a sheep nibbling the grass outside. The great difference in the real hut and the dream hut was the smell. This hut smelt of smoke, but otherwise clean. There was none of the rancid stuffy slept-in smell of the hut on the hillside.

Mr Fosse looked round.

'I think you will find all you need. William and Robert, you are the hunters, everybody depends on you for their supper. Grace is the wood-gatherer, and the water-drawer. Elizabeth will prepare the vegetables to go with the meat provided by the hunters, Selina is in charge of the fire. If you look round, Selina, you will find some hide bellows. On you depends a good fire to cook the hunters' meat and Elizabeth's vegetables. John, you will come with me, I have got something to show you, for your task comes later, meanwhile you can be the handyman and repair or sharpen the household tools. Is that all clear?'

Mr Fosse was not the sort of person anybody would want to look a fool in front of, but everything was not clear and questions had to be asked. William held out his dagger.

'Are Robert and I to kill our supper with these? I mean, of course we'll try, but I shouldn't think we'd get anything.'

Mr Fosse sighed.

'True. Such a pity, but you are perfectly right. You have not the skill of our friends. They can spear a running deer or bring down a wild duck with a stone from a catapult, but I am afraid your daggers must be for feel only. Outside the stockade you will find a couple of shotguns. You might have caught your supper by contriving a trap, but I hate traps, so firearms it has got to be, especially as you are both used to guns. I am afraid all that you will achieve towards understanding how our friends feel is the knowledge of an empty pot and four hungry and impatient people waiting for food.' He looked at Robert, who had cleared his throat nervously. 'Yes, Robert?'

Now that he had to answer, Robert felt certain the others would think his question idiotic.

'If we should put up . . . I mean to say, if we saw a grouse . . . I mean, it's not the twelfth, but . . .'

Elizabeth, John and Grace stared at Robert wondering what on earth he was talking about, but William and Selina knew. Selina said kindly:

'Of course it doesn't matter whether it's the twelfth or not, they didn't worry about special days to shoot things in A.D. 43.

William, apart from a natural inclination to disagree with Selina, was doubtful if she was right. He was torn between the ethics of the first century and the twentieth. He looked enquiringly at Mr Fosse, who laughed.

'A nice point, Robert. You are quite right, Selina, our friends on the hill had no special days for shooting things, but the law is the law, and I don't want our journey spoilt by our having to appear before the magistrates. In any case, I do not believe there were grouse.'

'What was there that we could shoot?' William asked.

'Deer, but there are none round here. Hares, but they were sacred so not killed; there were wild duck, pelicans, herons, boars and bears, not likely filling for your pot. There were no rabbits at that time, but I expect it will have to be rabbit stew, for you must do as they do, kill what you can. The same applies to vegetables, you must eat what you have, though there were no runner beans at that time.'

Elizabeth had been poking round the hut.

'Are we going to sleep here? Please let us, it would be such fun.'

'I quite agree with you. I had intended that you should. But Mrs Mummery has put her foot down, she says you do not belong to me, and she talked a lot of nonsense about your catching your deaths of colds.' Mr Fosse looked sadly at the beds. 'It was not a very good idea really, for you know there are six good beds waiting for you indoors, so you would be no nearer imagining how it feels to have no other beds than these. We can never put our minds back, however hard we try. To-night you are dressed rather as the hill people are dressed, and in little you can share their feelings because you are using only such things as they use; true William and Robert have guns, but you are dependent on their skill for your supper. I can assure you that this is true. I have fought

Mrs Mummery on this point, she wanted supper to be waiting for you in the house in case Robert and William were unsuccessful, but I said no, let them at least for this one evening share dependence on hunters with the hill people, for I can give them nothing else. I would like to say you are all alone, there is no one within miles, there is no means of transport, except horseback or small chariots over rough tracks, but you know it is not true. I would like to say if you are ill you must depend on yourselves for cures, and on herbs for medicine. You know it is not true. You know there is a telephone and if anything is the matter with any of you a doctor will be telephoned, and, if need be, a motor ambulance called to take you to hospital. I should like to tell you that the only education you receive is from your elders. What is the good of that when I know the moment you are alone you will talk of your different schools? Nobody, however hard they try, can cease to know what they know. We can only use every ounce of imagination we have to try and understand in the smallest way how it felt to be Britons when the curtain was going up on what is called civilization.'

William was used to rough shooting, but not with half as good a shotgun as the one that he found waiting for him in the ditch. Lord Ackroyd, determined that his son and heir, fool though he might be, should be competent to take part in sports suitable to his position, had Robert taught to shoot by his gamekeeper, and sometimes took him on a shoot. But this did not mean that Robert was a good shot; conscious of this he said:

'I . . . I say, William, do . . . do you think we shall shoot anything? I mean, I . . . I'm not likely to.'

There was a track up the field, William was following it.

'I thought we'd get up there and have a look round, I should think there's plenty of stuff about. I don't think it's any good fussing about what there was, we'll pot at anything we see, most likely a rabbit, but of course we might get a hare, or a wood-pigeon.'

Robert was enormously impressed.

'Might we! I say, I do hope we do. I mean, it's awful thinking of everybody waiting, isn't it?' He lowered his voice, for although there was nobody else about, he was conscious that what he was going to say would make the others think him even more of a fool than they probably did already. 'If . . . I mean suppose we get a rabbit or a hare, do . . . do you know how to clean it and take its skin off?'

William turned a searching eye on the countryside, and saw a promising-looking slope leading down to a wood.

'Of course I do. Come on.'

Elizabeth drew Grace away from the hut.

'I didn't like to ask Mr Fosse, because I thought he'd think it silly, but where do you suppose I get vegetables? I mean, they don't grow in fields and there aren't any shops.' She looked round the enclosure. 'They don't seem to grow anything except those red flowers over there.'

Grace laughed.

'Tha's gormless, Elizabeth, they'n't flowers, they'm runner beans tha' knows.'

Elizabeth tossed her head.

'All right! Proper Mrs Know-all, aren't you? As a matter of fact, beans don't grow much in London, and dad's never had an allotment. You better be stepping on it, or the fire'll go down, then you won't half catch it from madam in there.' She gave Grace a friendly nudge. 'Can't stand that snooty type, can you?'

Grace grinned.

'She's nobbut a blatherskite. She'll l'arn.'

Elizabeth was moving towards the beans, but she stopped, as a thought struck her.

'I say, you'll want water, you know what she is about washing.' She jerked her head towards the hut and Selina. 'Give me a shout and I'll come with you to get it. There's a bucket thing over there, but it looks heavy, I should think it will take two of us to carry it.'

Grace looked at a heavy wooden bucket bound with bronze standing by the hut doorway.

'It will an' all, I'll get t'wood, and lend you a 'and wit' t'beans, then we'll fetch a bucketful, reckon there's a runnel o'er yonder.'

At first Selina was glad to be alone in the hut. She prowled round looking at everything, thinking to herself how glorious it was to be on her own for a change, not to have to put up with that dreadful bouncy Elizabeth, or struggle to understand Grace's extraordinary accent. She planned in her mind how she would describe the others at Borthwick next term. She could picture everybody laughing as she described them and imitated Elizabeth, Grace and John. She could see herself sitting on a stool close to Miss Marion's chair, telling her all that had happened, and she could almost hear Miss Marion's shocked voice saying: 'How very unpleasant for you, dear child.' It would not be so maddening, Selina decided, having to waste her time with these strange people if they realized the difference between themselves and herself. Robert was all right, if only he wasn't so shy, and William ought to be all right, if he wasn't so stand-offish; but really, the others! She could not think what Mr Fosse was thinking of to expect her to mix with them. But she would show them, she would make them realize before this journey was over the sort of world she belonged to. It was at this moment that Selina came upon the loom. Because Miss Marion was keen on hand-weaving, it was the done thing at Borthwick to be keen on hand-weaving; Selina was not only keen, it was something she was good at. The loom was not a bit like any loom she had used, but it did not take her long to see how it worked. Two forked pieces of wood stuck firmly in the ground, held a crossbar, from which hung the warp-strands, some of red wool and some of blue. Lower down on the forked pieces of wood other bars were laid across, balanced on pegs, which, when moved, brought the reverse strands forward and back. At the bottom of the loom the strands of wool were securely threaded through to keep them in place, and each strand was held taut by a weight. Evidently, when completed there was going to be a

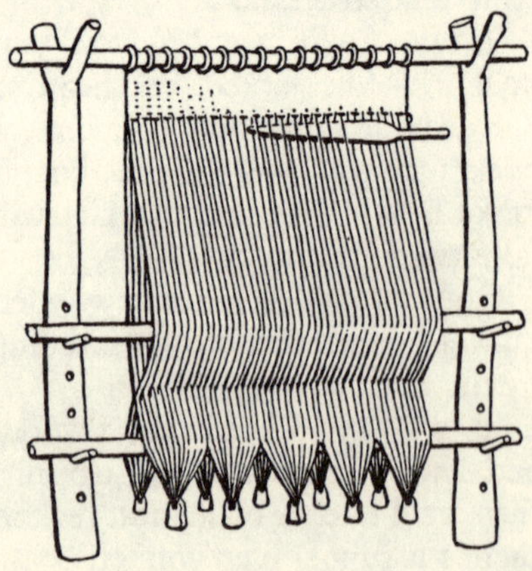

length of cloth of the same sort that had made John's trousers, for the design was a kind of tartan. At first Selina merely fingered the loom, the shuttles which held the two coloured wools, and a stick which she decided probably went through the strands of wool before the shuttle, and perhaps as well pushed the woof strands into place. But when you are fond of doing something just looking is not enough, so very soon Selina's fingers were working. Being fond of weaving was not the only reason she was attracted to the loom, in her mind she saw the others coming back tired and dirty from getting the food and sticks and things, to find her at the loom. She did not suppose any of them could weave, and she could imagine them standing round nudging each other, saying in respectful tones, 'I say, look at Selina!' or 'I say, Selina, show us how to do it.'

Selina was so absorbed in her weaving that she scarcely heard sounds outside, she did just catch Grace's shout of 'I've putten wood outside t'door, Selina,' and knew that Grace and Elizabeth must have gone off together somewhere, for their voices grew fainter, but she did not hear distant shots, nor John calling to William and Robert to know what luck they had had, nor all the others talking as they approached the hut, so she was only pulled away from the loom by a chorus of 'Selina!' not said in the tone of respectful admiration she had hoped, but in horror and dismay. She swung round to see what the trouble was. It was very real trouble; happy at her weaving she had forgotten the fire. There was not even smoke. It had gone out.

Although both John and William knew the way you were supposed to make fires when you had no matches and no lighters, in fact the way the hill people probably made theirs, the children could not get a fire going. Because it was her fault they made Selina work the stick way. For what seemed to her like hours and hours she sat on the ground rolling a piece of stick in her hands, the end of it in a groove in a log, while Grace, William and Robert stood by hopefully with dust, dead leaves, dried grasses and bits of bark to catch alight if she made a spark. Elizabeth, with another supply of dried grasses and bark, stood by John, who beat the top of the corn-grinder, which seemed to be flint, with the handle of a heavy knife which he thought might be made of iron sulphide and ought to produce sparks when knocked together. Either the handle of the knife was not made of what he thought it was, or the stone was not flint, or he did not know how to use one against the other, for no sparks came.

Selina's hands grew more and more sore, and at last she could bear it no longer. She threw the stick away.

'I won't try any more. It's a simply idiotic way of making a fire. I don't believe anybody ever made a fire like this. We'll have to do without one, that's all.'

Elizabeth went outside the hut and brought back some roughly hacked-apart gory-looking bits of rabbit in a pottery bowl.

'You may like to eat rabbits raw, but I couldn't fancy them myself. There are some nice raw runner beans to go with them.'

Selina shuddered at the rabbits.

'Take them away, they look revolting.'

'I don't want to rub salt in a wound,' said William, 'but I must say it seems to me funny you're the one to give up and talk about having no fire. After all, it was you who let it out. What on earth were you doing? You only had it to look after.'

'And tha' knows tha' were plenty'a wood,' Grace pointed out. 'I told tha'd put more be'int.'

Elizabeth looked despisingly at Selina.

'Yes, what were you doing?'

Miserably Selina pointed to the loom.

'I was doing some of that.'

Elizabeth groaned.

'Knowing we were only here for one evening just for supper, she did weaving! She must be cracked.'

John gave a final blow at the flint and laid down the knife.

'Cracked or not, we've got to get a fire somehow. The question is how. It looks as if we'll either have to go to the house and ask for matches, which makes us look fools, or have no supper.'

Grace remembered something.

'We'll not need t'matches. When Elizabeth and me'sen were seekin' water we saw a g'eat bonfire in a bit of a clearin'.'

The bonfire was their salvation. Selina did a little to redeem her character because she was the one who knew about the lamp. While she had wandered round the hut she had noticed a boat-shaped stone full of fat, with a piece of moss stuck in it. She would not have known what it was if in her school Bible there had not been a picture of the wise and foolish virgins with their lamps.

'I am almost certain that's a lamp. If it is we could light it at the bonfire.'

John picked up the lamp and examined it.

'That is what it is. That fat, when it's melted, would feed that moss in the same way a wick is fed by paraffin or petrol.' He passed the lamp to Selina. 'But it won't be "we" who light it at the bonfire, it'll be you.'

There was a good deal of argument about this, because although everybody wanted Selina to be punished for being such an idiot as to let the fire go out, they were hungry and did not want to trust her to bring them a flame. In the end a much-humbled Selina was sent off with an escort of William and Elizabeth, Elizabeth to lead the way to the bonfire, and William to see that when she had a flame she guarded it properly, and did not let a breeze blow it out.

In the ordinary way they would all have thought the rabbit stew, when at last they ate it, nasty. There was a block of salt in the hut, but it was in its crude form, rather yellowish-looking, and the children did not recognize it as such. Rabbits should be simmered slowly to taste good, and these rabbits were boiled furiously for an hour, so were tough as old leather. The beans, with some onions, were put in at the same time as the rabbits, with the result that the beans were soggy remnants. But eaten round the fire, for it was getting cold outside, the rabbit stew was a great success. It was a funny kind of meal, there seemed to be no plates, so they ate rabbit in their fingers, which they all agreed was the best way to eat it anyway, and they poured the so-called gravy into earthenware pots. There were some rough pottery spoons, but none of them used them, but drank the gravy out of the pots. When the last scrap was finished John got up.

'Mr Fosse said to tell you that some sticks show where another stockade is for cattle. There you'll find milk and fruit. I've got to go now, so keep my share of the fruit and the milk. One of you, or all of you if you like, are to keep an eye on the track to the top of the field, and shout when there is anything to see.'

The milk was in a bucket, just like the one Grace and Elizabeth fetched the water in. The fruit was a pleasant surprise: there were apples, wild strawberries and wild raspberries. They washed out the bowls they had used for the gravy and drank the milk out of them, and with some difficulty, because they had only cold water, washed out the pot they had cooked the rabbit in. When this was finished they stood outside, eating fruit, spitting out apple cores and watching the track. Suddenly it happened, just as it had happened to the people on the hill. A flurry of dust, a chariot drawn by two heavy solid ponies, and there, his helmet shining in the light of the setting sun, a man, his shield in one hand and the ponies' reins in the other. It was the queerest feeling seeing something only imagined, really happening, and though they all knew that it was John driving the chariot, without thinking they surged towards him shouting:

'What is it? What have you come to tell us?'

Outside the stockade John pulled up his ponies. Against the flaring rose-coloured sunset sky he was a fine sight, with his flowing hair, his big shield, and somehow his voice seemed to grow with the importance of the occasion. Although the words he used were different, and because of knowledge, the children's interpretation of the words utterly different, the dramatic effect could have been what it had been nineteen centuries before. He raised his head and shouted:

'News. I bring news. Invaders from Rome have landed in force on the coast of Kent.'

CHAPTER FIVE

# *Romans*

BEING Britons brought the six much closer together. Robert and William, while tramping after food, had become friends. Elizabeth and Grace had joined together in a common front against Selina, and had found there were lots of things they both liked. By the end of the evening, especially after she had the sense to find the lamp, they had all begun to find things to like even in Selina, not many, but here and there niceness poked through.

Breakfast smelt and tasted particularly good after the badly-cooked rabbits. Mrs Mummery filled their plates with sausages, bacon and eggs, and their cups with coffee, while in her fat warm voice she encouraged them to eat more.

'Eat up, me dears, you must be peckish after that nasty half-cooked supper. I told Mr Fosse we'd have you all ill this morning, but you've taken no hurt seemingly. Now eat plenty of bread and honey when you've finished what's on your plates; I must go to pack your lunch basket.'

At first there was silence round the table, broken only by the clatter of knives and forks and the sound of coffee cups. Then Elizabeth stopped eating. She looked across the table at John.

'Of course, I know there isn't magic, not in silk handkerchiefs with laundry marks, anyway; but when we were on the hill yesterday I did sort of see things, did you?'

They had all been turning over yesterday in their minds. It had been queer. John tried to find the right words to explain what he meant.

'Not exactly saw, just thought I did, I suppose.'

William stared round the table through his dirty tortoiseshell glasses.

'It was more than that, wasn't it?'

It was a surprise to him, but Robert found himself stammering out an idea which was only in the back of his mind, and which he had not thought of explaining to the others.

'I expect this sounds idiotic . . . I mean I'm sure there's nothing in it. . . . I was thinking of jets . . . when they get through the barrier of sound, anything can happen. . . .'

William, though he liked Robert, had not thought him particularly bright. Now he looked at him with different eyes.

'You might have got something there.'

Selina was glad to see Robert asserting himself.

'I bet he has. It was sound that Mr Fosse started on. I mean, don't you remember it was when he took away the everyday sounds that things began to happen.'

Elizabeth stretched across the table for the honey-comb.

'If you get through the barrier of sound you can break up, we didn't break up.'

John, Selina, William and Grace looked at Robert for an answer. Red to the ears with embarrassment, Robert tried to explain what he meant.

'Not us . . . our imaginations. . . . I can see it sounds absolutely idiotic . . . but if there is a barrier of sound on the other side of which a jet could break up and anything could happen . . . what I mean is, couldn't there be a barrier of imagination for people, on the other side of which anything could happen?'

Elizabeth was not going to show she was impressed.

'You mean, if our imaginations are broken into little bits there is no reason why one bit couldn't be in A.D. 43, and another bit somewhere else, and another bit eating breakfast here. I shall ask Mr Fosse.'

The other five felt, for no reason at all, that this would be a bad thing to do. Elizabeth was the sort of girl who would do exactly what she wanted whether anyone liked it or not. John ran his hand through his tow-coloured hair.

'We can't stop you, Elizabeth, but I wouldn't ask him, not yet.'

Elizabeth's chin shot up in the air.

'Why not, John Fish?'

Grace was sitting next to Elizabeth, she gave her a nudge.

'He's right, tha' knows.'

Robert nodded.

'Of course, none of us can stop you if you want to . . . but I think . . . I mean, what John means is, the sort of magic Mr Fosse makes. . . . I mean it wouldn't be there if he had to explain it.'

Elizabeth looked pityingly at the other five.

'I don't know what you're yattering about. Barriers of sound, and magic that wouldn't be there if Mr Fosse had to explain it; but I'll be big; if you'd all rather I didn't ask Mr Fosse, I won't ask him.. Miss Elizabeth Hamblett is quite capable of finding things out for herself.'

It was another glorious day. After breakfast the children were delighted to find the shooting-brake ready, Mr Fosse sitting beside Alfred, and Mrs Mummery with her picnic basket waiting inside. They drove to the same place as the day before, and soon the handkerchiefs were round their eyes. Either because of the conversation at breakfast, or because it was easier having done it before, there seemed quicker magic in the handkerchiefs that morning. Almost as soon as they were tied on it began. The whirling red balls, the rings of green and violet, the flashing stars, darkness. Then suddenly the change of sound, those that belonged vanishing like a mist before a breeze, and those of the past slipping into their places. Quietly at first, rather as if he were speaking on tiptoe, Mr Fosse's voice joined the sounds of the past and became part of them.

'As you can hear, we are back on our hillside, but we have moved on in time. It is another August day, but this morning the year is 250. There are a lot of changes. Can you see?'

Robert strained his eyes in the darkness. Suddenly a shape swam into sight below him.

'That's a town, isn't it? I mean where the trees were . . . it must be the beginning of Bath.'

William knew what he ought to see.

'Roads, good roads everywhere.'

Mr Fosse must have jumped up, for his voice came from above the children.

'That's not Bath, Robert, that is Aquae Sulis. We will go down and have a look round presently. Good roads is right, William, not everywhere, but a network of splendid roads is beginning to link the country together, one of them passes through Aquae Sulis.'

'Going where?' asked Elizabeth.

'The Fosse Way they call it. It starts at Lindum, now called Lincoln, leads to what you would call Exeter, Elizabeth, but our friends here call Isca Dumnoniorum.'

Elizabeth whistled.

'Goodness, what a name! Fancy having that for an address.'

Mr Fosse sat down again.

'I don't suppose the locals use it in full, locals never do. Think of a place like Weston-super-Mare. It hardly ever is called that, it's just Weston.'

John raised his nose and sniffed. The farm smells filled his nostrils. At once people were back, and it seemed to him sickening for them to have Romans building roads all over their land, and expecting them to learn the long names they called their towns.

'As they were building roads they might have built one for our lot up here.'

As John spoke the others felt some of the indignation he felt. It was not many hours since they themselves had dressed and lived a little like the people on the hill, and had heard the news of these Romans landing.

'I shouldn't think they'd want a road up here,' said Elizabeth, 'I bet they're glad the beastly Romans keep out of their way.'

Selina had a sudden vision of Roman women swaggering around, richly dressed, looking down their noses at poor Britons.

'Poor things, it must be hateful being conquered.'

'I don't want to interrupt this indignation meeting,' Mr Fosse said, 'but I don't think the Britons here to-day share your feelings.'

'I bet they do,' said Elizabeth. 'I learnt some poetry about it, "When the British warrior queen bleeding from the Roman rods." '

William knew the quotation.

'Boadicea, that was. What about her, Mr Fosse?'

Mr Fosse's voice slid through their anger.

'There were those who fought the Romans fiercely. Boadicea for one. But I doubt if these people here resent them, many have Roman relations. I daresay the people we met yesterday may have found their ways of doing things startling at first, but I doubt if they resisted.'

'I don't see them lying down under it,' said John.

Mr Fosse thought about that.

'Maybe you are right, but even so to these people to-day it's just a tale that is told; for myself I doubt if it is even that.'

Selina was collecting pictures of Romans in her head.

'How queer it must have been after the Romans landed, houses, clothes, everything changing.'

'But everything did not change, my dear Selina. Ruling lines across history is a mistake; we say solemnly that such and such clothes were worn in this period, and this was the architecture of that period, and these the conveyances of another period, yet all of us know that to be quite untrue. You remember the death of George VI, and Elizabeth coming to the throne. Did any changes take place in your way of life? Did you live in different houses, have entirely new wardrobes, stop riding in buses and trains and take to jets? Of course you did not, you went on living exactly as you had when George VI was on the throne, and any changes there may be will not be general for years, and for many there will scarcely be any changes at all. But if now we step forward even a little while in time, say a hundred years, and could hear what is being said about us, we would have a surprise. We would be likely to find great authorities asserting that we wore this, and our houses were built this way, during the reign of George VI, whereas these clothes and these types of houses belonged to the second Elizabethan age. Rather as if from one period of time to another everything was destroyed and everybody started again. As you will see when we go up to the farm there are enormous changes, but they have come gradually, and though the Romans have occupied the country for two hundred and seven years, and the effect of the occupation is tremendous, we shall still find objects in use unchanged from those we saw yesterday, for men of all time are apt to feel what was good enough for their old dad is good enough for them.'

'And I bet they're right,' said John. 'I thought they were doing pretty decently yesterday.'

Mr Fosse chuckled.

'I like your feeling for our friends, John, but I doubt if they need your support. Hard things are said about the Roman Empire, but the Romans give the countries they conquer some gifts of priceless worth, for one, where their legions go security follows, and security and happiness have a great deal to do with each other.'

John thought it very queer of Mr Fosse to side with the Romans.

'But the people yesterday didn't need soldiers to look after them, they had their own way of looking after themselves.'

'Having an eye on the horizon and an ear cocked for trouble is not security. Security is of course comparative, the security given by these Roman soldiers, together with good roads for them to move along so that they can get quickly from one point to another, is greater security than our friends ever knew. Naturally the size of the garrison changes, but there are always plenty of troops stationed in the country, for it is a good training ground for recruits, and a handy spot on which to keep reserves so that they can be sent across to France in a hurry in case of trouble in Europe. Barbarians are constantly on the warpath looking for living space where they can farm in peace, they are ignorant savage types and attack weak people, killing the farmers, seizing their land, crops and cattle. That Britain is comparatively free from barbarians at the moment is something for which Britons and Roman-Britons have to thank the legions.'

Grace had been lying on her back, now she rolled over.

'What's them barbarians, Mister?'

'Barbarian was a Greek word for foreigner, its meaning has changed, to the Romans it means enemies whose behaviour is barbarous. We have kept the Roman meaning of the word and use it in exactly the same way in our day.'

'I like soldiers,' said Elizabeth, 'but I suppose these Roman soldiers are different from our boys, or the Yanks.'

'Soldiers don't change much. Soldiers away from home make the best they can of life in the place in which they are stationed. They teach the natives a few words of their language, and speak their version of the language of the natives. This is made easier in the case of the Roman soldiers here for they have local recruits to practice on. Often they marry the native girls, and the children of the marriage become Roman-Britons. Like all soldiers they grumble a lot, but manage to have quite a good time on the side, and express their feelings by putting comic,

perhaps rather rude, words to old tunes.' Mr Fosse seemed to be moving. His high flute-like voice sounded excited. 'Come along, we have not all day to sit here, let's go up to the farm, you can have a look at things for yourselves.'

The children began to hear changes. The most noticeable was speech; evidently talking had become a habit, they could not understand a word but they could hear talk and laughter, a kind of essence of sound which had once been there, and was still lying on the air. Now that their ears were alert they heard road noises, close to them. They seemed to be walking up the hill beside the track which yesterday had led to the forest, now it was a sort of a lane down to Aquae Sulis. They could hear packhorses being led down it, and a cart full of hay rumbled by, pulled by two fat oxen. Then they left the grassland and were crossing the farmyard. Cows were being milked, they could hear the swish of the milk as it was directed into pails; there were farm smells around them, the unchanging smells of manure, and hot straw. Then they passed through the entrance and were inside a house.

The farmhouse, or villa, as Mr Fosse called it, faced south. It was built of bricks and was a long, rather narrow building with an entrance in the middle. It was so very much a proper house that it felt rude walking in without knocking or ringing, or anything like that, but Mr Fosse did not seem to mind, he just strode ahead as if the place belonged to him. Inside they found themselves in a stone passage, with rooms at either end of it. Mr Fosse led the way to the room on the right. It was a big room, Mr Fosse said it was not only the main family living-room, but used as the office for the farm. It was an awfully nice room, the walls were plastered and painted with a gay design in very bright colours. The floor was mosaic, little pieces of different coloured stones had been fitted together to make a recurring pattern. There were proper windows of glass, through which they could see the hillside where the farmer's sheep were grazing. In the middle of the room was a table made of bronze, with two benches drawn up to it. The whole room had a very lived-in look, it was as if the farmer and his family had only just that second left. On the table was a half-woven basket, apparently for fruit, and there were several finished baskets piled up in a corner. There was a weaving frame of much the same type as the ones used in '43, and somebody had been working on it, for on it there was a half-finished length of blue cloth. Somebody, too, had just been having a drink of wine, for there was a wine jar on the floor, and the dregs of some wine in a red-glazed bowl. The children were immensely impressed, even John could see there must be something to say for Romans. Elizabeth expressed her feelings by whistling through her teeth.

'Come up a bit in the world, haven't they?'

'Can we see the rest of the house?' William asked.

Mr Fosse sounded glad that they approved of the farm.

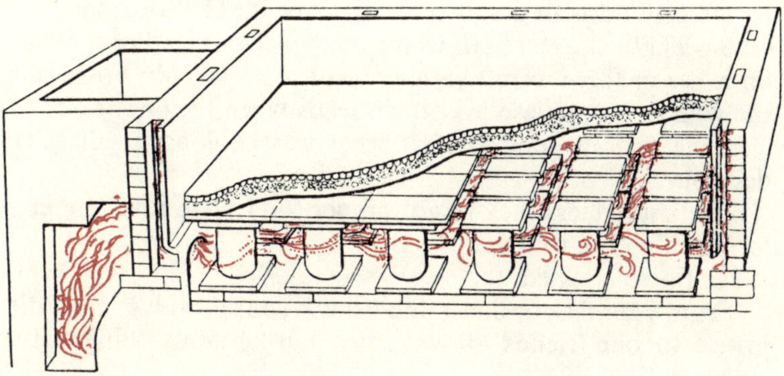

'Go where you like, but don't miss the central heating plant at the other end of this corridor.'

Central heating! Even Selina was startled, why at her home they did not have central heating. The kind of central heating the farm people used seemed simple and very sensible. It started under a hot room, and Mr Fosse said it was called a hypocaust. Heat was carried under the floors by pipes made of terra cotta. One big fire pushed under the hot room heating the main corridor and the living-room. The hot room had a mosaic floor like the living-room; Elizabeth was very taken with it.

'I should sit on my bottom in here all the winter if I had this room.'

The hot room and the living-room turned the corners to make the side walls of the house, the back of the house had bedrooms and a kitchen, in the middle was a courtyard. Because of last night and the fire going out and cooking their own supper, the children took a professional interest in the kitchen. The farm had a proper kitchen, there was not, of course, a gas stove or anything like that, but there was a very nice built-up stove of stone. Underneath it was a neat little arch in which the fuel was kept. On the top of the stove fires were lighted in holes and gridirons put over the fires for as many pots as were needed for the meal. The farmer's wife and one of her daughters seemed to be cooking the meal. They could not see the women clearly, but when they started to talk about their clothes Mr Fosse said that they were nearly right. The dress had not changed as much as everything else. There seemed to be a tunic of one colour to the ground with a shorter tunic over it. The top tunic had elbow-length sleeves, both women had well-cut leather sandals; on a bench there were two lengths of material, Mr Fosse said the women wore these over their heads when they went out.

Selina took a good sniff at what was cooking, it all smelt delicious.

Thank goodness they've got proper food now, it will make a lot of difference to them.'

Mr Fosse laughed.

'From your description I don't think your meal last night did justice to our friends of yesterday, but certainly things have come on.'

Elizabeth was trying to see the stove.

'They're frying, some sort of chicken I reckon, and a coupl'a veg.'

Grace saw the stove much more clearly than Elizabeth, and was not pleased with it.

'Stove's all right for fryin' or boilin' tha' knows, but what 'appens when they mon bake, Mister?'

'I am afraid they are not much good at baking, they have not got an oven. When they want to bake or warm up some left over food they have a makeshift arrangement, they use a pan on top of a pan, and a fan to regulate the heat.'

The boys were looking round the kitchen, it was full of sensible and convenient things, there was a shelf fixed to the plaster wall, underneath which a row of cooking utensils was hanging, and there were strings of onions and herbs. On the top was a dish of fruit, and several red-glazed bowls like the one used for wine in the living-room. On the floor by the stove were two large red-glazed wine jars, and on a sort of table next to the stove any amount of dishes full of partly prepared food. On a shelf at the end of the kitchen the dishes were waiting out of which the family would evidently eat. There were glass tumblers, the dishes were of the fine red-glazed pottery, but ornamented. John was not much impressed with the dishes.

'That ornamentation isn't done by hand, it's made by a mould.'

Selina, staring at the women, was at last beginning to see them clearly; she spoke in a whisper for it seemed rude to say what she had to say in front of them.

'They're quite clean. They don't smell at all. I should think their hair's clean too, it's done properly, piled up into a bun on top of their heads.'

Mr Fosse put his lips to Selina's ear.

'You're quite right, they are clean, and when you've done looking at the kitchen, I'll show you some startling advances they've made in that direction.'

Mr Fosse was right, the changes in hygiene were startling. The old spring from which the people of '43 had drawn their water was still being used, but it was no longer pumped by hand but sucked up through valves by pistons into a central reservoir.

'Many people have a bathroom,' Mr Fosse whispered, 'but our lot, who have no Roman relations, are a bit old-fashioned I think. The farmer probably calls a bath new-fangled nonsense, but, as Selina has noticed, they have got the idea that being clean is a virtue.'

'By looking at Romans, you mean?' asked William.

'Partly. Romans set great store by cleanliness and hygiene, they are a clean lot by instinct, but as well they have to be. No one can afford to be careless about hygiene when they are moving armies around. Nothing can so quickly thin the ranks as disease. Our friends here sell their produce in Aquae Sulis, and I don't suppose it took their ancestors long to realize that they would not be welcomed down there unless they cleaned themselves up. If you were a mole and could creep under this villa you would find jointed drainpipes, and underground sewers flushed with water connected to the lavatory.'

Elizabeth had been peering round.

'They buy things, what do they pay with?'

'Probably money, there is plenty of coinage about, and, as you can see, these people are doing well. Of course, sometimes they pay in kind, just as country people do to-day. "I'll give you a pot of my blackcurrant jam for that." '

'Do all the people round here live as well as this?' John asked.

Mr Fosse shrugged his shoulders.

'I don't know. More or less I should say. The ancestors of these people probably adapted their lands very well to Roman needs. Where there are soldiers the first need is corn, and when you go outside you will see fields of corn turning gold. They cultivate fruit and vegetables; Aquae Sulis has few residents, it is a town for visitors taking the waters, and what we call "summer visitors" staying in inns paying well for luxuries such as good fruit. But our farmer's main occupation is breeding cattle; it is good grazing land round here and he's probably been clever enough to cross-breed his sheep, cattle and horses with strains brought in by the Romans. There is more to it than being a good farmer; if he is known as a farmer, with sons and daughters working hard and productively, there is little chance of their being taken as slaves.'

Slaves! They all spoke at once, but John's cry of slaves had a note of triumph in it. So he was right about the Romans, they might build good houses and central heating, but they made slaves of people.

Mr Fosse was quite unmoved by the general indignation.

'I am afraid that Selina, unless she was generally useful on a farm, would almost certainly have been a slave; your skill at weaving would have been your downfall, Selina. Good cloth is needed, and slave weavers are used. I doubt if the rest of you would be disturbed, after all money is needed and our prosperous farmers here are good earners and therefore good tax payers; slaves do not pay taxes.'

Taxes! The children seemed to have heard all too much about taxation, it was a boring subject. They felt very sorry for the poor Britons that taxation had started.

'Why should they pay taxes, they don't get much for them, do they?' John asked angrily. 'I thought taxes paid for things like schools.'

'They do. As a matter of fact, there is education going on, though not free; our friends can probably "letter" a bit, and manage such adding and subtracting as they need for their business. But you can't say they don't get anything, look at the roads. Imagine what they mean. Constant traffic up and down, all the pottery and the glass that we saw in the kitchen, and cooking utensils, and all the rest of it, imported from the Continent and distributed quickly, easily and fairly inexpensively. Then look at the use our friends make of the roads. The wool from the sheep sold to the wool merchants, corn sold to the quartermaster's stores, animals driven along the roads to the markets, there's no end to what good roads mean.'

John sounded grumpy.

'All right, they have roads, but what else do they get for taxes?'

'Law and justice. The Romans rule the countries they occupy under governors, not always clever men, but well-meaning, and to the best of their ability they see justice, as they understand it, is done, and they try and allow for local rules. You have to accept it is no good appealing against slavery, because having slaves is an accepted condition of the Roman way of life, so the suggestion of doing away with slaves would shock them profoundly. But when it comes to taking another man's property, encroaching on his land, or whatever it is, I think that the people know that justice will be done. To me the best thing they get in return for paying taxes is something that they don't know they are getting, the feeling of belonging, of being people of one country.'

'I don't see why your country being occupied by Romans should make you feel all one country,' John argued.

Robert, absorbed by trying to see, had not spoken before.

'I . . . I think I do, it draws people together, being occupied, doesn't it?'

'It can, but that is not how it has happened here. Britain never had felt one country, because there was no person to draw the people into a whole. But the Romans have taught them to look to one supreme head, the Roman Emperor. Roman Emperors come and go, but there is always an Emperor. Looking to one head like that makes for a family feeling. I should say the Emperor is a cross between a father and a god; he is powerful, wise and directs the fortunes of everybody from the wealthiest man in the country to the poorest slave. As we travel you will see this idea of being one people started now.'

Selina wanted to have a look at Romans.

'Could we go to Aquae Sulis? I'd awfully like to see it.'

Mr Fosse seemed to give a little skip.

'Splendid idea, Selina, come along. We had better keep to the side of the track, or we will get run over.'

They were hurrying downhill, Mr Fosse springing ahead. Suddenly he began to sing and they all joined in at the top of their voices. The tune was 'The Cape Town Darkies sing this Song,' but the words came out differently:

'Off to Aquae Sulis we go
  Aquae Sulis,
For Aquae Sulis is a jolly little town
  Oh, doo-da day.
Going to Aquae Sulis
  Going to Aquae Sulis
Aquae Sulis is a jolly little town
  Oh, doo-da day.

Either Mr Fosse's handkerchiefs really had magic in them or the children were learning to see and hear better, but they all heard and saw Aquae Sulis. Sound came first. Sandals clattering, boots studded with nails clinking, the cries of street sellers, the hooves of oxen and the creak of cartwheels, the clip-clop of horses, and talk and laughter, not distant sounds, but the buzz of happy men, women and children on a fine summer day in a nice spot.

First they looked at the baths, for they felt possessive about them, having known them when they were hot mud in a forest before Aquae Sulis was thought of. Bath sounds are very unchanging. There was splashing and the slipperty-slop of bare feet on wet stone, and the odd echoing sound of voices calling across water. Evidently Romans bothered if they got too fat, for they could hear a masseur pummelling, and the grunts of a fat person enduring. And they could hear other men exercising, and the laboured puffings as they stretched down. The children envied the baths, they were so beautifully

built, it must be lovely to run down the broad steps to a great swimming pool of hot water.

Next they went to the temple, and thought better of the Romans because it was built in honour of both Sul and Minerva, 'And they could so easily have just called it after their own Minerva, and left poor Sul out,' said Selina. It was John who first saw the head carved on a shield which was part of a group over the portico. A huge bearded man gazing out of a circle of hair and beard, each strand curling out in angry S-shaped coils, the whole thing enamelled in brilliant colours.

'Goodness, look at that! What a splendid bit of work!'

Elizabeth stepped back to see better.

'I shouldn't care to meet him on a dark night.'

'It's more like the craftsmanship of the people yesterday than the design of somebody now,' said John. 'I had that sort of S-shaped engraving on my shield.'

William knew that John knew what he was talking about when it came to design.

'If the work of yesterday was good perhaps a Roman had the sense to think so and copied it, or perhaps it was carved by a Roman-Briton.'

Robert was staring fascinated at the head.

'It's a good idea remembering Sul . . . I mean, she is kind . . . she cures them, or they think she does.'

'They wouldn't need Sul to cure them now,' said William, 'the Greeks had doctors years before Christ, so I bet the Romans have too, haven't they, Mr Fosse?'

'Certainly they have, and apothecaries. Medicine, as taught by Hippocrates before Christ was born, was based on the belief that illness came from natural causes, but I suspect our farming friends still believe that diseases are a sign that they have annoyed a god or goddess. Of what good are doctors when you know only placating an angry god or goddess can cure you?'

Robert tried to find words for what he was thinking.

'Then security . . . I mean, you said it meant happiness. . . . I mean, they are still afraid.'

Mr Fosse's voice showed he was pleased Robert had said that.

'Of what good is all the might of Rome against angry gods? When your houses burn down, or there is an epidemic about, your parents deal calmly with the situation, knowing it has a natural cause. To children, whose parents believe in the vengeance of unpredictable-tempered gods, such happenings must be black shadows blotting out the sun, fear crouching in every corner like a savage beast.'

As Mr Fosse spoke for just a second the children knew what he meant; they had a cold dreadful feeling in their insides, then it was gone and they were looking at the shops.

The first shop they saw sold hot wine, it was opposite the baths, and the wine merchant seemed to be doing a roaring trade amongst those who felt in the need of a pick-me-up after bathing. All the shops were open-fronted with a store counter, behind which stood the shopkeeper, the shoppers standing on the pavement. There were all types of shops; food, cloth, jewellery, glass, pottery, in fact the sort of shops you would expect to find in a place where people went to drink the waters.

'I don't know that they sell ornaments with "A Present from Aquae Sulis" on them,' Mr Fosse said, 'but I daresay there is an equivalent.'

Selina was peering about.

'I wish I could see the people more clearly. I can't see their clothes.'

'You ought to be able to,' said William. 'You know about togas. Didn't you ever see *Julius Caesar?*'

Selina was annoyed with herself. Of course she knew what Romans wore, it was only that she had forgotten.

'I know about togas, but that's the men, I bet you can't see what the women are wearing, how their hair's done, and all that.'

Elizabeth, glad to be one up on Selina, spoke in a cocky voice.

'I can. They're wearing long-sleeved dresses with sort of tunics over them, and sort of cloaks made of oblong pieces of material. Oh, and they wear lovely necklaces and ear-rings, and their hair is done in simply masses of very fixed-looking curls.'

'Thank you for nothing,' said Selina crossly and untruthfully, for really it was too much being told things by Elizabeth. 'I meant Britons, and Roman-Britons, people who keep shops.'

Elizabeth was enjoying herself.

'Goodness! I thought you'd only be interested in posh types. If you want to know, the men have sort of tunics with proper sleeves, they are tied in at the waist with belts or cords, they wear kind of boots, and some of them have sort of hoods with capes. The women are dressed like the ones in the kitchen, only now they are wearing the shawl things over their hair. The children wear the same as the grown-ups, only the girls haven't anything on their heads.'

Mr Fosse was amused by Elizabeth.

'An excellent description. I had no idea you had begun to see so clearly, Elizabeth.'

Elizabeth sighed, it would have been gorgeous to pretend it was all seeing. But Mr Fosse was not the sort of person to pretend to.

'As a matter of fact it wasn't so much seeing, it was a film.

A pretty silly film really, but it was in technicolour and I specially noticed the clothes.'

'I could have told you it wasn't seeing.' Selina turned in a very grown-up way to Mr Fosse. 'Shall we look at the inns now, where you said visitors stayed?'

The other five could have hit her, but Mr Fosse thought inns a good idea, for they had not much more time and they ought to see them before they left.

The inn they visited was a charming-looking place, on the road in from Londinium. There were bedrooms on two sides of a walled paved courtyard. There was a big dining-room and reception-room for summer use, and smaller ones heated, from one stoke-hole, for winter. There was a great big kitchen, and three bathrooms at different temperatures, and as well a largish cold bath big enough to swim a stroke or two in. Selina, who knew how much staff was needed to keep up a place of that size, was puzzled.

'For somewhere people mostly come to only in summer, it needs an awful lot of servants, doesn't it?'

As Selina spoke the inn was full of scurrying shadows. The kitchen clamoured with cooks and their underlings. Servants ran with wine and dishes. The bathrooms were full of attendants. Everywhere there were scrubbers and cleaners.

'Slaves,' Grace gasped. 'Where do'st live, Mister?'

'At the back, they have their own quarters.'

Elizabeth shivered.

'Slaves! Are they ill-treated?'

Mr Fosse studied the running shadows.

'They are beaten, of course, if they are lazy, and they work, when necessary, for incredible hours, for they are only slaves, to be used as their master wishes. The great cruelty, and those who own them have not a glimmering of an idea that this is cruel, is that at any moment one of them may be sent to the market to be sold. It may be someone's wife, or it can be a child, for children of slaves are born slaves. If that happens the chance of ever seeing that person again is remote.'

Horrified, the children stared round, and the inn stopped seeming a pleasant place.

'Beasts,' said John. 'I knew they were beasts. I like their calling other people barbarians. I'd like to know what they are.'

'It is not only Romans who have slaves, all rich people of all races do, Britons who have married Romans included. It is barbarous, of course, but to them not wrong, for it is the natural order of things.'

There was a clatter of wheels behind them. A passenger van drawn by mules drew up. It was a light wooden vehicle, with a curved roof. As it stopped a man ran out of the inn. He was a Roman officer, very grand in his clinking uniform. Evidently the arrivals were his family, for he greeted the lady most lovingly, and he hugged the little boys to him as though he would like to eat them. Laughing and talking he led his wife across the courtyard to their rooms. The two little boys, obviously thrilled with everything, ran after them, their purple-bordered togas flying like little sails behind them. Mr Fosse said the purple border was the usual wear for freeborn children. The word 'freeborn' brought all their eyes back to the travelling cart. The lady's maid, a slave, was seeing the inn porters carried in the luggage. Then it seemed as if something made the driver, the maid, and the porters laugh, for laughter came dancing by on the wind as gay as if it were not centuries old, but had been made that minute. The children were glad to hear it, evidently even slaves could enjoy a joke.

'I don't know about you,' said Mr Fosse, 'but I am ready to leave Aquae Sulis and see what Mrs Mummery has for luncheon.'

It was a wonderful lunch, but eaten almost in silence. Bath, with its lovely terraces, looked strange standing in the place of Aquae Sulis.

'You're very silent, me dears,' said Mrs Mummery, dishing out a wonderful concoction of greengages, meringues and cream.

Elizabeth wriggled to make extra room inside herself.

'We feel silent. You didn't come, but we saw that,' she pointed down to Bath, 'when Romans had it.'

Mrs Mummery, living with Mr Fosse, was evidently used to that sort of thing.

'Did you now, very interesting I'm sure, but don't let it put you off your food.'

Mr Fosse waved away the plateful Mrs Mummery was offering him.

'I never eat such stuff, and you know it. There is some of Aquae Sulis left, Elizabeth. I thought that after lunch you should go with Mummery and have a look, all of you that is except Grace. I need her for something important.'

'Me!' said Grace. 'Why ever me, Mister?'

Mr Fosse looked mysterious.

'I am not saying. But I will tell you this much, it is to do with why I chose you to come on this journey.'

Bursting with food, the other five were driven down to Bath by Alfred. It was an odd experience, for of Aquae Sulis there was almost nothing, it was rubbed out so thoroughly the present lovely Bath seemed to be not even a relation; at least that was what the children felt until they visited what was left of the baths. They sat on the low wall round the great bath. Through the steaming green water they could see the lead floor laid down by the Romans. The terrace round it and the steps leading to the water were still there, but there were only stumps of the pillars that had held up the arches of the roof.

William swished a finger in the water.

'But why? It was fine here this morning when it was properly used. Why did people stop using it and let it fall to bits? It could be just as good now as it was when this was Aquae Sulis.'

'If it comes to that,' said Elizabeth, 'why have we stopped heating our rooms?'

Robert was hanging almost upside down over the water.

'I . . . I expect barbarians smashed everything up.'

'But even if they did somebody would remember all this. I mean, there are lots of things we don't really use now, but somebody still knows how to do them, like thatching.'

William was annoyed at stupidity.

'I must say it seems idiotic to get as far as having central heating, and good drains, and all that and then forget it. The farm people lived more comfortably than thousands of country people do now.'

Elizabeth lolled on the wall, both hands trailing in the hot water.

'And twenty million times better than most people do in towns. You ought to see the way some of them live round where I hang out in London.'

Alfred looked at his watch.

'We ought to be moving. Mr Fosse said to get you back early. There's great plans for to-morrow. We're going quite a distance.'

Elizabeth skipped off the wall.

'Real distance or Mr Fosse distance?'

'Real. Now I'm not saying anything, he wouldn't like it. But you'll see I'm right.'

Elizabeth hopped on one leg to join Alfred.

'Good. I'm all for getting around. Anyway, I want to get home to see what Mr Fosse wanted Grace for. Do you know, Alfred?'

Alfred looked very shut-faced.

'Maybe I do and maybe I don't.'

Elizabeth hung on to his arm.

'Darlingest Alfred, tell me. Come on, Selina, make him.'

Selina did not like joining with Elizabeth, but curiosity got the better of her.

'Yes, come on, tell us. What on earth could he want Grace for? I mean why Grace?'

John drew Robert and William back.

'Let them get on. Yatter, yatter. You know what girls are. I want to show you something, I found it as we came in.'

It was the bearded head from the Temple of Sul-Minerva. Not the violently-coloured head that had scowled down at them that morning, for the enamel had worn away, but it was the same head, though robbed of its majesty by being trapped in a museum, just as a lion is robbed of his majesty in a zoo. William said what they all felt.

'How beastly things look when they are only remains. Come on, let's catch up with the others.'

At the house Grace, who refused to say what she had been doing, and tea were waiting. Afterwards they were told Mr Fosse wanted them in the library. He was leaning over his big map, he had a finger on one of the small circles.

'Come here. Look, this is our next move.'

The children leant over the map.

'Whitby!' said Elizabeth.

Grace spoke possessively.

'That's Yorkshire tha' knows.'

William thought of the mileage.

'Are we going all the way in the brake?'

Mr Fosse sprang away from the map, and was over by the door before the children knew he had moved.

'No, my dear William, we are not. To-morrow we travel fast. I have chartered an aeroplane.'

CHAPTER SIX

# *In the Air*

A PRIVATE aeroplane! Only Robert had travelled in an aeroplane, and that was a public one. Travelling in a private one seemed to the children the grandest thing that would ever happen to them.

It was not a nice day for flying. The weather had turned grey and there were storm clouds about. For cold weather there were extra clothes, grey pullovers for the boys and grey cardigans for the girls, and navy blue mackintoshes with hoods and wellingtons for them all.

Mrs Mummery was not the sort of person who believed in people going long without food. They had only just unclipped their safety belts after the take-off, when she said, unpacking a basket:

'Nothin' much, me dears, just beavers.'

Alfred saw the children were puzzled.

'Elevenses, she means. Mrs M. is country-bred, her father always took what he called his beaver to work.'

Mrs Mummery passed round ginger cake and cardboard cups of lemonade.

'You get that down you, me dears.' She looked at Mr Fosse who was sitting near the pilot. 'You need to keep your strength up travelling with him. Never know where you'll be next. That's right, isn't it, Alfred?'

Alfred nodded.

'You never spoke a truer word, Mrs M.'

They had only just finished their beavers when Mr Fosse joined them.

'No handkerchiefs to-day, the clouds are our magic. Look how they blot out the land. Splendid, just what we want. See that purple cloud? That is this island as the Romans left it. Mind you, they did not leave it as we knew it yesterday. The

Empire crumbled slowly, and I don't doubt, as it crumbled, our Britons were first uneasy, and then lost that feeling of security the Romans had given them.'

'Then they stopped being happy,' said Elizabeth. 'Anyway, the slaves never were.'

'It would not be the slaves. The really poor are not as a rule worriers. When you have nothing much to lose you face losing it with the same stoicism you brought to living in poverty. It was the rest of the country who kept an anxious eye on Rome. The hastily put up fortifications, the ill-repaired public buildings, all spoke of tension. Probably towards the end there was much to be gleaned from the behaviour of leading Romans. Refusal to make long-term contracts, general jumpiness, waning faith in their country's greatness expressed in words or even more expressive gestures.'

William was staring at the purple cloud.

'Did they withdraw all their troops at once like Dunkirk?'

'Peer as I will I can never see those years clearly, but I do know in the very early days of the fifth century the Romans were gone, and the island, that purple cloud, with no Roman soldiers to protect it, had black clouds of invaders all round it, waiting to swallow it up.'

Fragments of cloud blown by the wind became semi-detached from the purple cloud, they looked like drifting smoke.

'What's oop?' Grace asked. 'Who's burnin' t'island, Mister?'

Mr Fosse shivered.

'Barbarians! They had been making raids on the island for loot for a long time. Now the raids grow fiercer. Men, women and children are being killed. Listen!'

There were screams on the wind. Age-old screams of hopelessness, despair and terror. Then Mr Fosse pointed to a huge cloud blacker than the rest, sweeping in from the east towards the purple cloud.

'Look at that.'

As is the way of clouds when looked at properly, the huge cloud took shape, and the children saw it was full of light wooden ships rowed through gigantic seas by twenty-eight rowers. As they watched they began to see the men at the oars, tall men with bright hair and moustaches, and very savage they looked.

'Goodness,' said Elizabeth, 'I bet they're pirates.'

Mr Fosse was leaning forward to see better.

'Fierce types. The Romans, who were not afraid of much, described them as sea wolves. They come from the North Sea coast, Saxons, Jutes and Angles.'

'Beasts,' said John. 'Poor Britons!'

'Beasts is right, savage, ignorant beasts, but those men when they settle will be the first Englishmen.' The children gasped in horror. 'It is true. Angles or Engles, it is after them our land is named England.'

William half stood up and pointed at the black cloud. They watched horrified as the first swarm of invaders was succeeded by another and another until the purple cloud disappeared.

Selina turned a shocked face to Mr Fosse.

'Did they kill everybody? It looks like it.'

Mr Fosse put a hand on her shoulder.

'Watch.'

The black clouds thinned for a moment and through them they could see parts of the purple cloud. They were looking at the great Roman roads, and the trackways; everything that had wheels seemed to be on those roads: farm carts, waggons, barrows piled with household things, tools, crates of chickens, and sometimes babies. There were cattle and sheep being thrashed along in an effort to make them hurry. Behind, moving as fast as possible, came people, the whole sorry procession moving westward. Not all succeeded, many fell by the way, and where they fell they lay.

'Got a nerve not stopping to pick them up,' said Elizabeth.

'They are driven by panic, and panic is a terrible master. Look what is happening now.'

It was only a quick look the children had before further black clouds blotted out their view, but it was enough. Horse-drawn chariots and travelling waggons loaded with rich possessions were whipped along the roads at a furious pace, with no regard for the other travellers, carts were overturned, people mowed down.

William was not easily upset, but he turned away in disgust. 'Where are they trying to get to?'

'As far from the invaders as possible, which is west. You cannot blame them for being afraid, these barbarians come from a barren part of Germany, from which they have never been able to scratch a decent living. They never came under Roman influence, and by the standards of Roman Britain are utterly uncivilized. No barbarian can write, and most of the inhabitants who can write you have seen taking to the roads, so there is no history of what happened, as there was when the Romans came. The Romans could record events as they occurred, but without records we can only have a pretty good guess. Look at our clouds, perhaps we shall see something.'

The children could see, and seeing, understood why so much that the Romans gave was forgotten. The invaders were a good-looking lot, but utterly primitive in their behaviour. They rushed through towns and villages howling with joy at loot, but half the time unaware of the purpose of what they found. What was drainage to people who had never conceived a purpose for drains? They had dishes of a type in their homes, but they bore no resemblance to what they found, and in any case they were living off the country and did not want home refinements, so they smashed much of the pottery and glass. They knew what kitchens were for, but thought nothing of the Roman-British ones, for meat was their diet, and there were no arrangements for cooking joints. As a sea-going race they were used to water from the transport point of view, and had fun splashing about in baths, but how could they guess people existed who had baths in their homes, and heated water so that they should be clean? Still less could they guess what the heating arrangements were for; they crawled under the hot rooms, searching amongst the terra-cotta pipes for loot which often they found, and as well unlucky creatures who for some reason had not fled with their families, and these they usually murdered, though the stronger might be kept as slaves. It was a horrid picture of blood, and smashing for smashing's sake.

Selina was the first to give in.

'I can't look any more.'

'Nor can I,' said Elizabeth. 'I should think it's hateful there now.'

Robert had turned quite green.

'It . . . it must be terrible . . . they may be the beginning of us, but they were beasts. . . .'

Mr Fosse sounded as if he did not think much of what he had seen either.

'They were hard times. But wait a moment, let about a hundred and thirty years blow by.'

They waited. Then it happened. The south-eastern edge of the cloud turned silver, then slowly a soft glow began to cover the whole.

Elizabeth, who still felt Mr Fosse would fool her if he could, spoke firmly.

'That's only the sun breaking through the clouds.'

Mr Fosse's eyes twinkled.

'As you say, Elizabeth, but I myself am not looking at the sun, but at Augustine landing at Kent with forty missionaries.'

'What a lot happens in Kent,' said John. 'That's where I told the '43 people the Romans had landed.'

Selina did not like the way John said 'I told.'

'I suppose you've never been abroad, but if you had you'd know that Dover to Calais is still the quickest sea route.'

The others, even Robert, had their mouths open to squash Selina for that, but Mr Fosse spoke first.

'The head of the Church is by now called Pope, it came from Papa or loving father, and it is he who has sent the party over to make Christians of the heathen Anglo-Saxons.'

William knew some Church history.

'But there are Christians here already, haven't any of them stayed put?'

'Probably, but my guess is the first Christians were mainly the better off and better educated, and many have evacuated to the west. Those that are about are not likely to have spent their time trying to convert the Anglo-Saxons, they probably like thinking they are among the damned.'

The sun struggled to shine through the clouds and for a moment or two there was nothing but a bright mist. Mr Fosse told them to look down when that mist cleared for they would be crossing the Humber in the year 664. He said the country by now was divided into seven parts, and as they flew across the Humber they were in the part called Northumbria where, at Whitby at this very moment, a synod or meeting was being held to decide whether the Anglo-Saxon Christians converted by Augustine and his missionaries, or Christians from Scotland, Ireland and the west who were followers of a man called Aidan, were the best sort of Christians.'

'Who won?' asked Elizabeth.

'The followers of Augustine.'

William sounded annoyed.

'So that was how we all became Roman Catholics, was it?'

'Very idiotic of us to have two sorts of being Christians,' said Selina. 'Only 664 years after Christ you would think there would be only one way.'

Elizabeth looked scornfully at Selina.

'I wouldn't. Look at all the sorts there are now, you can be Salvation Army, or Church, or Roman, or Chapel, or . . .'

Grace interrupted.

'M'auntie's a Plymouth Brethren.'

'There's a lot round us are Quakers,' said John.

Mr Fosse nodded.

'There are endless kinds of Christians. So strange, for Christ was clear as to how his followers should live, but it is not on a way of living that the various types of Christians differ, but the way of worshipping.'

Robert hesitated before he spoke.

'I would think that living . . . I mean that living like a Christian matters most. . . .'

'So would I, Robert,' Mr Fosse agreed, 'but it has never been so. Anyway, after that synod at Whitby the Roman form of Christianity is the accepted form, and a very good thing too, because if the form used by the followers of Aidan, called the Celtic form, had been accepted, it would have cut the island off from the rest of Europe and so from learning.'

William did not think being a Roman Catholic could be a good thing to be.

'I bet there are some who don't follow the Roman way.'

Mr Fosse was amused.

'I expect you are right. There are always people who feel they show they are captains of their souls by worshipping God in a different way from other people.'

John saw he must now accept the Anglo-Saxons as the beginning of England, but he still felt a fondness for the Britons, and thought Mr Fosse had forgotten how well the hill people had lived.

'A very good thing too, I should think, the people in '43 did more things the way they liked doing them than anybody has since.'

The others disagreed. The Romans might have kept people as slaves, but they felt that so far the Roman occupation was the best period of time in which to have lived. Mr Fosse understood why John stood up for the '43 people.

'John's got a right to his own opinions. I daresay if he had lived after the synod of Whitby he would have been one of the originals who worshipped in a different way from his neighbours. And why not? Freedom to pray in your own way is a very important part of being free.'

The pilot signalled they were landing, and were to fasten their safety belts.

Elizabeth looked down at Whitby, round which they were circling.

'When we land who are we going to see this time?'

Mr Fosse finished fastening his belt.

'Wouldn't the pilot be surprised if he knew he was landing us in the year 866?'

## CHAPTER SEVEN

# *Whitby*

THEY stayed in what Elizabeth described as 'a posh hotel.' It was full, so four of the children had to share rooms. Mr Fosse had told Alfred they were to draw lots for who had the single rooms. Grace drew one and Robert the other. None of the boys wanted the single room as it was dull being alone; Grace and Elizabeth would have liked to have shared and given Selina the room to herself, but Alfred said that Mr Fosse had said there was to be no deciding amongst themselves.

'Oh, my goodness,' Elizabeth grumbled to Mrs Mummery, 'I only hope we don't stay long, I don't fancy being shut up with Miss High-and-Mighty prancing around giving herself airs all over the place.'

Mrs Mummery's fat laugh rumbled out.

'Who knows but what she's thinkin' the same thing, me dear, but you may have a surprise comin'. It wouldn't startle me if you and Selina finish up proper good friends.'

'Wouldn't it?' said Elizabeth, 'well, it would me.'

'We'll see, me dear, anyway what's sharing a room for a night or two? It'll all come out in the wash.'

After a lunch the children thought splendid because there was duck, but Mrs Mummery, who despised food that was not home-cooked, considered unhealthy, the children, wearing mackintoshes and wellingtons, explored Whitby. They shared buying a guide-book.

'What d'you suppose we ought to look at?' William asked.

John turned over the pages.

'There's nothing left of 866 as far as I can see.'

'Good,' said Elizabeth, 'then we can look at to-day, which will make a nice change, and I want to buy a postcard to send my mum.'

William too wanted postcards, but he did not want Mr Fosse to think they had wasted their time.

'Isn't there one important ruin we could just look at?'

Elizabeth made a face at William.

'Come on, worry-guts, what's the good of looking if there is? It won't be a ruin when the handkerchiefs are on us.'

'And he'll rub out all to-day's Whitby,' Selina added, 'he always does.'

The postcard-buying, followed by slot machines on the pier, followed by ices, won. The afternoon made quite a hole in what was left of their money, but they none of them cared, they had enjoyed themselves, and came back to the hotel in roaring spirits.

Mr Fosse did not ask how they had spent their time. He came into their sitting-room while they were finishing an enormous shrimp tea.

'I had not thought we could go out to-night but the rain has stopped so we will leave in half an hour. We are going to a party.'

Mr Fosse's magic did not only happen with seeing and hearing, it happened with shooting-brakes, for there was one outside the door just like the one they had left behind. The children were most impressed. They were impressed, too, with the grand way Mr Fosse did things. Most people would not be able to build on somebody's estate, but that was what Mr Fosse had done. He had built a great barn. It was made of wood; Mr Fosse said he should have used oak, but good timber was scarce and he had to use what he could get. The roof, which was thatched, was supported by wooden rafters, in the centre was a hole. Inside the barn it was not easy to see clearly, for only a little light came through the glassless windows, but peering upwards the children saw a fine building, which did not look like the work of barbarians, but the work of craftsmen with good eyes for proportion. There was dignity in the height, and grace in the way wood was used to fashion the beams and rafters. They had come in under a porch and stood just inside the entrance peering round rather puzzled.

'It's a barn,' said Selina. 'I thought you said there was going to be a party, Mr Fosse.'

Mr Fosse chuckled.

'So there will be, and this is not the first time you will have been to a party in such a place, Selina, for this is the Hall. Nowadays we call it the Village Hall, or perhaps the British Legion Hall, but whatever we call it, it is a distant relation of this Hall, for although this one has been built by a settlement of Anglo-Saxons, or Saxons, as we will call them for short, for their chief to live in, it has a double purpose, for it is intended, just as halls are to-day, to be the centre of the lives of the community living around it.'

John fingered one of the great beams which supported the roof.

'They are good craftsmen, these chappies, they've come on a lot since they landed, haven't they?'

Mr Fosse gave the beam a little pat as if he loved it.

'They have indeed, I suspect they seldom mention their savage ancestors nowadays, they are Christians and have lived down their shady past.'

William looked at the glassless windows, and the hole in the roof obviously intended for smoke to escape. It seemed a fine Hall from what he could see of it, but it did not appear to have half the comfort the Romans had known.

'What I can't understand is why once they settled down and all that they haven't used the Roman towns and villas. They didn't smash the lot, you would have thought somebody would have had the sense to look round and put things together, and see what they'd been used for.'

Mr Fosse called to Alfred to fetch some torches from the brake, then he turned to William.

'Ghosts. That was the trouble. Most of them were scared of any place people had lived in, they thought they were haunted and called them cold harbours and left them severely alone.'

William thought it pretty idiotic of the Anglo-Saxons to be afraid of ghosts.

'Did they leave the roads alone too?'

'Not because of ghosts. They often left the roads and tracks alone for fear of their leading invaders to their homes. This avoiding of Roman roads has had a lot to do with the layout of England. If you notice many of our villages are not on main roads, but are reached by lanes, and this is because these Saxons or Angles, I hate hyphens, they sound so unfriendly, have cleared living places for themselves on moorlands, hillsides and forests, as far as possible from tell-tale roads which could lead invaders to their doors.'

A question had formed in Robert's mind while Mr Fosse was speaking.

'Then . . . what I mean is . . . I mean, if they are scared of ghosts it hasn't helped being Christians. . . . I mean they're still afraid.'

Mr Fosse smiled.

'You will find plenty of people to-day, possibly good Christians, who are afraid of ghosts, Robert.'

Elizabeth had been prowling round, now she skipped back to the entrance.

'Of course there are, Robert. I bet you wouldn't stop alone in a house where somebody had been murdered.'

Elizabeth said 'murdered' in so dramatic a way that the Hall seemed darker and more full of shadows than it really was. They were glad to see Alfred with the torches. Mr Fosse signalled to him not to hand them round for a moment.

'Becoming Christians has cleared away some fears, but freedom from all fear is something we are still groping for, and is still only won by the few whose faith is really great. Give them each a torch, Mummery.'

The torches were strong, and by their light the children saw the barn was partly furnished. Down one side ran a sort of platform, on which was a wooden table and chairs, and sideways to the table on the platform were trestle-tables and benches. The corner to the right of the platform seemed furnished as a separate room. In the middle of the Hall was a stone, obviously for the fire. At the far end, away from the platform, were little cubicles made of wood. Round the walls were iron brackets. Mr Fosse seemed proud of his Hall, and led them round to be sure they missed nothing. He said they were only looking at bare bones, everything else, such as tapestries, they would see when their eyes were covered; he could have put up imitations, but he was not going to insult the ladies, who were most beautiful weavers, or the craftsmen, by showing fakes when soon they could see the real work.

Selina wanted to see where the weaving was done. This took them to the corner of the Hall furnished like a separate room.

Mr Fosse said it would be curtained later, it was a bower or bur for the ladies. It was obviously a bedroom, for there were wooden bunks built into the wall rather like bunks on a ship. There was a table, stools and wooden clothes' chests.

'Again bare bones,' said Mr Fosse, 'no people, no furnishings, no bed linen, no knick-knacks, no curtains, all these will come.'

Selina found the loom. It was a better loom than had been used before. Weights had gone out of fashion, and instead a roller was used at the bottom, a great improvement, she thought, because it meant longer lengths could be woven. Mr Fosse stroked the loom as if he loved it.

'Glorious materials they make, Selina. They have a splendid colour sense, as you will see: scarlets, blues, purples flare together, they even use gold, mostly for head-dresses.'

'Does 'ter mean real gold, Mister?' Grace asked.

'Certainly real gold. Thin sheets beaten flat and cut into the finest wire.'

Elizabeth thought of her mother who was always doing something: cleaning the house, shopping, washing-up, there was no end to it, certainly no time to sit and weave tapestries and gold wire into head-dresses.

'Who does the house if they're weaving tapestries and stuff all day?'

'This Hall we are in is the home of the landowner. Each group of Anglo-Saxons live round a hall like this, and call themselves either a Tun, a Worth or a Ham. Make a list sometime of the Hams, Worths and Tuns you know of, and you will usually find they were once Saxon settlements. Thanes are well-to-do important fellows, and it is their ladies who weave fine tapestries and such.'

'But where do people who aren't important live?' John asked.

Mr Fosse swept his arms out, as if drawing an armload of people to him.

'Just here. This site was selected of course because there is water nearby, which not only provides for themselves and their animals, but fills a moat which runs outside the defences, which surround the settlement. First they cleared the land, then they built this Hall, and round it farm buildings and storage sheds. Then they laid out gardens for fruit, vegetables and herbs and quite possibly put some beehives in the herb garden. Then, and this is very important to them, at the side of this Hall they left a piece of land clear. This is common land, they call it the Moot-Green. In the middle of the green their ancestors, as soon as they became Christians, built their church. The people livė in huts round the green, their huts are this Hall in miniature, made of wood with a hearthstone in the middle and a thatched roof with a hole instead of a chimney, but the walls are mud, not wattle and daub, as these are. We would have visited a hut but the Hall is the right place for us to-night, for all the people in the huts are coming here to the party.'

Selina thoroughly understood everyone being invited to the Hall.

'What sort of party?'

'To entertain important visitors. These Anglo-Saxons are great ones for feasts.'

John was puzzling over the layout of the settlement.

'Just those gardens can't keep everybody going. What about their cattle? Where are they grazed?'

'Outside the defences, looked after by herdsmen. Farming goes on inside the defences, they have a good farming system: all land suitable for crop growing belonging to these people is the property of all free men in the settlement, but of course they want their own pieces of land, so it's divided up. The thane sees to the dividing, but it is planned what all shall grow. What they grow, of course, is what they most need: grain for bread, barley for beer, flax for the linen they weave, and so on; but whatever the crops grown, all crop-growing land has a rest year, for they know about starved land. Just now, as it is August, the working fields are probably being harvested, but the resting fields will have cattle grazing on them, so that they get manured for next year. Crop-growing land is divided into allotments, a fair arrangement, for they draw lots for which allotment in each field each has, so that nobody gets pushed off with only bad patches.'

William's mind had turned with interest to the church.

'Where does the parson live?'

Mr Fosse chuckled.

'They have what seems a splendid arrangement for him, but it is one that has caused a lot of trouble ever since. You ask your father. They give him a piece of land to live on, which is called his glebe, and everybody gives him one-tenth of their crops to keep him, and that tenth is called his tithe, and is stored for him in his tithe barn.'

'What I can't see,' said William, 'is what the earth defences and the moat are for. There's nobody about, is there? Who are they afraid of?'

Mr Fosse turned to Grace.

'You tell him.'

Grace, which puzzled the others, flushed.

'Vikings.'

The moment Grace answered, William saw what a silly question that was. Vikings . . . he had forgotten about them.

'Of course. I knew really, but seeing things when they happen, I forget what's going to happen.'

Mr Fosse seemed pleased.

'So you should. Live in the present, that is what we want to try and do. Just a snatch of time, we don't see much, but enough to titillate the appetite I hope, and tempt some of you to real meals later on.' He gave one of his cat-like springs. 'Come along, come along. We shall be late. Mummery! Mummery! Bring the handkerchiefs.'

It was so odd, they had not been conscious of any to-day noises in the Hall, but the moment the handkerchiefs were on they found that there had been, because they noticed that a train, an aeroplane, and from somewhere a wireless playing popular tunes faded out of earshot. With the handkerchiefs new sounds filled the air. Such a bustle was going on. Copper pans clattering in the kitchen. The slop-slop of running feet. Light laughter from women and children behind the curtains of their bower. Then smells came. Before the Hall had smelt of new clean wood, now it was full of smells. First good cooking smells. The kitchen was at the side of the hall, there was a smoke smell, so obviously the cooking was done on an open fire. Only too clearly too, washing did not mean much to Anglo-Saxons, for there was the rancid smell of unwashed bodies. Mr Fosse heard the children sniffing.

'Better get used to it,' he whispered, 'it'll be much worse when the feast starts.'

Evidently it was getting near the time for the feast. Round the high table on the platform the tapestry was hanging. Lovely work in gay colours. Below, the children saw pegs, Mr Fosse said they would be used by the thane and his guests to hang their shields on. Then suddenly the Hall was full of servants. Robert nudged Mr Fosse.

'Slaves?'

'Those who are not free men; either descendants of Britons who were here when they landed, and have not come up in the world, or Saxons who have gone down in the world.' He spoke so that all the children could hear. 'The kinsmen of a free man are paid if he is killed. Free men have a value on their lives in money. That is to say, if a free man is killed the punishment for the man who kills him is having to pay his kinsmen what he is worth. The amount is fixed, from a king down to a tradesman. Herdsmen and such are not free, and so have no price.'

The children were indignant.

'Ought to be ashamed of themselves,' said Elizabeth. 'Call themselves Christians.'

Mr Fosse's reed-like voice cut through their anger.

'Patience, patience. Be fair. It is the custom of the time. No one, not even the slaves themselves, think a sin is being committed. In fact, a sin is not being committed, a man only does wrong when he knows what he does to be wrong. If you could speak to these people, they would not know what you were talking about, when you said having people to work for you for nothing was wrong. At times they all work for nothing. A king—and there are kings at this time—call on men like this thane here to bring his men, when called upon, for special service, especially to fight if need arises. The parson takes as his right part of the work of every man. There are farmers, you will see some here to-night, who either own their land or farm land owned by their thane, and they work for and give service to the thane, and so do those who work for them. The peasants living here get no wages, merely those strips of land, and they have any amount of free service to give, especially keeping the earth fortifications and moat in order, and, of course, they must go with their thane when he orders them. Even the men with a trade: potters, carpenters, fishermen and so on, who have taken service with the thane, and receive payment in kind and wages, will probably have to render service as well.'

William felt Mr Fosse thought they were being a bit dense, seeing things only from the point of view of their own day.

'It must be so awful having nobody on your side. No laws to help you.'

Mr Fosse stuck to his point.

'There is law. This putting a value on a man in money works as well for injury. Even if a toenail of a man is damaged it has got its value. As well, there is a very pleasant right belonging to all free men, and women, they must be allowed to enjoy their homes without interference.'

'Good job too,' said Elizabeth, 'nobody wants snoopers sticking their noses in other people's business.'

'That's right,' Grace agreed. 'Sends me dad mad, that does.'

John remembered his father and mother's rage at being asked to fill in a questionnaire about their home.

'A very good law.'

'But who decides if he is guilty?' William asked.

'It is decided by something called "ordeal." Tests by fire and water, not being blistered or drowned. To them I think this means leaving it to God to decide.'

William hated to nag, but he had to.

'But they don't think God will decide if slaves are guilty? I call that a bit thick.'

Mr Fosse patted William's arm.

'I think the law does help slaves indirectly. Punishments, especially for stealing, are pretty severe, you can be outlawed, or you can be made a slave. Where you can go down you can climb up. There will be freed men about.'

The Hall was now full of flickering light. Rush torches soaked in tallow had been placed in each of the brackets.

'They have candles,' Mr Fosse whispered, 'but torches are used for this sort of thing.'

Grace screwed up her nose.

'Don't half smell, do they?'

Selina put her handkerchief to her nose.

'The whole place smells terrible.'

They all agreed with her, but they were not going to tell her so. Mr Fosse chuckled.

'You boys had better be ready to carry Selina out when the Hall fills up. There are no bathrooms, Selina, no soap, and no system of drainage.'

The slaves were strewing the earth floor with fresh rushes. Grace watched them with approval.

'That's a champion idea, that is. Quick ter sweep up, an' it'll take most of t' muck out wi' it.'

A new sound came on the evening wind. Very faint at first, but a little clearer as the children's minds knew what it was they were hearing. Selina, used to the hunting-field, recognized it first.

'That's a horn.'

William felt he could almost see the hornblower.

'It will be the visitors coming to the feast I expect. That horn sounds an awful long way off.'

Mr Fosse, at the sound of the horn, had sprung towards the entrance with one of his little cat-like jumps.

'It is. The stone on which the visitors are standing to blow the horn is called the Mark, it is at the edge of a clearing, which is the boundary to the whole estate, and Heaven help the stranger who tries to enter without sounding his horn on the Mark.'

The horn seemed to have been waited for by everybody. There were shouts, and the clip-clop of horses' feet breaking into a canter until the sound died in the distance. There was a gabble of excited voices outside. There was a crescendo of laughter and talk from the ladies' bower, and as for the servants, they were rushing round like madmen, urged on by shouts from the cooks. Mr Fosse was amused by the cooks; he said it was a pity Mrs Mummery was not with them, she would see that cooks did not change much.

The Hall began to fill up. The first to arrive, pressed forward

by those outside, were a band of musicians. The children did not see them at first, it was only when they settled down and blew into, or pulled on the strings of their instruments and they heard them that they saw them. They were a rather raggety-taggety party, but cheerful-looking. There was a harpist, a fiddler and a flautist. The flute was played by a boy of about ten, who by his looks was the son of the harpist. All three wore long-sleeved tunics, one was dull green, one brown and the boy's was bright red. They had shoes of skin, fastened with thongs, and leather belts. The musicians had no sooner settled themselves than the benches began to fill up; the children did not see this at first, it was their noses told them, but when they accepted what their noses had to say they could see pretty clearly. The Saxons seemed a primitive, savage-looking lot, but full of good spirits. Most of the men had beards and moustaches, though some of the younger ones were clean-shaven. The men and boys' clothes varied from the simple tunic with a cloak, such as the musicians wore, to more elaborate tunics with leggings with cross-gartering, or with leggings cut off at the knee, and then starting again at the calf with cross-gartering to the ankles. Every man, and even boys of about fifteen, were armed, in their belts were daggers and battle-axes, some carried spears and a few had swords.

Selina whispered in William's ear.

'How odd to come to a feast with all those weapons. If I was the thane I'd tell them to leave them outside.'

William thought that a particularly Selina-ish remark.

'Not if you lived now, you wouldn't. You never know when you're going to need them, suppose the Vikings come while they're having supper.'

The fashion of the day for women and girls seemed to be a

tunic to the feet of a gay colour, on top of this some wore a sort of cape in a contrasting colour, with a hole for their heads, so that it fell with folds back and front to the knees. Round many of their heads was a coloured handkerchief worn like a hood. They had girdles, a few with a kind of handbag attached. A good many had jewellery of a sort, necklaces of fine lumps of colour, and some had brooches. All had made some attempt at following the fashion, but Mr Fosse said some of them simply had not the time to do much about beautifying themselves, apart from looking after the children, doing the housework and feeding and waiting on their husbands, they had outside work such as looking after the animals and chickens. Not that they must get the idea the men were not fair to women, they were, treating them in most ways as partners.

The effect when the tables were full was a brilliant mass of colour. Robert had his nose lifted to detect a special smell from the mixed smells circling round, and suddenly he had it. He leant forward, as if he could see more clearly that way.

'Look—dogs. They've brought their dogs to the feast.'

It was quite true. The moment Robert spoke they saw them. Lying under the tables, or prowling round the hall were any number of dogs, most of them looked as if they were great-great-grandfathers of to-day's sheepdogs or greyhounds.

The thane, followed by his wife, family and guests, stepped up to the high table. The lady of the house looked magnificent. She had two tunics, one worn over the other, the upper one and her cloak handsomely embroidered. Her head-dress, with gold threads running through it, was of blue silk, held in place by a gold fillet, and as she stepped on to the low platform she lifted her skirt, and the children saw beneath it she wore what looked like a petticoat of white linen. But it was not her dress which

caught the eye so much as her accessories, which were very rich-looking. Her belt was gilded, and its buckle shimmered with jewels, and from it hung a gold hanger on which there was a big key. She had two fine brooches, and a necklace of great lumps of amethyst. Elizabeth was impressed, and to cover this, muttered:

'Doesn't half think she's somebody.'

Mr Fosse was amused.

'She is somebody. A lady of considerable importance in her community, for it is she who is responsible for the distribution of bread, and as well she has a lot to do with the running of the estate.'

The thane was a fine-looking man. Very fair, with hair to his shoulders and an important beard and moustache. He wore a tunic of iron rings, a yellow cape edged with blue; grey leggings and a round helmet, with an iron frame and horn crown, on the top of which was a small metal bird. When he came to the table he was carrying a shield of iron and wood, but before he sat down he hung this on the peg on the wall above his chair. From his belt hung a wooden scabbard for his sword.

The thane's family, at least those old enough to come to the table, were two boys and two girls. The girls were dressed much like their mother, but without her fine jewels, and they wore nothing over their heads, their hair was plaited and kept in place with fillets round their foreheads. The boys wore brightly-coloured tunics, which had hems and necklines of contrasting colours.

The guest was obviously an important man. The children did not think he was as good-looking as the thane, but he was more grandly dressed. He had a son with him, a boy of about eleven or twelve, which seemed to be about the age of the thane's eldest boy. Evidently quite a number of the guest's people had travelled with him, for the thane's people moved up and down the trestle-tables to make room for them. It was while this was going on that John noticed wells cut in the tables, and asked Mr Fosse what they were for. There was so much noise that Mr Fosse did not have to whisper.

'Salt. It's a sort of social register. Look at the visitor's men, see, some of them are finding places above the salt-well, and some below it; seems funny to us, but it means a lot to them.'

The priest was the last person to come to the high table. His head was shaved at the crown, and his hair left in a fringe all round. He was wearing a long-sleeved tunic to his feet, of a greyish colour, and a dark cloak, but he took the cloak off and hung it on a peg intended for a shield. Before he sat down he said a grace in Latin.

It was amazing what Saxons could eat. Food was waiting on a service table, and the moment grace had been said it was passed round, and what food! The children gaped at what was eaten. The showpiece, and that was carried to the high table, was a huge boar's head, but what was placed on the lower tables seemed enough to feed a large town. There were joints, some roasted, some boiled. There were great plates of fish,

mostly eels. There was soup and all kinds of eggs, and in case anyone had any space left, cheese, butter and flat loaves of coarse bread. The food was eaten off wooden plates, either cut up with the daggers from the men's belts, or eaten in the fingers. To drink there was buttermilk for the women, and something, judging by their rising spirits, far stronger for the men. Mr Fosse said it might be mead, made of honey, or it could be ale. Whatever anybody drank, it had to be tipped straight down, for drink was served in horns, which would not stand up. At the high table the drink was taken in blue glass tumblers, ornamented with a nice bubbly design, but they could not be put down either, as they had no stems but rounded bottoms.

The Hall grew hotter and hotter, and the men grew gayer and gayer. As the food disappeared, and it was eaten in an eager, wolfish way, tongues loosened, laughter rose, and there

was singing to the musicians' music. Belts were let out, belching was general, the floor was covered in bones thrown to the dogs; in fact, of manners, as the children knew them, there were none at all. After the meal, when the feast seemed to be turning into what the children thought was meant by the word 'orgy,' the lady of the house rose and, followed by her daughters, went into her bower, and presently the women at the trestle-tables left the Hall for their homes.

Elizabeth looked at the curtains separating the ladies' bower from the main hall. She was yawning from the heat and the smell.

'What a place to try and sleep in! Poor things, might as well try to sleep in Piccadilly of a Saturday night.'

Grace stifled an enormous yawn.

'What 'appens if there's bairns?'

Selina was cross from trying to keep awake.

'It's disgusting, such behaviour, such a row and such a smell.'

For once nobody argued with Selina, for nobody could say it was not noisy and smelly.

John's eyes were trying to close, but he was still interested.

'Where do the guests and that sleep?'

Mr Fosse turned him round to look at the cubicles. In each was a rough bed covered with an animal skin. John laughed.

'I shouldn't care to sleep here when this feast's over; shocking state the Hall will be in.'

Mr Fosse laughed too.

'Funny mixture these Anglo-Saxons. Slow, stupid, stubborn lot in many ways, and greedy eaters and drinkers, but, bless them, great believers in the right of the freeborn to enjoy the fruits of hard labour, and in their right to have their say in the running of their affairs. A bit backward, there is so much they could learn from Europe, but will they? Not a bit of it, they stick to their own ways and are quite satisfied.'

John, for all he thought their behaviour rather crude, liked what he had seen of the Saxons.

'And they're good craftsmen. Look at the jewellery, and the armour, and all that, and look at this Hall.'

Mr Fosse spoke softly.

'And look at all of you, you are nearly asleep.'

All in one second, as the handkerchiefs came off, 866 disappeared and the present swept back. The rain had cleared off, the sky was full of stars. Overhead an aeroplane light twinkled, the distant wireless was still blaring popular music. The children blinked, the change was so sudden that their minds were still in the past.

'I wonder what the guest came for,' William wondered.

'I can tell you that,' said Mr Fosse, 'for you will see him

to-morrow. He came to bring his son who, with the thane's eldest boy, is to be sent to the monastery near here to be educated.'

* * *

The next day was gloriously fine. Mr Fosse almost skipped he was so pleased. The children were finishing breakfast when he came in. Elizabeth spoke with her mouth full.

'Where are we going to-day?'

Mr Fosse, with one of his quick cat-like movements, came round the table to behind her chair.

'Let us see if you can guess.'

Elizabeth turned her head and gave Mr Fosse a wink to show she was hoping to get a rise out of Selina.

'I can't imagine. Can you guess, Selina?'

Selina felt Miss Marion's approving pat on her shoulders. 'Borthwick girls do not show off, Selina, but answer quietly, displaying both in words, and by their behaviour, where they were educated.'

'I should suppose we were going to the monastery.'

Elizabeth turned wide amazed eyes on Selina.

'You wouldn't!' She looked round the table. 'Whatever made her think of that?'

They all laughed. Selina forgot Borthwick and gave Elizabeth's leg, which was within reach, a kick.

The kick did not hurt Elizabeth much, but it gave her a chance to ask in a most aggravating tone:

'Where *were* you brought up, Selina Edgecombe?'

Mr Fosse did not appear to have noticed there was an argument going on, but he heard Elizabeth's last words.

'That is a very proper question for this morning, for we are going to see what we can of the manner in which those boys will be brought up. Hurry now, the brake will be outside in a quarter of an hour.'

It was just like being at Mr Fosse's home. Alfred drove and Mr Fosse sat beside him; inside was Mrs Mummery, the big picnic basket and the children. The only thing extra was a large groundsheet. Mrs Mummery kept it beside her.

'No lunch for anybody, and that means Mr Fosse too, who sits off this sheet. I don't want you all in bed with chills, me dears. No better way to get upset than sitting on damp ground.'

The groundsheet was laid out on a hilltop where they could look down over Whitby's miles of sand, busy harbour, promenade, sea-wall, hotels, houses, streets and shops, to her distant moors. They heard the hum of traffic, a babble of voices from nearby picnickers, aeroplanes, the siren of a pleasure steamer, then the handkerchiefs were on, and the magic began, the whirling rainbow-coloured lights, then blackness and silence.

The monastery crept slowly to their ears, as if it were difficult for it to force its sounds through the barriers of time. The first recognizable sound to reach the children was a bell. Clang! Clang! Clang-clang! William recognized it first.

'That's a church bell.'

Mr Fosse sounded as if he too were listening.

'Certainly a bell calling to prayer, but it may be rung by hand.'

The next sound was footsteps, the unhurried tread of country people who know what has to be done with the working hours of the year, and so go quietly from task to task.

'Field-workers,' Mr Fosse whispered, 'that bell is calling them to the early afternoon service, Sext they call it. Shall we follow them? You must use your ears, noses and eyes well, for look as I will, I can never see this monastery clearly.'

Seeing came slowly, and when it did they had a surprise. John was the first to spot it.

'There are nuns as well as monks.'

Mr Fosse explained that there were mixed monasteries at this time. That this mixed monastery was called Streanaeshalch. The church from the outside was something the same shape as the Hall, but it had a cross on the roof. Inside, it was clearly a church, it even, as Robert pointed out, felt like a church, which Mr Fosse said was to be expected, as it had been prayed in for over two hundred years. There was a stone carved font, an altar covered in exquisite tapestry, with a linen altar cloth, and on it a gold cross. At the side of the altar a fine linen cloth lay over a chalice and paten, which Mr Fosse thought were probably made of gold. The windows were small and high up, so not much light came through them, but hanging by chains from the middle of the roof was a sort of wooden chandelier, with candles in it, and as well there were bowls, also hanging by chains, which had wicks in them burning in fat. There were fine carved chairs for those who took the services. Mr Fosse said that if they could look in the chests belonging to the Order they would be sure to find splendid woven altar frontals, vestments, fine linen and valuable church plate, for monasteries were always receiving expensive presents.

The service was in Latin, and anyway none of the children could hear it clearly, so they looked round at the congregation. It was not all nuns and monks, for there were a few ordinary people there as well, and amongst them they saw the thane and his lady, and the eldest boy and last night's guest and his boy. Robert thought of his first day at school and was sorry for the boys.

'I . . . I should think they feel pretty awful.'

Mr Fosse had guessed how Robert felt about his school.

'They won't have so bad a time, we will have a look presently.'

Grace's nose made her turn her head.

'Eeh, look!'

They looked and a sad sight they saw. Men, women and children, thin, dirty, in rags, most of them diseased, some were blind, some had lost a leg or an arm. The children drew together, hating such misery, and yet forced to look, and as they watched they grew angry. Robert was so shocked he spoke without stammering.

'People like that thane over there have got plenty of food, you would think nobody need be beggars.'

'Selfish beasts,' said Selina, 'ought to be ashamed of themselves; if I could I'd tell the thane what I thought of him.'

Grace nodded.

'He'd 'ave a piece of my mind, he would an' all.'

Mr Fosse's whisper silenced them.

'There have always been poor and helpless. There has been no room in anybody's life for passengers, everyone has had to work. Each family has their own problems, an old person to care for, a cripple perhaps. These people were nobody's business. There is plenty of room for the strong, but precious little for the weak.'

William was frowning.

'Where do they come from? They must be somebody's relations.'

Mr Fosse said if it came to that where did any beggars come from? The forefathers of these could have been outlawed, or descendants of Britons, or Roman-Britons, who were too poor stock to be worth using as slaves; whoever they were they were fortunate in the date in which they lived. A few hundred years ago they would have had little hope of survival, there were always generous people who helped them, but to the majority, people such as these were vermin who would be better dead. With the coming of Christianity the outlook on the poor and humble completely changed.

'Everybody joining a religious order vows to be poor, for it is living as Christ lived. So all monasteries certainly feed, and to a certain extent care for, these beggars, and people outside, such as our thane, will probably give them food and a night's shelter if they want it, because it is accepted as a Christian duty.'

The children looked again at the beggars. They did not look cared for. Selina turned away in disgust.

'They don't look as if anybody bothered about them much. Dirty torn clothes and those horrible sores, somebody might bandage them up.'

Mr Fosse, in his gentlest voice, stilled Selina's impatience.

'The problem of vagrants has never been settled. They will take so much help, but they shy away from anything approaching restraint. There may be an infirmary, we will have a look later, but none of these people would stay in it for treatment. Medicine, I think we shall find, apart from very rough surgery, is mainly faith healing, backed by some admirable herb remedies.'

'Then a monastery is a sort of town hall,' said Elizabeth. The others, not having her London knowledge, looked puzzled. 'You go to the town hall for everything; you know, like when sombody thinks they're paying too much rent or that.'

Mr Fosse laughed.

'Scarcely a town hall. Monasteries are distant relations to all those societies, religious and otherwise, who, through the centuries, have tried to help people such as these.'

Robert caught the idea.

'You . . . you mean this monastery, and all monasteries, are the first sort of social service. . . . I mean, somewhere people like these beggars can go and be sure of people being kind and . . . well, I mean, anyway trying to help them.'

Mr Fosse was moving.

'That's the idea. Now come along, let's go and see what else we can see.'

The first place they visited was the kitchens. The children were surprised at what a lot of food there seemed about. Mr Fosse said, as a Benedictine order, the monks and nuns should only have one meal a day, and that not meat, but every monastery was not as strict as it ought to be about keeping the rules of the order, but it might be most of this food was for visitors. In any case it was the main meal that was being prepared for, being summer time, it was eaten directly after Sext.

Meat was being cooked over an open fire, which meant the smoke which did not escape through the hole in the roof swirled round the kitchen. The meat was being cooked on long forks which were used by the holders as spits, they spun the handle round so that the meat revolved over the flames. There was fish, too, ready for cooking. Mr Fosse said that the monasteries were largely responsible for good cooking of fish, because they ate it most days and nothing else on fast days; so important to them was fish that they had special ponds which were fish farms, so that they always had farmed fish to fall back on when fast days came along, and they had been unlucky at catching wild fish. As well they salted a lot of fish down, and possibly, though he was not sure of this, cured herrings; certainly they had to have a lot of preserved fish by them for periods like Lent.

Ready to serve were piles of the round flat coarse biscuity things they used as bread. A monk was throwing a lot of these into baskets; Mr Fosse said that he would take them to a table outside where they would be served to the poor, together with pieces of meat, and probably the poor would have their drinking horns filled with ale from the monastery's own brewery.

From the kitchen they went through an arch to the refectory. This was very like the Hall they had seen the night before. There was a high table where probably the abbot and distinguished visitors ate, and trestle-tables for the rest. There were no cubicles, no bower, no elaborate tapestries, just a plain carved cross on the wall behind the high table. Mr Fosse said they would not be interested in seeing the meal served for it would be taken in silence, the monks and nuns making signs for anything they wanted, and while they ate a book would be read out loud. The children thought it sounded a most depressing way to eat.

From the refectory they walked quite a distance and came suddenly on a small hall which was used as an infirmary. They did not stay long, or see much. There appeared to be beds in cubicles and some nuns in charge. There was none of the cheerfulness the children connected with hospitals, but a sort of oh-well-I-suppose-it-can't-be-helped atmosphere. When they remarked on this Mr Fosse said they were probably right, for when those who looked after them had done all they could, they just accepted it was God's will the person should die, and did not try any more. They had good reason to feel that sudden death might be what God intended, because there were constant outbreaks of plague, caused, as the children had seen for themselves, by the habits of the people, which were unhygienic, to say the least. In this monastery there was drainage, even lavatories, but few outside thought such refinements necessary.

'Probably think them sissy,' William suggested, 'the sort of thing monks and those types use, but not ordinary people.'

Mr Fosse kept the school side of the monastery until the last. He said the boys they had seen in church this morning and at the feast last night were starting their education late. The great scholar Bede had been sent to a monastery when he was seven, and there was a case known of a boy who started at three.

'Three!' said Elizabeth. 'How silly, he wouldn't learn anything at three.'

Mr Fosse said no monastery would agree with her. Although of course most of the boys who came to monasteries to be educated had no intention of becoming monks, much of their upbringing was based on the rules of the order. Absolute obedience for one, which meant not doing things as you wanted to do them, but in the way that authority dictated you should do them. For another, constant occupation, for idleness was

the enemy of the soul. There was no reason why a child should not begin to understand these things at three, or even earlier.

The children thought of their schools. Constant occupation had a familiar ring, and so had absolute obedience, though there were times when doing things your own way was popular because it was supposed to show individuality. William asked Mr Fosse about this; he said he quite agreed modern schools did go in for worrying about individuality, but he doubted if these monasteries did, they probably knew their tough Saxon pupils would turn out individuals without their help.

Lessons, the children saw, were taught by monks. The boys learnt amongst other subjects Latin, how to read, writing in Roman characters, illuminating, arithmetic, scripture, astronomy, carving and religious poetry. Mr Fosse said this last had a very special place in the education of this monastery, because the first English poet, called Caedmon, had been a lay brother there in the days when Hilda was Abbess. He said Bede had written about Caedmon: 'None could ever compare with him, for he did not learn the art of poetry from men but from God.'

A lesson the children enjoyed watching was the one on illuminating. The boys were learning such lovely delicate work, the letters exquisitely trimmed with scrolls and curls in scarlets, blues and golds. Best of all they liked the lessons on carving on bone and wood. An old monk taught this, and whatever the order might decide about training boys he evidently saw no harm in individuality when it came to wood or bone carving, for he enjoyed it enormously when a boy, who was carving a bone casket with a scene in the church, put in a dog praying behind the monks and nuns.

Suddenly, in the middle of watching, the children stopped seeing clearly.

Elizabeth fiddled with the handkerchief round her eyes.

'I can't see them now. Has my handkerchief slipped? They're fading away.'

Mr Fosse put his arm through Elizabeth's.

'That means it is time we were moving. Come along, they are going to have their meal, so let us go back to our day and find what Mrs Mummery has for us in her basket.'

* * *

There seemed to be no end to the things Mr Fosse could arrange in a very grand way. Plenty of people showed films in their homes, but who other than Mr Fosse would have a special film made for him in technicolour, and have it shown by the company who made it, just for himself and six children? Even the Mummerys were not there.

It was a gorgeous film. First there was a caption to explain that what they were seeing took place in the year 867. Because of only one year having passed since they had visited the monastery, the children expected to see a film about the Saxons, but they had a surprise. The first shot was of Vikings. Since the journey had begun they had been getting acquainted with strangers, but everybody knows about Vikings, so the moment the winged helmets appeared they felt they were meeting old friends. Although it was silent and only had captions when it was necessary to explain something, it was a proper story. The hero was a good-looking young man with flaming red hair, beard and drooping moustaches.

The film started with a picture of the funeral of the young man's father. If a caption had not said so the children would not have realized it was a funeral, because nobody, not even the son, looked sad exactly, more proud and lifted up. First the father's body, dressed in full armour, winged helmet and tunic of chain mail, with his two-edged sword, with a hilt glittering with jewels, buckled to him, and his battleaxe, two-edged like the sword, in his right hand, and his wooden shield on this left arm, was put on a sledge, which was dragged in procession to the beach. Drawn up on the beach was a Viking ship with its dragon-headed prow facing out to sea. Every other Viking ship the children had seen pictures of was being rowed by numbers of oarsmen, but this ship was evidently going under sail, for there was a mast and a blue woollen sail ready for hoisting. First certain things were carried on board. The caption said that these Norsemen were heathens worshipping gods such as Odin or Woden, and Thor, from whom we got our Wednesday and Thursday. That they believed the dead man was voyaging to the home of the gods called Valhalla, which meant he must have died in battle, for if he had died in his bed, which they called a cow's death, he would not have been worthy to live in Valhalla. They put plenty of food and drink on board in case the dead man should be hungry or thirsty on the way. The next thing was horrible. The horse and dog of the dead man were killed, the caption said this was because they thought he might want them for hunting expeditions in Valhalla. The children thought this rotten luck on the horse and the dog. Finally several chests were carried on to the ship. The caption said that these were the warrior's valuables, that he wished them to journey with him so that his son would have no temptation to give up being a Viking. The son looked at the chests, but he did not seem to mind seeing them go, in fact he threw back his head and his eyes seemed to say, 'Good, I need nothing, thank you, father.' When everything was in place, the dead Viking was carried on board and laid on a pyre already prepared, and there, one by one, his friends took leave of him. Then the sail was hoisted, a torch put to the pyre, and the ship pushed out to sea. It was a magnificent sight, the blazing ship, the blue sea, the white whirling seagulls, but it looked a lonely journey to Valhalla.

The next scene showed the young man's ordinary life. He seemed well-to-do, in spite of not inheriting his father's valuables; he had farm land, on which all the work was done by slaves, whom, the caption said, he had probably acquired on raiding expeditions for loot. There were some shots of his land, which showed it was poor in quality, so it was hard to make it yield sufficient food. The young man had a red-headed wife, and it was she more than he who seemed to trouble about food, for there were several shots of her in the fields, sometimes lending a hand herself, but always anxiously examining the crops. Well-to-do Viking ladies seemed to work very hard; she had not only the food to prepare and the house to see to, but she brewed the drink and carded and wove wool for the household needs, as well as looking after her three babies, and really her husband was a fourth, for he did not seem to expect to do anything for himself, for there was a shot of her looking after his hair and beard, and another of her starting to undress him for bed.

The next shots showed what the young man did with his time. Many days he spent hunting, but according to the caption you had to be immensely strong and fit to go on plundering raids, so that when Vikings were home, which was usually in the winter, though there were a great many feasts and much singing of rather boastful songs, there were as well many tests of skill. There were fine shots of these, some on horseback, some running and jumping, some with weapons, in fact, a Viking's home life seemed to be rather like a continual Olympic Games. But Vikings did do other things than keep themselves fit, for when they were home they took their share in running their country. The caption said landowners and free men attended meetings called 'Things.' There were shots of the young man and many other men leaving what they were doing, and going to a 'Thing' which had been called because a murder had been committed. They were notified they had to attend by arrows being brought to them.

Oddly enough, in spite of being such tough types, Vikings seemed very home-loving. There were shots of the young man playing with his children; he was a bit fierce with his baby boy, but gentle as a kitten with his little girls. He was very quiet and loving with his wife, there was a shot of them sitting together playing a game which looked uncommonly like draughts.

Suddenly all the games, feasting and domesticity came to

an end. There was a new fierce light in the young man's eye, and in the eyes of his fellow Vikings. Great work went on carrying stores on to the ships. There was much overlooking of weapons, which, as might be expected of so warlike a people, were of very fine quality. There was a last great feast, there were last farewells, the women in floods of tears, then the dragon ships were rowed out to sea.

Up till this moment the children had been so interested in the young man and his wife and children they had not thought what all these warlike preparations might be for. But now the scene changed and they knew. They were back with the Saxons, where life appeared to be going on much as it had done when they had left it. It was only passing shots that they saw: field-work on the allotment strips, the ladies weaving, the craftsmen, potters, metal workers and so on, with rapt expressions, bent over their lovely work. The Hall being prepared for a feast, cows milked, animals fed, everything apparently as usual, though Mr Fosse said later that everybody was nervous inside, for they knew the Vikings might raid them at any time. Because the children had known the Saxons first, and everything looked so ordinary, it was all they could do not to shout to warn them of their danger. The only hope was that whoever the Vikings were going to raid it was not their Saxons. But as dusk fell on England that hope died. The dragon ships came into view, no lights showing, slipping quietly through the waves. The ship with the young man in her was in the foreground, they could see his hair and beard had been given an extra brushing, he had washed, that he was fully armed and looked ecstatically at the shore as if the thought of what was before him made him feel so excited he could hardly hold himself down on the deck. The camera moved to show what it was at which he was looking The children gave horrified gasps. It was the monastery.

The next scenes were all caught in the light of flames. The monastery burning. Nuns and monks running. A fight with dead Saxons lying around, and an apparently almost mad Viking slashing away with his sword as if using it was a joy. There was a shot of a wounded Viking; knowing from the funeral that all Vikings prayed to their gods to be allowed to die in battle, it was natural they should fight on until they dropped, but what was odd was that this one seemed to feel no pain; blood streamed from him, by his colour it was clear he was dying, but his eyes still glowed, his sword slashed until his last heart-beat. There were shots of the looting of the abbey. The rich treasure of which Mr Fosse had spoken being carried in armloads to the ships. There was a shot inside St Peter's of the abbot being murdered on his altar steps. The last scenes were the worst. The longer the fight lasted the madder the Norsemen grew, until there was an orgy of killing. Men, women and children, and the nuns and monks killed by spears, or mowed down by sword. Fires sprang up everywhere as homes were destroyed. Before dawn there were only Vikings in view; the Saxons who had survived, taking advantage of every shadow, were flying westward.

The picture faded out, and a caption came on the screen. It said some years passed during which King Alfred had beaten the Vikings in battle at Ethandune. This so surprised the Vikings, unused to being beaten by anyone, that after the battle many of them decided Alfred's god was obviously worth worshipping, and so they were christened. A little later there was a treaty between Alfred for England and the Vikings. This treaty partitioned England more or less in half. The Romans had built a fine road called Watling Street, which ran between Canterbury and Chester; this was the dividing line. Alfred ruled south-west of it, and the Vikings north-east of it. The Viking half included London, and was called the Danelaw.

The picture came back. It showed their Viking and his wife much older, perhaps as old as fifty. The place where they lived was near where the monastery had stood. They had built themselves a fine home not unlike the Hall of the thane, for it was of wood and it was thatched. But what amazed the children was their guests, for they were the thane and his wife, who were really old by now, and must have escaped when the Vikings landed. A caption said, which the children found it hard to believe, that those Vikings who had settled down in Danelaw had become very good settlers, and got on well with their Saxon neighbours. The eldest son of the thane had married, and had settled on land they called Thwaite. Before the children had time to look at each other, and to nudge Grace, they saw the entrance to the home on the land called Thwaite. Sitting in it, teasing wool, was the granddaughter of the thane and the Viking. She had red hair like her Viking grandparents. Presently the girl raised her head and smiled. There was a howl from William, Selina, John, Elizabeth and Robert. The girl was Grace.

CHAPTER EIGHT

# *Normans*

THE next day they flew to Kent, and landed at an airport called Lympne, where a very surprising thing happened. While the children and Alfred were gouging Mrs Mummery and the picnic basket out of the aeroplane, Mr Fosse disappeared. At first the children thought he must be hiding, but when they got to the brake and found no Mr Fosse, and the Mummerys quite unconcerned about his absence, they were thoroughly shocked. What odd manners! Mr Fosse to behave like this! How queer to invite people to come on a journey, then leave them alone without a word. Mrs Mummery's warm, strawberry-jam voice interrupted their thoughts.

'Come on, me dears, no good worrying after Mr Fosse, is it, Alfred?'

Alfred, having counted the children and the luggage, started the shooting brake.

'You never spoke a truer word, Mrs M.'

They stayed in Hythe, in a lovely hotel with a big garden, tennis courts, even a private golf course. As soon as they were settled, Alfred gave the children a letter from Mr Fosse.

*Dear Six*

*I have to leave you for some days to superintend details of our journey. In any case I think a rest is indicated. Too much of our way of travelling can cause aches, the kind you get from overthinking, not overeating. There is plenty to amuse you in and around Hythe, I hope, and as well the hotel has resources. Look for me in six days' time.*

*Your friend,*

*Fosse*

The weather was gorgeous. The days slid into one another, like pink ice cream sliding into yellow ice cream. It was hard to remember afterwards where one day began and the other ended. There was the day they sat on the cliffs of Dover, and watched a Channel swimmer arrive. There was the day they went fishing in a rowing-boat. Every day there was bathing, every evening before dinner all six played a rough, any-cheat-allowed game of golf croquet. They were queer golden days, but they did not seem quite real somehow.

'It's because we weren't expecting to be here,' Elizabeth said. 'I was absolutely sure when we flew this way we would be in 1066 and all that, with Harold and Editha with the swan neck.'

The day they remembered best was the day they went to Dungeness on the miniature railway. It began by being the sort of day when nobody could stop laughing. Getting Mrs Mummery and the picnic basket into one of the tiny carriages was enough to make anyone laugh, and to hear her puff 'Oh, me dears! Who'd have thought it at my time of life?' 'Oh, well, it'll all come out in the wash,' was enough to make anyone laugh. It was a specially good day for getting to know each other. Already John and William were friends, and got on well with Robert, but that day they all began to see things to like in each other, even the others found niceness in Selina. It could have been laughing so much, or it could have been the sun, or the miles of beach, or the fun of a day in the open, but each of them seemed to melt a little. Selina was less stuck up, Elizabeth less bouncy, Grace softer, Robert less shy and William and John more willing to laugh at silly things.

Alfred met them with the shooting-brake and drove them to a place called Lydd, which Mrs Mummery wanted to look at because her mother had been born there. After a splendid lunch, which Mrs Mummery despised because she had not cooked it, they went to look at the house in which Mrs Mummery's mother had been born. It was while looking for the house that the children saw the church, and it was a great surprise for Lydd seemed a smallish place, but the church was enormous.

William, used to ordinary country churches, was particularly impressed.

'Goodness! Look at the tower with those four pinnacles. I shouldn't have thought there were ever enough people here to want a church this size. Did your mother ever tell you about the church, Mrs Mummery?'

Mrs Mummery shook her head.

'I can't say that she did, William. But while me and Alfred are looking at the house, why don't you look at the church?'

None of the children were particularly fond of looking at old churches, but they guessed Mrs Mummery wanted to go into the house where her mother was born, so they agreed.

In the churchyard there was an old man doing something with a rake. William went over to him.

'Excuse me, do you know anything about Lydd? Was it an enormous town once? I mean, if not, why is the church so big?'

The old man scratched his head.

'It do be a big church, they calls it the cathedral of the marshes. Hit by a bomb, it were, in the last war. They say a mort of history were blowed away by that bomb.'

The others had joined William. Selina said:

'When the church was built there must have been enough people to fill it.'

The old man nodded thoughtfully.

'Maybe. They say the sea come close once. This tower were built as a landmark all seafarers could look for. There's sheep a' course, famous the marsh is for sheep.'

Elizabeth giggled.

'Sheep don't go to church.'

The others frowned at her for being rude, but they need not have bothered, for the old man went on without seeming to notice Elizabeth had spoken.

'They say there 'ave been fine sheep on this there marsh since the Romans . . .'

Mrs Mummery's voice came next.

'Come, me dears, you must have done with staring at the church by now.'

Twelve glazed eyes looked up at her. Then six heads turned to look at the old man. He was quietly raking, and yet . . .

They left the churchyard oddly silent, and it was half an hour later before they got back to their usual noisiness.

That evening, as they were coming back from their game of golf croquet, Elizabeth blurted out in a rather awkward way:

'D'you think Mr Fosse's magic sticks? I mean, did we do it?'

The others stood still. Selina said:

'Did you think you saw something too? I thought it was only me.'

Robert stammered with excitement.

'No—no, of course it wasn't only you—I bet it was all of us. I—I think we're beginning to know how.'

Grace twisted one of her red plaits and scowled.

'Don't be sackless, Robert. T'weren't nowt that a drop of me auntie's brew for spring spots won't cure.'

John spoke in a worried voice.

'It doesn't make sense though—I mean what I thought I saw doesn't. That chappie was talking about sheep and Romans, but . . .'

William's eyes behind his dirty glasses were like candles in a window.

'What did you see, John?'

John wriggled.

'It wasn't seeing exactly, more feeling like. You remember all those who came to the feast in the Hall . . . ?'

Elizabeth skipped forward.

'That's what I thought, I didn't see them exactly, but I knew they were there. . . .'

Selina was torn almost in half trying to live up to the standards of Borthwick, which told her to stand firm against hysteria, and her real self, which was pushing up inside her like a bulb coming into flower, saying, 'Go on, go on, tell them what you saw, I'm sure we're finding out something exciting.' The real Selina won.

'You remember all that lovely, lovely embroidery they had in the abbey? Well, I saw some of that, not in any place exactly, more folded as if it was in a chest.'

The piece of mouse-coloured hair at the back of William's head stood up more than ever, as it did when he was interested in anything. He fixed his eyes on Grace.

'You saw something, didn't you, Grace?'

Grace kicked up a bit of grass with the toe of her sandal.

'T'weren't nowt.' Then suddenly, in a rush, 'course I did, leastways I felt them, not my folk, nor Romans, these was Saxons. I smelt 'em.'

Robert was so sure that they were on the edge of something wonderful that he was trembling.

'But didn't you hear? It's hearing that comes first. There was a bell. . . . I'm sure I heard a bell, like the bell at Streanaeshalch, and . . .'

Elizabeth stamped her foot.

'We must need seeing to. We're letting Mr Fosse and his magic handkerchiefs get us down. What would we see Saxons for? You heard what that man said, he never said anything about Saxons . . .'

William could contain himself no longer.

'There *was* a Saxon church there. I read about it while Elizabeth was buying postcards. It said there was a bit of wall left, part of a church that was probably here more than a thousand years ago.' William paused, trying to remember. 'I didn't hear the bell, and I didn't see the embroidery, but I think I saw them building the church. . . . I wonder why we saw them there, I mean, why not here, or. . . .'

Suddenly Elizabeth felt scared. It seemed so odd to be standing in the garden of a posh hotel agreeing that they'd seen or smelt or heard people who had been dead for over a thousand years. It didn't make sense and she'd had enough of it. She snatched Grace's hand.

'Come on. There's been enough blatherskiting, as you call it. Let's have supper.'

It was a long time before any of them spoke of Lydd again.

On the day before Mr Fosse came back they wrote a theme song for Grace. William woke up one morning with the idea. He was sharing a room with John, so he put a foot out of bed and pushed it into his behind to wake him up.

'I say, as Grace is a Viking let's make a song about her and serenade her.'

As soon as Grace had gone to the bathroom the others got together, and after much smothered laughter stood outside the bathroom door and sang, to the tune of *From Deutschland I Come:*

Our Gra-ace is a Viking, a Viking, a Viking,
  Our Gra-ace is a Viking from Thwaite in Daneslaw.
She'd a Norseman for a father and a Saxon for a mother,
  Oh—oh come, pretty Viking, oh come shake a paw.

Singing this jingle made Selina think about Grace; she thought about her all the time she was dressing. Mr Fosse must have made up Grace's history. People like Grace did not have family trees, only people like herself and perhaps Robert had those. The walls at home were covered with portraits of ancestors, and she would bet Grace's home had not one portrait of an ancestor, so how could her history go all the way back to the Vikings? After breakfast, casually, so Grace should not think she was really interested, she asked:

'Mr Fosse made that up about you being a Viking, didn't he?'

Grace was trying, while she had the opportunity, to learn to swim; William was teaching her. Not to waste time she practised when she was not in the sea. She paused in the middle of an overarm stroke.

'No. Mr Fosse said he was well-nigh certain it was true. "That's where you come in, Grace," he said. He said us Thwaites, Becks, Gristhorpes and a lot a' folk with names ending in "son" mebbe has the blood of Norsemen in us.'

'What did he mean "came in?" '

Grace stopped practising swimming. She sat up.

'In our history. He said how as everybody came in somewhere—were part of the pattern like. That's why he picked on us six. Each belongs to different place in pattern, tha' knows.'

That evening, roaring with laughter, after a particularly silly round of golf croquet, the children almost fell over Mr Fosse. He was sitting on a chair outside the hotel looking as if he had never been away. Mr Fosse was not the sort of man you would expect to say ordinary things like being pleased to see you, and noticing how brown you were, so they were not surprised when all he said was:

'Ready for to-morrow's journey?'

They sat or lay on the grass round him.

'I bet I know where we're going,' said Elizabeth. 'It's Hastings, isn't it?'

John chewed a piece of grass.

'Could be the time when the Danes ruled, Canute and all those.'

Mr Fosse looked at Robert.

'Who do you think we are going to see?'

'I—I thought perhaps Normans. I mean to see how they live before they came here.'

Mr Fosse turned to Selina.

'And you?'

'I thought we'd be somewhere just after the Normans land.'

'And you, William?'

'I think it will be sooner than 1066. An awful lot happened between then and 867, didn't it?'

Mr Fosse stretched himself. He looked like a cat enjoying the sun, almost he seemed to purr.

'A lot happened, indeed. I hope some day you will visit those years, for on this journey we can only visit so few, just picking one here and there, to give us a taste of what is going on. To-morrow we shall be in the latter half of the twelfth century.'

There was silence, while the children racked their brains to think what they knew about the last half of the twelfth century. Elizabeth found she knew nothing.

'If you don't mind my saying so, Mr Fosse, that's rather mean of you. I wanted to see William the Conqueror.'

Mr Fosse gave one of his funny chuckles.

'I am afraid you will not meet great personages on our journey, Elizabeth, no matter what years we choose to visit, but since you have a fondness for them, you should visit them yourself some day, quite a journey that will be, from throne to throne, so to speak.'

Selina could not hold back her question another minute.

'Grace said you told her that being a Viking was where she came in. She said it was because we all come in at different places to be part of the pattern, that you chose us six. Which of us comes in next, Mr Fosse?'

Selina's face was close to Mr Fosse's knee. He looked into it in a pleased way, it was as if he was thinking how much nicer it looked now than the first time he had seen it. He stroked her hair.

'It is not where each of our threads joins the pattern that matters, but of what the thread is made; its colour, its strength, its durability, the something which makes it different from other threads, that is what is of importance. Now off to your suppers, all of you, we have an early start to-morrow.'

* * *

The next morning they drove into Sussex through some of the loveliest parts of Kent. There were whole orchards of red and purple plums, acres and acres of apple trees, gardens flaming with flowers, and fields of hops almost ready to pick. They picnicked on a hillside. Below them was the most marvellous view. As far as the skyline there was a patch-work quilt made of squares of gold from ripening corn, green from grazing fields, and patterned squares from little villages snuggling round their churches. Mr Fosse seemed as pleased with the view as if he had invented it.

'Nice, isn't it? Pity to shut it out really, but it will still be there when we come back.'

The magic seemed to come faster than usual, and there was something different about it. Almost from the moment the handkerchiefs were on to-day's sounds died and yesterday's were there. Because of the lovely view there had been a lot of traffic on to-day's roads: motor cars, motor buses, charabancs, motor bicycles, ordinary bicycles, a jet aeroplane overhead and the usual wireless blaring. Usually the sounds of yesterday had come dropping into their ears, one by one; this time it seemed to the children that they had shot through a sort of tunnel to come out almost breathless into a world in which the clop of horses' hoofs was at first the only sound. Then slowly, as if they were fumbling in the dark, they began to see. They were riding on large clumsy horses, wearing the most extraordinary clothes. John and Elizabeth were on one horse, Robert and Grace on another, Selina was riding behind a stranger, William did not seem to be with them.

Selina was the first to think clearly. Who was it she was sharing this horse with? Was it a stranger? He did not turn his head, but he could be a younger Mr Fosse. He was wearing what seemed to be two tunics, one on top of the other. The underneath one, which had long sleeves, was of brownish coarse linen, and the one on the top a reddish colour. Round his waist was a leather belt. On his legs were sort of tights made of cloth, kept in place with crossed leather thongs. On his feet rather clumsy shoes. Oddly enough, it took Selina longer to see herself than the stranger. She was riding side-saddle, keeping herself steady by holding on to the stranger's belt. She found she was wearing what at first she thought was a long dark-blue linen dress, with white linen sleeves; but when she picked up her dress to see what she wore underneath she found that her sleeves were evidently part of a white linen underdress. Round her waist was a leather belt, with two tails hanging down rather like a dressing-gown cord. Hanging from her shoulders, kept in place by a brooch, was a dull-red cloak of coarse wool, which, once Selina was conscious of it, seemed a ridiculous thing to be wearing on a hot day. On her feet were leather shoes. Her hair was in plaits, and round her forehead was a metal band. The moment she saw herself clearly she could see the others, and they could evidently see her, for when she looked at them they moved up closer to her. John and Robert were dressed much like the stranger, and Elizabeth and Grace like Selina, except that Grace's linen dress was brown, and Elizabeth's a dirty red. It was the colour of the clothes that shocked Selina out of feeling that she must be dreaming and made her speak.

'If this is the twelfth century, give me the colours we saw at that Saxon feast.'

John was puffing from being jolted about. He forced his great clumsy horse forward.

'I can't think why they don't do something about their roads. If you can call this a road.'

Selina looked down. It was certainly terrible going. A rough track stamped out by the feet of horses and men. It was dry now, but it must be solid mud in wet weather.

The stranger spoke. His words at first meant nothing at all. The children could not understand a syllable; then slowly, as if they were twisting and turning in the air before they reached their ears, the words began to make sense. The stranger said the lands through which this road passed belonged to his lord, they were his manor. He was his lord's reeve; this, he explained, meant that he had been chosen for this year by his lord's bailiff to parcel out the work that had to be done amongst the other serfs or peasants. He spoke proudly of his possessions. His lord had allowed him, and evidently he thought this a great favour, to hold quite a tract of his waste-land, and on this he was allowed to grow what he liked. It was evident he thought a great deal of this privilege. He had, of course, as had all, a garden, in which he grew leeks and cabbages, and he had a quince tree, but on his free land he grew apples, herbs and many other plants that he had a fancy to grow; and he also kept pigs and hens, and he had two hives of bees. On the other land he possessed he could only grow, of course, what his lord's bailiff ordered should be grown.

Elizabeth said:

'Do you mean to say you can't grow what you like on your own land?'

John thought he understood.

'I expect it's like the Anglo-Saxon arrangement, it's probably gone on ever since.' He spoke to the reeve. 'Aren't the fields divided up in allotments, and though you all grow the same crop in a field, you keep the crop grown on your land?'

The reeve hesitated. Certainly, he said, that was the way things were done in these parts, but he had heard tell that it was not always so. It was told by travellers that there were villages where there was no lord, and all land belonged to the people of the village, and they were free to do as they would, having no master other than the king. On this manor they were particularly fortunate. Theirs was a good lord and none starved, but this was more than could be said for some living on other lands; still, who should complain, you were what you were in this world, and if you suffered you could comfort yourself that poverty was a virtue. At this time of year none would starve, the weather was good and harvesting of manor lands would soon begin; at such times it was the custom to give a meal to the harvesters. Meat perhaps, soup, rye bread, cheese and ale.

'But won't you want to harvest your own bits of land?' Elizabeth asked.

The man looked rather sadly at the sky at that, and said that of course they would, but perhaps this wonderful weather would hold; there were years when harvesting their lord's corn took all the good weather there was, and their own corn was beaten flat. Still, that was the way of life, wasn't it, and they must not get the idea that the harvesters would get nothing from their lord. He was a generous man and there might be as much as two sheaves for each when the harvest was gathered.

'I—I think it's all wrong,' said Robert. 'If it were me I should run away.'

Again the man showed a queer acceptance of conditions as they were. It was very difficult, he said, for a man to live if he ran away, for who would hire him? Imagine the trouble this would bring on the hirer's head. Yet there were cases, he had heard, where a man had escaped and reached a town, and it was said that after a year, if he were a good workman, he might join a guild, and then he would be free, but it did not happen often, and maybe was only hearsay.

'I don't see why anybody need be so poor,' said Elizabeth. 'With your gardens, and even bad bits of land, there ought to be enough to live on; I mean you grow what you need to eat, and flax for your clothes, and I suppose you have sheep.'

'And no taxes, I should hope,' John added.

John's remark did at last get a spark of resentment out of

the reeve. No taxes! What about tallage? Tallage was a levy which his lord and all other lords could claim at any time, without warning, from all peasants. His own lord claimed it seldom, but there was the terrible fear that at any time he might, for that was the time when the thrifty man, and the man who had done well, suffered the most. For what tallage could be got out of a man was based on how much he held or owned. He hoped very much his lord would have no need of tallage in the next years as he was saving to buy his freedom. If ever he could buy that he would be able to go wherever he chose, for there would be no one from whom he had to get permission, that would be a wonderful thing; but it was clear from the way he spoke it was a kind of pipe-dream, he was not caring deeply if he were never free. He added quite casually it was hard to save, for there was much to pay out all the time, not necessarily in money, but in kind. There was a payment for grinding corn at my lord's mill. Selina gave the reeve's tunic a pull.

'Why do you send it to the miller to be ground? Do you know, what must be nearly a thousand years ago to you, people had found a way to grind their own corn. It was an awfully simple way, but I should have thought that would be better than paying someone else to do it for you.'

John thought proudly of the people in '43.

'Pay a miller! You could easily do what people used to do, just a hole in a stone, and another one on top to grind with.'

Back came the man's patient tone. All could grind, they could of course build their own mill, but no man might grind his own corn. There was a law which gave the right to grind people's corn to the lord, just as it was his right to bake all bread in the bakery of the manor.

On either side of the road along which they were riding had been grazing land, but now they were on the edge of a wood. Robert saw the scut of a rabbit, a pheasant, and where the trees were thick he guessed there would be deer. Then what about rivers? There had been plenty of fish. At the monastery there was even a fish preserve.

'Even if—I mean, if you do have to pay the lord for grinding your corn and baking your bread, I can't see why anyone need be hungry. There must be masses of game in these woods, and fish in the rivers.'

The reeve agreed this was true, but, he said—and this time he sounded really bitter—that these woods were his lord's, as was all the land through which they were riding, and the punishments, if the keeper caught you poaching, could be terrible.

John knew something about poaching.

'But I bet most of you get what you want all the same. I mean, why not? Your lord can't want all there is, and however many keepers he's got they can't be everywhere.'

The reeve did not answer this, but instead gave a very Mr Fosse chuckle, which showed that he thought it was a poor pot that had not something poached cooking in it.

At that moment a man came running towards them. The reeve drew his horse to the side of the track, and signalled to Robert and John to do the same. The man did not seem to see them, for he ran past them without giving them a glance. He was a miserable-looking creature, dressed in what looked like a sack, with holes cut in it for his head, and arms, and a rope round his waist. Selina whispered:

'Who is he? Where's he running to?'

The reeve gave his horse a kick with his heel to start moving again. He did not seem particularly interested in the man. He said, by his clothes, he knew he had been outlawed. There was no saying what his crime might be, he might be a felon or a murderer. He must have taken sanctuary in a church, and while there must have refused to stand trial. Since he would not be tried he had to leave the country from a special port in so many days, most likely this man had been ordered to sail from Dover.

'Poor beast,' said Elizabeth. 'I hope somebody takes him in and gives him another chance.'

The reeve clearly saw no reason for sympathy. The man, whatever his crime, had escaped his proper punishment, by claiming sanctuary in a church; he was very lucky if he

reached Dover safely, for if anybody wanted to kill him on his way there, they could do so safely. There would be no punishment for the man was outside the law.

They rode in silence for a while after this. Talking to the reeve was muddling. He seemed to take so much for granted that seemed to the children unfair. Of course, if the man was a murderer he was lucky to escape, but suppose he was not? Suppose he was innocent?

Robert had to find out.

'If he wanted to . . . I mean, could he have had a fair trial?'

The reeve sounded doubtful. He said kinsmen could come forward and swear he was innocent, and if it had to be proved he could hold a red-hot iron bar, or be thrown into water, and if he was guilty, pay the proper price.

'Ordeal!' Elizabeth was scornful. 'Fancy, still that old way!'

The reeve said that used to be the end of the matter, but now there was a new-fangled law, kings-law they called it. Twelve common men must decide whether a man were guilty or not, and those they thought to be murderers, robbers, those who stole, and those who hid those who stole, were sent to a king's court. These king's courts moved about, he thought, but he had never known anyone who saw one working. He only knew of them from the talk of travellers, pedlars and such.

The forest thinned out and became open land with only a few trees standing amongst bracken, ling and bushes. John, used to collecting vegetables and fruit from the farmers for his father's business, looked round in a puzzled way. The land did not look farmed, yet there was a big ditch dug round it, and all sorts of animals feeding on it: scraggy small cows, goats, sheep, and a few chickens. He called out to the reeve:

'What's happening here?'

The reeve explained that this was his lord's waste land, it was the custom for such land to be free for the use of all from Lammas, the first of August, until the beginning of the following

February. It was a strip on land such as this that he held, and hard work it had been clearing it.

The children looked at the waste land and hoped that the reeve did not pay much for his piece, for it did not look good farming land. All the same, evidently the peasants seemed glad to use it, for most of the men, women and children of the place seemed to be on it. They were dressed in poor editions of what the children and the reeve were wearing; the majority seemed to have no under tunic but one garment of coarsely-woven material, often patched, and sometimes torn. In spite of all the reeve had said about the goodness of his lord, the children privately thought that he was not doing half as well by them as the thane had done by his people. Of course, it might be partly the much duller colours of the clothes, but the people looked less gay somehow, as if just getting enough to eat was a full-time job, and left little leisure for fun. Most of the peasants seemed to be gathering wood, the men cutting branches off the small trees, and the women and children collecting firewood. The reeve explained by custom the men could cut what they needed from the small trees, such as the holly, to mend their tools, and all could get what firing they could find; if they looked they would see that the women and children were pulling down or raking out firewood, with hooks and crooks. This was because it was customary for them to keep anything they could get by hook or by crook. The children thought this very funny, they had often heard people say by hook or by crook, but they had never known where the expression had come from. The reeve said there were other things besides wood to be had off the waste land; they were allowed to cut any turves they wanted to mend a shed roof, and then there were plenty of worts, or whortle-berries, to be had, and very good eating they were, and there would be nuts later on; and for those that liked them, sloes. Come November all the bracken would have died, and a nice bit of bedding that made for an animal. In fact, if you put your mind to it, and worked hard, there was no end to what you could get from the waste, including fillings for your cooking pot. Like everything else, what you got out of it depended on the amount of work you put into it. He ordered his wife and all five children, even the youngest who was four, out on the waste every free hour of daylight, for they seldom came back empty-handed. But there were others, usually the grumblers, who complained they had not got this, and couldn't have that, and yet made poor use of the waste. He had no time for that sort.

Selina had stiffened at the word ordered.

'Do you mean to say you order your wife to do things?'

The reeve evidently did not know what Selina was fussing about. He answered in a general way, saying he was lucky in his wife, who was hardworking and thrifty by nature, and brought her children up to be the same, it was seldom necessary for him to beat her. Selina said no more, but made a very expressive face at the others. Beat his wife! This was a change for the worse, from the Saxons and Vikings, who had treated their wives as partners, wasn't it?

The reeve pulled up his horse. Neatly, without kicking Selina, he dismounted. He said he was afraid he must leave them, he must find the bailiff, for whom he had been to the shepherd with a message. Elizabeth, who was scared of the country at any time, gave a dismayed squeak.

'You can't leave us here, it's terribly empty and we might meet a bull or something.'

A quite different voice answered, that certainly they must not be left alone. The children were surprised, for no one had seen the reeve go or anybody else arrive, but there, leading Selina's horse, was a priest. They could not see his face, but he was an old man, for the little bit of hair left in a fringe round his shaved head was grey. He had a thin old man's voice, very like Mr Fosse's, for it had the same wind-across-the-reeds sound, and the same warm, seeing-everybody's-point-of-view tone. Once more it took the children some time to understand what was being said. However, when their ears did get used to his voice, they found he was using more or less the same words as the reeve had used with now and again French and Latin words popped in. Their pace was, of course, slowed down to the old man's speed, and as he stepped and sometimes skipped over the ruts and stones on the track, he chatted gently in a I-am-sure-this-will-interest-you way, which the children fouud very nice and friendly. He was, he said, the parish priest; he hoped he was doing his duty, but he doubted whether he and his bishop saw eye to eye about things. Bishops, and high-up people like that, seldom understood the difficulties of those below them, hadn't the children noticed this? His bishop seemed to forget how poor a man he was, that if he was to eat he must see to his glebe land, his pigs, feed the chickens and all the rest of it, and that did not leave as much time for the care of his people's souls as the bishop thought he ought to give. While he was talking the children tried to remember how priests had lived in the thane's time. Robert asked:

'Don't you . . . I mean, haven't you a tenth of what everybody grows?'

'Your tithe,' John added.

The priest, skipping from rut to rut, agreed that in principle he certainly had a right to tithe, as indeed he had a right to every man's second best possession when he died, but they knew how it was, a right was one thing, and taking a right quite another.

Elizabeth raised her voice, for skipping about the way he was she was not quite sure if the priest would hear her.

'Why do you only get a man's second best?'

The priest explained that the best possession belonged to the dead man's overlord, in this place the knight who held the lands through which they were passing. The knight here was a good man according to his lights, and seldom claimed his right, for the people were poor, and the best possession often as not was a cow or a pig, and how would it serve the knight if the dead man's family died of starvation, for after all, the dead man's children had to work for him. They would see that if the knight, either from charity or common sense, refrained from taking the best possession, it would be very unseemly if the priest took his right to the second best.

The children certainly could see that, but though they liked the priest their sympathy was with the peasants. They seemed to have a hard time, and certainly a very insecure one: it must be awful for a widow not knowing if she would lose her two best possessions or not.

'Does the same thing happen to your tithe?' Elizabeth asked.

The priest shook his old head, and made clicking, worried noises. It was often difficult to ask for tithe, the land here was not rich as it was towards Canterbury, nor had they the good grazing for sheep, such as it was said there was on the downlands. Most years were bad in some way. If the harvest was poor, or animals died, then there was near starvation, followed of course, as was natural, by plague. His people came to him for everything. He knew which of them were really poor. Who was having to buy from the knight a son's freedom from service, so that he might become a priest. Whose farming had been delayed by illness. Knowing these things it was difficult to go from one poor little slip of land to another claiming the best sheaf of corn, or whatever it was. He had his tithe barn, of course, but often there was little in it. He took what tithe he could, because, as the children would know, people were quick enough to claim a custom, and it was certainly not his place to make a custom of not taking tithes, for tithe was what the Holy Church decreed was his right.

Selina, looking at the priest's shabby brown cassock, wondered if he was not being a bit too generous.

'The reeve ought to be able to pay, he seems to be doing all right.'

The priest chuckled. He was not thinking of such as the reeve, he explained, for the reeve was a richer man than he was, though often it was those who had most who were least willing to part with their possessions. But this reeve here deserved his success, he had worked very hard at raising pigs, and after all, what greater wealth could you have than pigs? Unless of course it was sheep. If you had pigs, and a hard winter came, and starvation stood outside every man's door, it was surprising what could be got in barter for salted pigs' meat.

Robert was shocked at the word 'starvation.'

'I say, doesn't the knight . . . I mean, he must have heaps of everything . . . I mean, he wouldn't let the people starve, would he?'

The priest, though his sympathy was clearly with the peasants, seemed to see the knight's point of view. The knight, they must remember, was a Norman, French-speaking in his home, and without understanding of peasants, such as a man like himself possessed. He said that according to his grandfather, his people had owned lands such as this until the Normans conquered the country. His grandfather, when he was a little lad, had given him nightmares telling him of the days of the Conquest, terrible times they must have been. One day a landowner living comfortably, and the next everything taken away by King William, and divided between the Church and the great lords. His grandfather had told him that in France great men had such rights over their peasants that they were little more than slaves. Nowadays the Normans were changing their ways, but it was still hard for them to believe it mattered what happened to a peasant, that he had a soul to be saved, just as they had themselves.

'Did the grandfather of the knight fight in the battle of Hastings?' Elizabeth asked.

The priest did not know about that, but he did know how the knight came to hold his land. 'All the land round here,' he said, 'belonged to a monastery.'

'What!' said Selina. 'Doesn't it belong to the knight?'

The priest tried to explain, but it was rather difficult. The abbot, head of the monastery, had, of course, to pay the king for his land, not in money but in knights, who had to fight for him for so much time in each year. When this was first arranged the abbots, and most of the great lords who owned a lot of land, settled these payments by giving away parts of their lands to knights, who in return for the land had to fight for the king when wanted.

John scowled as he struggled to follow.

'Do you mean the abbot uses this knight, and the other knights who have bits of his land, as rent?'

The priest said that was exactly what he did mean, only nowadays the knights mostly paid money direct to the king, and with this money the king could hire fighting knights.

'Fighting knights!' Elizabeth spoke quite angrily. 'All knights fight, didn't you know that? They travel all over the country looking for maidens in distress, tied to trees, and sometimes they kill dragons for them.'

The priest was amused about the dragons. He said he knew there were those amongst his flock who believed in dragons, but he himself had never met one, and he doubted if they existed. As for the knights, there were two sorts: there were knights such as the knight here, who was really a farmer, and there were knights who liked fighting and did nothing else.

At Borthwick Miss Marion often spoke to her girls on Sunday

evenings, and one of the subjects about which she loved to talk was the great days of chivalry; what inspiration maidens in those days gave the world. Selina could not imagine what Miss Marion would say if she could hear this priest talking about farming knights.

She spoke with the whole weight of Borthwick behind her.

'If you don't mind my saying so, I think you've got your facts wrong. The knight here can't really be a knight when all he does is farm. I mean, haven't you ever heard of chivalry?'

The chuckle the priest gave was so like Mr Fosse's chuckle that they were all startled. Chivalry, he said, of course he had, and when they reached the house of the manor they would see a boy learning chivalry, for by chance the knight's son was home. As was the custom, the boy had been sent as a page to a great household. There, by example, he was learning how to behave himself, waiting constantly on his lord, and also on his lady in her bower. This last part was very important, for it was teaching the boy the proper way to honour a lady. As well, he had daily lessons from the chaplain in Latin, reading, scripture, and so on. Naturally, from the time he could toddle, he had learnt a little of the arts of war from his father; but now, while serving as a page, he was learning further skill with the sword and the lance, and of course riding came into it, for he attended on his lord at hunts. He was having lessons from the falconers in how to look after his lord's hawks. The boy was only twelve, and was still in the middle of this simple training, but when he was a year or two older he would become a squire, and then would start to train properly. He would have to wear chain mail, and the simple lessons he had had in spear-tilting and fighting with the sword he would put to use on a great war horse.

The children felt as if they were coming to a stretch of time that they knew. Selina could almost hear Miss Marion's voice; she leant over her horse towards the priest.

'That's when he chooses a maiden, isn't it? And wears her glove or her rose in his helmet when he's fighting, for she is his own true love.'

The priest chuckled again. It was quite true that about

this time the youth chose a lady, and often enough carried her tokens, but he was not so sure about the true love. After all, a marriage was not a matter of chivalry or tokens, it was a business affair to be arranged by the boy's family. Elizabeth couldn't bear it another minute.

'You are the most miserable man, I shan't ever like this part of history so much again.'

John was a little surprised at the term 'business affair.'

'Do you mean to say they don't marry people they love?'

The priest didn't think so, nor did he seem to think that this was an important part of a marriage. He said that often marriages were arranged when the boys and girls were children; there had to be sense in these matters, sometimes it was the question of combining lands so that they would march together, sometimes a dowry. Elizabeth thought they had better get off the subject of marriages in case any further shocks were coming.

'Well, what happens to the squire next? You aren't going to say he doesn't become a knight, are you?'

The priest hopped across a large stone. Certainly he becomes a knight, he said, then his tone grew solemn. The church had arranged a beautiful ceremony for that day. After a bath, and having been well instructed in the meaning of being a knight, the young man spent twenty-four hours in his lord's chapel, praying for help to keep his vows. Then he must make his confession, and after attending Communion, wait quietly in his room for the ceremony. The ceremony itself was a very moving one, and he wished the children could see it. He described the crowd in the big hall, and the young man who was to be a knight receiving his spurs and his sword, and being tapped on the shoulder with the flat of the sword, and how after that he went to the chapel to lay his sword on the altar, as a sign to God that he intended to be his true knight.

Partly because it was a story they knew, and mostly because the priest spoke of the ceremony as if he liked it, the children made pleased noises when he had finished. Even Grace, who had been too stunned since she found herself riding on a horse behind Robert to open her mouth, murmured:

'Eh, it's fair grand.'

Elizabeth was utterly carried away.

'How simply splendiferous, bit of all right for everybody having so many gorgeous boys to defend them.'

The priest gave another very Mr Fosse chuckle. He said that he liked Elizabeth's simple faith, but he was afraid nothing was ever perfect in this sinful world, and chivalry was no exception. There were those, and he praised God for them,

who kept their knightly vows: they honoured their church and the priesthood, protected the poor and the needy, fought against treachery, endeavour to see that there was peace on their lands, and were always ready to fight and, if necessary, die to protect a brother. But this was not true of all knights, there were those who, he was afraid, brought shame on the word 'chivalry.' Still, for the few who shamed it there were the many who brought fame to it, and in so doing led their fellow-men to a more Christ-like way of living.

While the priest was talking they turned a corner, and in front of them lay the village, if you could call it that, for it was more like a camp really, huts spread higgledy-piggledy on either side of the track. To enter the village it was necessary to cross a stone bridge over a stream. The children held their noses as they crossed the water, for it smelt terrible, and were nearly sick when they saw a mother and her little girl fill earthenware jugs and drink some of it. The homes were poor little places, one-roomed, built of wood with wattle and dirt between the framework; they had thatched roofs with holes in them for the smoke to come out, and as well there were tiny glassless windows and smoke curled out of them too. At the back there were small fenced gardens. As most of the huts were empty, John asked the priest if it would be all right if they looked in. The priest thought it was a good idea, so the children slid off their horses and had a look round. On the whole they thought the peasants lived pretty miserably. Outside each home was a horrible manure heap, buzzing with flies and bluebottles, which, of course, got into the houses. The whole village seemed to be full of pigs, snuffling around for food, and many of the houses had a pig or two in them and, as well, chickens perched on the beams or, worse still, on the sides of bacon which were hanging from the beams. What with the pigs and the chickens the floor, even where the housewife had thrown down fresh rushes, which was seldom the case, was in a horrid mess. The fire was still in the middle of the room, and even on a hot August day evidently had to be kept smouldering, so the huts were full of smoke, which made the children cough and their eyes run. There seemed little change in the way of cooking; there was much the same cauldron on a tripod over the fire as they had used when cooking their rabbit in A.D. 43. Most of the houses had a simple wooden trough in which to knead bread, and a few of the smarter huts, which the priest said belonged to craftsmen, good well-carved chests. In every home there were tools hung round the walls and in a corner the wife's spinning outfit, usually with some sheep's wool on it. All the better homes, and a few of the poorer ones, had a loom. The huts were probably very much the same as the Saxons had lived in round their Hall, but certainly there was no improvement. John, climbing back on to his horse and pulling Elizabeth up behind him, tried to explain what he felt to the priest.

'I suppose it's all right, but they don't have much, do they? I mean, not much to be proud of!'

The priest waited until they were all mounted before he began to move. He said that he was afraid there was no advance in the way the people lived. From what he had heard, if those who had died at the time the Normans conquered them could come back, they would find little change in the condition of the peasants, certainly no improvements; but he was glad to say that discontent was rising.

Robert was surprised that a priest should talk like that.

'Do—do you mean you'd like them to be angry and discontented?'

The priest thought for quite a while before he replied. He did not want them to misunderstand him, he said, he did not approve of violence, it was a poor way to get what you wanted, but it was a poor thing too, that men built in the likeness of God could be satisfied to be the chattels of a fellow man. For even here, where conditions were good, the knight had complete power over his peasants; they might not even go on a journey without his consent and they had an immense amount of labour they had to give him. There was such a thing as divine discontent, which meant being discontented with something because in your soul you knew it to be wrong. It was that sort of discontent that he meant, and it was for that sort of discontent that he prayed.

The children said no more, but they looked at the priest, or rather the back of his head, in a surprised way. Robert was glad his father was not there, for he was sure the priest was the sort of man he would describe as 'One of those so-and-so agitators.'

The village had a bend in it, and as they passed the bend they came to the church. They pulled up their horses to stare at it. For what seemed a very small community it was enormous, almost as big as the church at Lydd. It was an imposing-looking building. It was built of stone with two transepts, which made it the shape of a cross. The walls were very thick. There was a handsome doorway and many narrow windows with rounded tops. The priest was evidently very proud of his church, for there was a note in his voice which sounded as if his eyes were shining. He said that it had been built by the people, naturally craftsmen must have been used as well, some belonging to the manor and travelling ones who must have been hired. He was trying to persuade the knight that the time had come when more work should be done on the church. He had not travelled much of recent years, but those who had told him that there was beautiful decoration on many churches, stonemasons were doing splendid mouldings and carvings in plain designs, though sometimes figures were used. Of course the knight would not pay for it all, the people, as was right, would take their share, and of course

he would pay his. He must think of some way to raise the money. He was always in need of church funds and the people were tired of direct giving. Still, it would please them to see their church beautified for it was the centrepiece of their lives. They were in it daily at mass. No man, woman or child could fail to look at it when they rose in the morning; they could see it from almost any spot where they worked, and they must see it as they returned in the evening.

Considering the size of the church the children thought the poor priest had a miserable little home. They thought of the vicarages they knew, and felt very sorry for him. He evidently did not feel sorry for himself, for he said with pride that it was as fine a house as any of the knight's craftsmen owned. Elizabeth only just bit back: 'I should jolly well hope so.' The one thing the priest did have that the others hadn't was that, instead of a garden, he had a little farmyard. It was very dirty and smelly, but he did not seem to notice that. He smiled affectionately at his cows and pigs, his tithe barn, and even at his manure heap and said, and obviously meant it, that he was a lucky man. The children would have liked to have gone into his house and seen how he lived, but they had no chance, for just as they were getting off their horses the priest pointed to the sun. It was evidently his clock for, on looking at it, he said it was getting late, and they must hurry.

'Where are we barn for, mister?' Grace asked.

There was no need for the priest to answer. He had led Selina's horse back to the track, and there ahead, very imposing after the huts of the villagers, lay the home of the knight.

CHAPTER NINE

# *The Knight's House*

AFTER the way in which the reeve had vanished it seemed quite natural to find that the priest had disappeared and taken the horses with him.

The children were standing outside the knight's house. It had a stone wall round it, and there was a simple drawbridge over a wide ditch. The whole effect was rather like the forts they had played with when they were smaller. The drawbridge was down, so they could look through the rounded arched entrance into the house. It was more like a to-day's house than any buildings they had seen since they had started their journey, for it was built of stone, it was two storeys high and it had a sloping, slated roof. In other ways it was quite different: the windows were tiny and had no glass in them, though there seemed to be wooden shutters for use in bad weather, and there were no chimneys, for the smoke still came out of a hole in the roof. There was a big yard round the house, with lots of outbuildings; the children saw stables and kennels and there were other buildings which looked like workshops and stores. The house seemed a very self-contained affair, as if the drawbridge could go up, and there you would be safe inside with probably everything you needed enclosed in its stone walls.

Selina felt it was beneath her to be peering over a drawbridge at the house.

'What are we hanging about for? Why don't we go in?'

The others were embarrassed. Robert said:

'We—we don't know anybody there. Isn't it rather rude?'

This made Elizabeth remember who they really were and why they were there.

'Robert Ackroyd, you really are the silliest boy. What d'you think we're doing here, if we're not meant to go in? This is just a new kind of Mr Fosse magic.'

Robert looked down at his cross-gartered legs and clumsy shoes.

'I . . . I suppose you're right, but it's a very strong sort of magic, I . . . I feel more here than there, if you know what I mean.'

Selina felt the house looked more or less the sort of home she was used to, and was certain, dream or no dream, she would be a popular guest. She walked proudly towards the drawbridge.

'Whatever you others are going to do, I'm going in.'

Naturally they weren't going to let Selina go in alone, so they followed her.

Either because of the clothes they were wearing, or because they looked like people who belonged, nobody stopped them. On either side of the rounded arch which supported the drawbridge were little stone houses for the gatekeepers. The children supposed that if there was fighting, robbers, or other dangers, there were probably armed sentries in the gate-houses. The man on guard that they passed seemed to be an ordinary servant, for he was dressed very much as they were, and his only weapon was a stick. In the courtyard, and in various buildings, people were working. They saw a cart, full of vegetables and fruit, and drawn by oxen, go round to the back. It was an odd sort of cart, rather like a basket on wheels. They saw something which looked like a wooden box with windows with poles running through it, being repaired outside a shed. Selina saw

there was harness attached to the wooden poles. She pointed this out to the others.

'That's to ride in. I'd rather ride pillion than ride in that thing. Do you know, I believe it's carried by horses, one in front and one behind. Imagine it on a track like we were on. I bet I'd be seasick in five minutes.'

There seemed to be two ways into the house. An imposing sort of front door leading to the ground floor, and a sort of stairway ladder, roofed over, which led to the top storey. They tried the ground floor first. The door was open, so they peeped in. It was clearly not the part of the house that people lived in, for it seemed to be mostly a place where food was stored, so they decided to try the stairs.

At the top of the stairs they came to a passageway off which was evidently the kitchen, for there were gorgeous smells and cheerful kitchen noises. At the end of the passage they had a surprise, for it seemed for a moment they had moved back in time, and were in the hall of the thane's house. It was another great high room. A little light crept through small rounded windows. There was the platform with the high table. Against the walls they could see trestle-tables stacked ready for the ordinary people to eat off. There was the fire still in the middle of the room with the smoke trying to escape from a hole in the rafters. On the floor were the revolting dirty rushes, mixed up with bits of bone, dogs' messes, and goodness knows what else. Then their eyes grew accustomed to the light and the smoke, and they saw that this hall was not really so like the thane's hall, there were quite a lot of changes. The thane's hall had been built of wood; this hall was of stone, though there were wooden rafters. The thane's hall, except for a curtained-off part for the bower, had been used for everything. This hall had other rooms, the kitchen for one, which they had passed coming in.

A voice was speaking. At first they could not hear the words, nor see the speaker. Then slowly they began to understand and see. A nice-looking man in a rough countrified way was talking. He was rather better-dressed than either themselves or the reeve, for his blue linen under-tunic and his blue woollen over-tunic were more finely-woven than the materials they had so far seen. The man said that he was his lord's steward; this was a small household with no marshal such as big household's kept to see after the lord's affairs, so he was in charge of everything. He said he controlled his knight's people, though his special business was running the house of the manor. The farm and the handling of the peasants were left to the bailiff. He said he had more than enough to do looking after his lord's personal staff. You needed eyes at the back of your head, for they were a lazy lot and needed watching, or goodness knows what state the house would be in. Hearing him say this made Selina look at the floor. If the floor was a sample of the state the house was in he did not seem to be running the house particularly well. The steward either did not notice where Selina was looking, or took the state of the floor for granted, for he paid no attention, but said there was time before the meal was ready to show them round. It was a good moment, for his lord and the lord's son were out hawking, and his lady amongst the peasants. It was clear from the very down-his-nose way the steward spoke that he thought nothing of his lady being amongst the peasants. His lady, he said, was very charitable. Naturally it was right to look after the poor, but it was also well to remember that to be poor was a virtue, and it might be a mistake to better a poor man's condition. He said his lady at this particular moment was troubling herself about a beggar. For himself he thought such cases were suitable for the priest, but his lady would see to things herself. The children must not think that he didn't believe in charity; when wayfarers passed he was the first to see they were fed, and a place found for them to lie down in the hall. He himself gave what he could to lepers and other poor and needy, but in his opinion his lady's charity went altogether too far.

John had been listening to the steward's voice. It was less broad than the reeve's, but it had none of the French words embroidering it, such as the priest had used, yet he supposed he must be a Norman, or how would he have got such an important job.

'I suppose you speak French, don't you, when you are talking to the knight, his lady and their son?'

The steward laughed. He said, try as he would, he could never manage to get his tongue round French words; his own language was good enough for him, and he saw no reason to try and speak it the fancy way the Normans did.

'But I thought only Normans could get important jobs like yours.'

The steward was leading the way back to the kitchen. He said he quite understood John thinking that, and so it had been at one time he believed, but, after all, men were men wherever they came from, and to-day it was sometimes hard to say whether a man was born Norman or Saxon.

The kitchen was a fine big room, reached through the place where drink was kept and the place where the food was kept. The steward said the drink-place was his butlery, and the food-place his pantry. In his pantry he also kept his torches and candles. At this season of the year they were not used much, as, unless there were guests, the household usually went to bed when it was dark, and got up again when it was light. He said his bakery was outside. It was a big place, for they not only baked for themselves but baked for all. There were baskets full of bread on a table. Bread was getting, the children noticed, much more like the sort of bread they were used to. The steward said that a lot of the loaves were four days old, for they were used to serve the food on. Trenchers they called them.

'You mean, instead of plates?' Elizabeth asked. 'I must say that's a good idea, for I suppose you eat them afterwards. No washing up. My mum wouldn't half like that.'

The steward, who, like the reeve and the priest, had something about him that sounded Mr Fosse-ish, said they could eat their trenchers, and did if they were tasty, but more often they were thrown into baskets and given to the poor.

The kitchen fire was in the middle of the kitchen. The steward said that when they could get craftsmen for the work the fireplaces were to be altered. Travellers told how great fireplaces were now being built against the walls, and the smoke escaped through the walls behind the buttresses. It was, they said, a great improvement, leaving far less smoke to hang about the roofs, and the fires gave out greater heat. It might not be possible to put such a fireplace in the great hall, but his lord was considering having one in here for cooking, one in his own room, and there might be one built in his lady's bower.

Cooking was going on in iron pots, some hung on chains and hooks over the fire and some had three little legs. As well some meat was being turned round and round by hand on a spit, so it cooked all the way round and not just on one side. The knight's household evidently ate just as much as the thane's household, for there was a tremendous amount of food being cooked: soups, meat, game, venison and fish, and there was cheese and butter as well as the baskets of bread waiting to be eaten. There also seemed to be some sort of sweet, at least that is what the children thought it must be going to be, because they saw one of the cooks mixing honey and cream and fruit. The steward asked if they would like to have a look at his butlery. The children agreed but only out of politeness, for they were not particularly interested in drinks. Elizabeth whispered to Grace:

'I hope the knight asks us for supper. I'm starving.'

Grace nodded.

'Tha's right. Me guts is fair cracking.'

The drink for the meal was waiting in large glazed pottery jugs. The steward said they brewed all their own ale and, as well, their wine. They made their wine, he said, of honey and spices and grapes. The steward took them next to see the knight's room, which he called his 'solar.' To get to it they had to cross the great hall. Evidently it was getting near supper-time, for two men were beginning to move the trestle-tables from against the wall. Some of the household had come in and were filling up the time while waiting for the knight and his lady to come home, gossiping and playing dice. The steward said they were all fond of games of chance, but of course he himself had little time for amusements, but the children noticed that he threw a wistful look at the dice players, and they felt sure that if they had not been there he would have found time for a game.

The knight's room and the lady's bower were at the back of the raised stage. In the knight's room there was only one piece of furniture—a bed. The walls were covered with some rather dull-coloured stuff; instead of cupboards the knight used his ceiling, for some armour and his spare suits of clothes were hung on a rod from it. On another rod sat a lot of birds, of a sort the children had not met before. The steward said they were some of his knight's falcons and hawks, though his finest, a jer-falcon, was out with his lord. They ought to see it, the falconer said it was the finest bird he had ever trained. The odd thing about the knight's room was that there was a window, which did not look out but looked in. The steward saw the children staring at it, and explained that it was where his lord could look down upon his household to see that they were behaving properly in the hall. Sometimes he had to call for order, especially when there were many visitors and the horse-play got rough. They had had a lot of visitors recently. The great lord, whom the knight's son was serving as a page, had passed that way on pilgrimage. The boy would be with him, but he had seemed to his mother to look pale, and the lord had agreed to leave him behind and pick him up on his return.

'I should think that's a bit of all right,' said Elizabeth, 'it must be nice seeing strangers. I should think it gets a bit boring just being yourselves, doesn't it?'

The steward said they could be very isolated, especially in the winter, the track often got waterlogged and it was hard for people to reach them; but of course entertainers got through: minstrels, jugglers, acrobats, as did pedlars, and so on. As he spoke the children began to see how lonely a house like this could be. The reeve had used the expression that 'he had heard,' and so had the priest, and now the steward used it. How odd to depend on gossip and hearsay from passers-by, not expect to find out for yourself what was happening. How important roads were.

'I . . . I should think having visitors makes all the difference,' said Robert. 'I mean, that's how you find things out—like fireplaces against the wall.'

The steward said that in the summer there were all too many people passing, going on a pilgrimage to Rome, merchants, farmers selling wool, those joining crusades, those on pilgrimages to Canterbury. They must not think his lord was lacking in hospitality, or that the household, and indeed the peasants, did not know their duty to strangers; but of course, if too many visitors came, it made them all anxious. They were a small community, and though they stored everything they could for the winter months, and kept a good table going, food could become short if there had been too many visitors. The great lord, whom the knight's son was serving as page, who had just visited them, had been travelling with a party of over two hundred and fifty, and they had eaten them out of house and home. For himself he hoped they would not stay too long on the homeward trip.

'Do you mean to say,' said Selina, 'that he came with over two hundred and fifty people without being invited?'

'Where did they all sleep?' asked Elizabeth.

John simply could not visualize so many guests.

'Do you mean you have got to put them all up? Aren't there any inns or anything of that sort?'

The steward could not understand that they thought it a bit hard to be expected to put up two hundred and fifty guests, for it was evidently the custom. There were inns, he had heard, in the towns, places where a man could pay for a night's lodging, but there were none in the villages, nor did great men travelling the roads expect to use them, they went from castle to castle, or castle to knight's house, as the case might be, and were without question made welcome. The steward grinned there at a memory; he wouldn't like to say, he said, that the hospitality was always what the fine gentleman hoped, there were no spare beds in the house, and they could take their choice between lying on the floor of the great hall on the rushes, as they did themselves, or, if that became too crowded, they could claim hospitality from the villagers. Of course the visiting great lord, or abbot or whoever it was, would share the knight's solar, and usually be given his bed. Together, after they had eaten, they would come up here, and would talk privately sitting side by side on the bed. The steward clearly thought sitting in a room of your own talking privately was a very great luxury.

The lady's bower was next to the solar; it was like the lord's room except that there was a fine carved chest for the lady's clothes, and a loom, and an embroidery frame. On the loom there was a length of red woollen cloth being made; the embroidery frame was covered with a linen cloth, which the steward removed with great care. Under it was a beautiful piece of embroidery on linen, vestments for a priest, the steward said. Selina was full of admiration.

'It's perfectly lovely, I should think the priest will be awfully pleased with it.'

The steward said he doubted whether that piece was intended for their priest, he believed that when harvest was over the knight and his lady were making a pilgrimage to Canterbury, and she was giving it to the church there. He said that the lady spent a lot of time embroidering, and so did the women who waited on her; she was, they gathered, a domesticated type, and liked being in her house rather than riding out on hunting expeditions with her husband, which many ladies in her position were fond of doing. She enjoyed music, and it was a great pleasure to her when visiting musicians played in the hall, she was particularly fond of the harp. When a great lord came visiting, amongst his following, of course, was a musician, sometimes two, and his lady would spend half the night listening to them. It was a pity his lord could not afford to keep a musician on his pay roll, it would certainly brighten the winter evenings, and would please his lady very much.

The whole house was pretty smelly, but coming out of the lady's bower the children smelt such an awful smell they all put their handkerchiefs to their noses. The steward pointed to a corner of the passage, where the smell was coming from; he called it a garderobe, but it was a lavatory. No proper drains,

just a shaft in the thickness of the wall. The steward said in a most casual way that his lord had said it was smelling rather high and needed clearing, did the children notice anything? Selina, speaking as if she had a cold, because she was holding her nose so tight, said:

'But it's tebbible!'

The steward seemed surprised that it seemed to them so bad as all that, he added that in the summer months it was apt to get smelly, but he doubted if they could spare a man to clear it until the harvest was over.

Not too quickly, after passing the garderobe, in case of sounding rude, Robert said:

'What happens if anyone's ill? Have you hospitals and doctors and things?'

The steward hurriedly crossed himself. He said it was not lucky to talk of illness, there were of course physicians at the monasteries, and some places had pest-houses. Sometimes there would be a traveller skilled in medicine, and of course they had their own herbs, but when real illness came there was very little they could do. Three times in his lifetime there had been outbreaks of plague; he had caught it once himself, why he had lived he never knew, for most people had died. Plague seemed to arrive in the village like an evil spirit, stalking here and there, killing off whom it would, then, just as suddenly and equally for no reason, it would go. The children exchanged looks. Going by the dirty water they had seen the woman and the child drink when they came into the village, and the awful smell from the lavatory, it did not seem to them odd that there was plague.

'But there are doctors in the towns, aren't there?'

Once more they were back at the heard-tell conversation which seemed so much part of everyone's life. The steward had heard tell of a very great doctor in the town of London, his name he thought was Rahere, and he had founded a hospital in honour of St Bartholomew. He did not know whether

Rahere was still alive, for they knew how it was with travellers' tales, they spoke of what they had heard and seen, and been told, all in one, as it were.

Suddenly a noise and bustle arose over the whole house. The children looked round in surprise, for they could hear nothing to cause it. Then a servant ran up to the steward; the knight and his lady, he said, had met in the village, the family were riding home together, they would be crossing the drawbridge in a few minutes.

It seemed as if the knight and his family were the key which wound up the works of the house, for from the moment the household knew they were coming home they all seemed to have something to do, and a feeling that it had to be done quickly. The trestle-tables in the hall were up in a flash. In spite of its being a warm evening, wood was thrown on the fire. A coarse linen cloth was spread on the high table. The women servants, who had been watching the dice game, ran to wait for their lady in her bower, and a manservant to the knight's room to wait there for him.

'Funny,' said John, 'I don't hear horses. I wonder how these chappies know they're coming.'

Country-bred Selina understood.

'People in the country always know things like that. My father says they have what he calls a grape-vine, they always know what's happening before it happens. I expect that's what they have here.'

Elizabeth was longing to see the family.

'I'm going outside, in spite of all that old priest said, I bet the knight looks simply marvellous. Oh, I hope he's on a great white horse wearing glittering armour.'

As the children reached the top of the stairs the family rode over the drawbridge. The lady came first. She was riding pillion behind a servant. She wore a blue tunic, laced at the sides, over a yellow linen under-tunic. The neck of the top tunic was cut low enough to show the under-tunic. Round her waist was a good solid belt, it seemed to have some jewels in it, and there were jewels in the heavy brooch which fastened her brown cloak to her shoulders. On her head she wore a white veil held in place by a metal band. Elizabeth was disappointed in her.

'Doesn't look very smart somehow.'

Selina recognized the type.

'That sort wouldn't. If she lived in our time she'd wear lumpy tweeds and a down-in-front, up-behind hat, they do.'

The knight was a much worse disappointment to Elizabeth. Far from shining armour he wore no armour at all, and by no stretch of the imagination could he be said to look an imposing figure. He was a little man, with black beard and hair, and he wore a nondescript-coloured over-tunic and a felt cap, in fact the only thing which distinguished him from his servants were some rather good leather boots. Far more impressive than he was, was a big bird sitting on his leather-gloved wrist.

'I bet that's the jer-falcon,' John whispered.

Several servants followed the knight, then, some way behind, came the boy.

It had been clear since the lady and the knight had arrived that, though from what the priest had told them they were not considered great people, they were very important amongst their own people. Most of the servants were not wearing anything on their heads, so they could not take off their hats, but they did the countryman's equivalent of a half bow, together with what looked like pulling their front hair. When the boy appeared, these bowings and pullings were increased, but they might not have been going on for all the attention he paid to them. They could not see his face, but there was something very proud about the way he rode his horse. He clattered over the drawbridge, talking to his falcon, which was fastened to his wrist, and whom he obviously thought much more important than the bowing servants. He was dressed more or less as his father was dressed, with a green over-tunic and cap, but his clothes looked utterly different. Selina nudged Robert.

'They go in for good tailoring at the great house where he's a page.'

Robert was trying to see the boy's face. He spoke vaguely.

'I . . . I expect they would, I mean the knight is mostly a farmer, the priest said so, and farmers aren't . . . I mean, farmers don't care how they look.'

'Young lad needs takin' down a peg, if you ask me,' said Grace.

Elizabeth let out a slow satisfied sigh.

'To me he looks simply marvellous. Oh goodness, I do hope they ask us to supper with them, just fancy sitting at the high table next to someone who is learning to be a knight.'

It was as if the boy had heard Elizabeth for he turned his head and looked straight at her. The westering sun shone on his face. Gasps and whistles came from the five children. In spite of his rather long dark hair, and no dirty horn-rimmed spectacles, and little differences all over, there could be no mistake. The boy was William.

CHAPTER TEN

# *The Years Between*

THE children came back in the way they usually started their journeys. First there were sounds: the bumbling of heavy buses, the chug-chug of motor bicycles, the scream of a jet plane, the blare of wireless, the sound of modern voices. Then came the smells, or rather lack of smells. Finally they could see. Their first reaction when they looked at Mr Fosse was annoyance.

'You are mean,' said Elizabeth, 'I was just going, at least I think I was, to sit at the high table with . . .'

Ten eyes were turned on William, and very disappointing he looked. His blue shirt was crumpled, his mouse-coloured hair more sticking-on-end than usual, and his grey eyes looked more shortsighted as they stared back at the others through his dirty horn-rimmed spectacles. John said:

'Where were you? I mean, it was you, wasn't it?'

Selina, getting a grip on the present, felt a prick of jealousy. Did William really belong to the Normans? Had his ancestors been knights? He was quite poor now, his father was only a parson, he couldn't have an older family than hers.

'It was only made up, wasn't it, Mr Fosse?'

Robert ran his hands through his hair till it stood on end.

'But it wasn't . . . I mean, we were there . . . we saw him.'

William suddenly seemed to realize he was being discussed.

'What are you jabbering about?'

John leant forward. He spoke slowly.

'Where do you think we went to-day, William?'

'Where Mr Fosse said we were going, of course, the end of the twelfth century.' He turned to Mr Fosse. 'They weren't bad days, those, and things have come on a lot, haven't they? I mean, it's a fine training chivalry, and they have a good time too.'

That was more than John could bear.

'All right for you beastly Normans, but the poor Saxons weren't having much of a time. Of course you don't care how your peasants lived.'

William did not yet seem himself, which must have been why he gave so un-Williamish an answer.

'Poor creatures! But I don't think they expect much.'

Mrs Mummery interrupted by putting a large plate of chicken on every knee.

'Eat your food now, me dears, it's not cooked as I could wish comin' from a hotel kitchen, but it'll fill you, and you must be peckish, for you've been gone a long time.'

As Mrs Mummery spoke the magic of the past was gone and the present was properly back, and they realized they were starving. As they ate they looked round them. There was the patchwork quilt of ripening corn, grazing fields, little villages linked together by winding roads and lanes. John pointed to a bus climbing a hill.

'What a difference roads make. It's so easy for us climbing on the old bus, or on the back of someone's motor bike, or hitch-hiking on a lorry.'

'Or going on the train,' said Robert.

Selina pointed to the sky, where an aeroplane was passing.

'Or flying.'

William spoke with his mouth full.

'Getting around is one of the great differences. I mean all those villages have good roads, and those roads join main roads, and apart from newspapers, wireless and all those things which of course they hadn't got, it's awfully easy for us to get around and find out for ourselves, but it was much more difficult for them, so much depended on what travellers, pilgrims and all those types told them.'

Elizabeth passed her plate to Mrs Mummery for more chicken.

'From what they said there were plenty moving around. I suppose England was getting fuller with all those Normans living there, wasn't it, Mr Fosse?'

Grace swallowed a mouthful.

'An t'Vikings.'

'And Saxons and Angles,' said John, 'and, if it comes to that, what was left of the others.'

Mr Fosse had been listening to them all with an ears-pricked look.

'Enjoyed yourselves? I'm sorry I had to take you away before the meal, Elizabeth, but I don't want to tire you, and now you know how to find your way I want you to travel alone, for you will not always have me to guide you, nor by our journeys' end will you need me.'

Robert said:

'But you did. . . . I—I mean, weren't you the reeve, or . . . ?' He tailed away, not knowing what he meant.

Mr Fosse, in his cat-like way, had jumped to his feet.

'I may have been, or I may not. One thing is certain, you are learning to find the road back for yourselves, that is what is important.'

'Where are we going next?' asked Selina.

'The year will be 1495.' Mr Fosse saw the children were going to protest. 'Yes, I know, quite a distance from to-day's journey, but the years between will not run away, visit them yourselves any time.'

Elizabeth wriggled to make room for the gorgeous food.

'Where do we go to in 1495?'

Mr Fosse looked mysterious.

'I am not going to tell you yet, because the one of you who belongs to that part of our story still lives in that part of the world.'

The one who belongs! How aggravating Mr Fosse could be, thought Selina. Then an idea struck her: perhaps the others knew where they belonged.

'William, did you know you were a Norman?'

William shrugged his shoulders.

'Sort of. I knew there was a place we came from which belonged to us from the twelfth century, it's National Trust now. It was always miles away from belonging to my part of the family, but I supposed we began there.'

Elizabeth looked at him enviously.

'How gorgeous to be you. Don't you feel in your bones you were once a knight?'

William laughed so much he choked over his helping of greengage tart.

'Idiot! Of course I don't As a matter of fact, if you want to know, I thought we were grander, I mean lived in a castle. It was a bit of a come down really. Wait until I tell my father.'

Mr Fosse was in a skipping-about mood. First in one place, then in another. He answered William, but he looked at Selina.

'What home you had does not matter. It was hard for you Normans not to do pretty well for a time, William, for after the Conquest you could all have land, and for a time all of you were the ruling class.'

John had to interrupt.

'But they didn't all go on ruling, William hasn't. I bet there's heaps of Normans about now who are beggars.'

Mr Fosse nodded.

'Quite right. Up one minute, down the next, that's how it goes for many. But, mind you, going down in the money sense has never mattered, plenty of families have done that, to-day so many you could not count them. Nor is going up in the world important, it is what you are, whether up or down, that matters.'

Elizabeth pointed her spoon at Grace.

'You've slipped a lot, my girl, from where you began.'

Grace grinned.

'Tha's a blatherskite, Elizabeth.'

Mr Fosse chuckled.

'Isn't she! From what I have seen of Grace her forbears would not be ashamed of her. Fine stout thread and stalwart design, that is what your kind has brought to our pattern, Grace.'

Elizabeth sighed, partly from food and partly from a let-down feeling.

'Of course, I know your father's a reverend, William, but I must say I think that's a bit sloppy after starting off as a knight.'

Mr Fosse gave another chuckle.

'If ever you see our pattern clearly, Elizabeth, you will be surprised how much it owes to families such as William's. On the looms we have seen, you saw the lengthwise threads called the warp. . . .'

Elizabeth was sitting next to William, she dug her elbow into him.

'William the warp, that's what I'll call you.'

'He ought to have a song tha' knows,' said Grace, 'same as you made for me.'

They all tried to make a song for William, but it was not easy. It was John who found a tune for him. He was good at imitating bugle calls. He whistled the officers' mess call. Then he sang it changing the words:

Normans born have puddings and pies
While Saxons born have nothing.

That made the others laugh. They sang it several times, looking meaningly at William and howling the word 'nothing.'

'We'll all have a song, won't we?' said Elizabeth. 'I do hope I come in soon, but I bet I don't, nobody could say my family was warp, I should think the moths have been at my bit of the pattern.'

Mr Fosse skipped over to Elizabeth and gave her hair an affectionate tweak.

'That's what's so exciting. Sometimes it does seem that the threads are so weak that they will break, then the miracle happens, the thread strengthens, perhaps stronger than before, the colouring is vivid, the design more interesting.'

Selina looked at Elizabeth. Surely Elizabeth could not be coming in next? She would be unbearable if she did, it would make her more bouncy than ever. She tried to sound as if her question was unimportant.

'If you can't tell us where we're going to, Mr Fosse, could you tell us the sort of place it'll be?'

Mr Fosse sat down.

'We are going to have fun, I hope. We are going to a town for a great fair. I think you are ready now for a town, and, I think, for changing time. The great fair we are going to visit is part of the celebrations for the feast of Corpus Christi, which is in June. So far, as this is August, we have journeyed back in August. Then we have been looking at country folk, and, allowing for changes in method, the country folk we visited have been doing much what the country folk we left behind us were doing, and the birds, scents and so on have been much the same. Now we have to adjust a bit. Every month smells and sounds are different from those of other months, so we have to leave the smells, sounds and feelings of August and arrive at our fair smelling, hearing and feeling June-ish. Quite easy when you get the hang of it.'

'I bet we'll find a lot of changes,' said William, 'a lot can happen in nearly three hundred years.'

John was staring at the view. The villages looked so cared-for it made him think of the peasants' poor little strips.

'I hope the people are standing up for themselves a bit better.'

Elizabeth had stretched out flat, for lying down her inside seemed to have more room.

'Some of them will be outlaws, like Robin Hood. Goodness, I wish I could meet him, Mr Fosse.'

Robert hugged his knees, trying to remember.

'There's . . . there's been a war for a hundred years, hasn't there?'

'Hope roads is better,' said Grace. 'That road to your place, William, was nobbut a snicket.'

Grace talking about the road made Selina feel again the motion of the horse she had ridden; she saw in her mind the priest skipping over great stones, and across such ruts that they were small valleys between mountains of hard mud. She saw the bridge they crossed, and at that memory, what she had learnt in history lessons came to her mind.

'Plague. They've been having the Black Death in the years we aren't there.'

Mr Fosse looked so pleased they could almost hear him purr.

'Quite right, all of you. There were outlawed men, and a war which lasted for a hundred years, and a civil war, but I doubt if these made as much difference to the life of the commoners of the country as you would expect. But the Black Death, though it was not seen as such at the time, was to affect everybody's life, particularly the lives of those peasants you are worrying about, John.' Mr Fosse pointed to the view below them. 'Many little villages like those down there, after the plague, had no able-bodied person left in them. The population of the country, and remember it was still small, was cut by at least a third. Now, think for yourselves what that has meant. Think of your schools. If the headmaster or mistress wants a job done, and is prepared to pay for it in some way, he or she will not have to pay much, will they, because there are so many of you to do the job, but if they want it done in the holidays when labour is scarce you would expect them to have to pay through the nose.'

John saw, and was delighted.

'Of course, only one-third left and everybody wanting them . . .'

Elizabeth looked at William.

'That stopped you grinding the faces of the poor, my boy.'

William, looking very like an owl disturbed by a sudden light, blinked at Mr Fosse through his dirty glasses.

'Then, in a way, was the Black Death a good thing?'

Mr Fosse took his time before he answered.

'There's very little in our pattern that is black or white, in fact there is very little in any pattern that is either. Things that seem black as pitch when they are happening have a surprising way when looked at as part of the general pattern of seeming more grey than black, and then in time they seem not only part of the bright colours round them but as if bright threads started from them. If we had visited the Black Death years we should have come back wretched. Heart-broken husbands, wives, fathers, mothers, children; burying your own dead is a miserable business, and then, of course, everybody was terrified, and there was precious little help, and, as men died, cattle were not fed and crops were not planted, and starvation was always round the corner. For the people those were dark years, yet looking at the pattern now, those dead, and the tears which must have streamed, were not wasted, for from them came better times for those who worked on the land. When times were bad many people trekked to the towns to see if things were easier there. . . .'

'I thought they couldn't go without permission,' said John. 'That's what the reeve said, he said no one would dare take on somebody else's peasant.'

'He was quite right, but there again shortage of labour helped. Everybody needed labour, so were willing to pay and ask no questions, and sometimes, provided the runaway paid his lord a fee, he could stay away.'

'I . . . I think it's awfully queer,' said Robert. 'I mean that bad things could ever be good.'

Mr Fosse jumped up.

'Well, you had better get used to the idea, for it is not only true of England's pattern, but of your own, and all patterns, and a very comforting thought it is when you are in the middle of what seems a hopelessly black patch.' He signalled to the Mummerys to pack the picnic basket. 'Time we were going.' Then he clapped his hands. 'How I look forward to to-morrow. I do so love a fair.'

That night after the children were in bed Mr Fosse had a talk with Alfred.

'Mummery, has it struck you that our six are changing?'

Alfred considered the question.

'Mrs M. and I were speaking of it yesterday, sir; maybe it's the dress, but they do seem more one family like, than when we started.'

'Would you say they influenced one another, took their opinions from each other?'

Alfred laughed.

'Not them, sir. Course young Elizabeth is a bit bossy, but it doesn't get her nowhere, not even with Robert. Selina, for all her fancy talk, doesn't count for more than Grace, if as much. Maybe William and John are the leaders like, being the sort you can trust, but I reckon, and so does Mrs Mummery, they each think and act for themselves, same as children should do in a family.'

Mr Fosse's eyes sparkled and he clapped his hands.

'Splendid. Splendid. Just what I hoped . . . but I will tell you something, Mummery, I noticed when we were chatting after luncheon that our family, when it comes to the rights of man, thinks remarkably alike.'

Alfred thought it was time Mr Fosse was in bed.

'So they would, sir. After all, we all know what those ought to be, don't we? It's not a thing you can argue about.'

CHAPTER ELEVEN

# *The Fair at Norwich*

THEY flew in a helicopter from Lympne and landed in a field outside Norwich. Long before they landed John had begun to think that he knew where they were, and where they were heading, and when they circled Norwich he knew for certain. Mr Fosse had been watching his face.

'Yes, John, we are visiting your home town, finding out where your thread joins the pattern.' He turned to the other five. 'I thought we would not waste time, we would go straight to the fair. Have a good look at Norwich as she is now, for in a very few minutes much of what we are looking at will not be there, for we shall walk into her in the year 1495—and do not forget the month is June.'

Mr Fosse's magic was very strong that morning. Talking it over afterwards none of the children could remember getting out of the helicopter, having the handkerchiefs tied on, what happened to the Mummerys and when they lost John. Nor could John remember when he lost them, but the first thing that the other five knew was that they and Mr Fosse were in Norwich.

Sound, as usual, came first: the rattle of wooden wheels, the clop of horses' feet, laughter, talk, the shuffle of feet and, in the background, the cries, music and shouts which were unmistakably a fair. Smells came next: cooking smells, garbage smells, river smells and an ever-growing smell of human beings. Then they began to see.

They were walking up a city road. They were not alone, but part of a crowd who pushed and jostled, and laughed, like crowds do on a holiday. The first thing they noticed, of course, was what everybody was wearing. Many of the people around were puzzling, for they did not seem important in the way the thane or the knight had been important, for they were not at all stand-offish, but laughed and shouted jokes to each other, and yet were obviously well-off. It looked as if there were a new sort of middle people.

Clothes of the well-off were made of wonderful materials. Afterwards, when the children had seen really grand clothes, they realized that from a fashion point of view the clothes they saw first were only fairly good copies of what the great wore, but at first sight it looked as if nobody, not even kings and queens, could be better dressed. One thing was queer: men were more grandly dressed than women, and wore gayer colours, in fact no colours seemed too gay for them, nor did there seem to be any colours they did not think would go together. They wore short tunics with fancy vests, and long loose top-coats rather like dressing-gowns, and the idea seemed to be to look conspicuous, which the children thought very odd, for they knew their fathers had fits if they stood out in any way from other men. The 1495 men liked exaggerated clothes, tunics being short; some of them wore them so short they were just little frills. Fussy sleeves on the overcoat were the fashion, sometimes slashed to show the sleeves of the tunic, sometimes falling away at the elbows, in fact all shapes, but whatever design they chose the idea was clearly to have odder sleeves than anybody else. On their legs the men wore woven tights, and on their feet immensely long pointed shoes, except for one young man who was wearing very square shoes, held on with a strap across the instep. Evidently he thought himself no end of a dog in those shoes, for wherever there was enough space he strutted around and showed them off. All types of hats were in fashion, from large feathered affairs tied under the chin, to little square turned-up hats. Whatever was worn it was of beautiful workmanship, and all kinds of lovely materials were used. The women looked like queens on playing cards, for they all wore head-dresses built like the roofs of houses, the roof part made of black material with a veil hanging down behind. It was obviously a time when materials were bought to last, for the dresses looked as if, when not worn, they would stand up by themselves. The over-and-under dress idea was still in fashion, for nearly all the dresses were made so that the top dress was cut away, or fastened up to show the under dress.

Both the over and the under dress were often of enchanting colours. It was disappointing, after eyeing all this glory, for the children to realize that they and Mr Fosse were wearing dull clothes. In line they were more or less what everybody else was wearing, but less exaggerated, of less good materials, and of drearier colours. Only Mr Fosse wore a hat, and his was a very drab little edition of the small turned-up felts some of the other men were wearing. They were noticeably badly shod. Smart people's shoes were of fine cloth, damask, velvet or leather, often beautifully embroidered, whereas theirs were poorly cut and made of coarse woollen materials and had no embroidery. Elizabeth, looking at themselves and then at the other people, complained to Mr Fosse.

'I take it you choose the sort of people we are, so do remember next time when you're choosing I would like to be the most smashing girl in the town.'

Mr Fosse said he quite saw Elizabeth's point of view, but he chose poor backgrounds for themselves because he wanted them to be able to talk as equals with the less grand people. Then he beckoned to them to come closer so that he could talk more quietly.

'If you listen carefully you'll be able to follow what these smart people are saying.'

It was quite true: up till then everybody seemed to be talking in a foreign language, now, though the words spoken did not change, they twisted and turned in the air until they reached the children's ears in a shape they could follow. At once they learned something exciting. It was not just the fair these people were visiting, they were on their way to see what they called the Corpus Christi plays or pageants. From what they could pick up the well-dressed people round them either belonged to, or were in the party of three families, who made their money in different businesses. One group seemed to be in the worsted-weaving business, another were dyers and colour-makers, the third brewers and vintners. The children found this out because they talked about play-pageants, each group seemed interested in a play-pageant which had amongst the actors people belonging to the guild of their craft. The colour-making and dyeing guild were evidently connected with a play-pageant about Hell, for there were lots of jokes tossed to them about the fires of Hell being kept alight and not going out like they had done last year. The brewers and vintners' craft were to be represented in a play-pageant about Noah, and the worsted-weavers a play-pageant about Heaven.

Mr Fosse said the Corpus Christi fair and the play-pageants were the great events of the year, they would not have time to see them all, but they would try and have a look at one. They must be prepared to be a little shocked, for although they were religious stories, not all the parts were played seriously, there were certain characters that were meant to be funny, so the audience could jeer at them, Judas Iscariot for one, and

Pontius Pilate for another. They might find the fun a bit rough, and they would not be alone if they did, for the plays were originally acted in churchyards and got turned out because they were so rowdy. Now, though they were part of the Corpus Christi celebrations, they came under civic authority. They must not be surprised if some advertising crept in. He was certain that the dyers' guild would see to it there were some startling colours in the play-pageant about Hell, that water would not be the only liquid in the vintners' display about Noah, and Heaven, as seen by the worsted-weavers, was sure to include lengths of their finest materials. But they must not think any irreverence was intended. The players and audience had a deep simple respect for God, but that did not mean they thought He could not enjoy a joke, or that He was not sensible enough to see that if you spent a lot on your play-pageant it was only reasonable to get a little advertising out of it.

The fair was very well arranged, the different sort of goods for sale were kept in rows, so that you could go straight to the part of the fair that sold what you wanted, and when you got there compare prices and quality. Fairs did not seem to have changed much; there were no electric-driven merry-go-rounds, of course, but the stalls could almost have belonged to the children's own time, especially those that sold sticky sweets and cheap presents to take home to those who could not come to the fair themselves. The hangers-on you usually find at fairs were all there: the man who offered to take out teeth without hurting, the man who had a medicine which would cure absolutely anything, the man who had stuff to rub on your head to make your hair grow. Then there were the side-shows, which did not seem to have changed at all: the cow with two heads, the mermaid, the fat woman, the dwarfs, and all the other freaks, including strong men and contortionists. As always with fairs, everybody seemed to be in the wildest spirits, and in the mood to buy rubbish, even when they knew it was rubbish. But there was one way in which this fair was different from any fair which the children had seen before, it was not only a fair but a meeting-place.

Mr Fosse explained that.

'The three weeks the fair lasts people come to it, and other fairs like it, not only from all over the country but from abroad. It is at fairs like this that everybody gets a chance to hear how things are going on in different neighbourhoods: how towns are run, what the fashions are, what the news from Europe; they are the big get-togethers, and many, especially people from villages, feel, when they have been to a fair like this, that they are part of the great world, and what they learn at this fair will be the main topic of conversation until they go to another. It is a way, too, of getting things done locally; the news of how the city fathers in a town like this are doing is carried home,

and people say: "If they have that in Norwich why can't we have it here?" '

When they got into the thick of the cooked food stalls the children found that Mr Fosse seemed to be quite well known. People called out to him, asked him how he was keeping and said they were glad to see him again. He acknowledged these greetings, but did not stop but led the way to a stall selling boiled eels. This was kept by an enormously fat woman with a big broad smile and very Mrs Mummery voice. Her name was Joan. She saw Mr Fosse coming long before they reached the stall, and greeted him with what was evidently the 1495 version of ' 'ello me old duck.' Mr Fosse seemed equally pleased to see her, and asked for news of Norwich. Joan had two small sons helping her, and she left them to serve eels while she leant against her stall to talk to Mr Fosse, though that did not mean she took her eyes off the boys. She said that things had not been bad since the last fair; were they going to see the pageants? Mr Fosse said he thought they would have a look at one, Joan said she recommended the one the worsted-weavers had a share in, it was a lovely sight, so she had heard. They had got into a bit of trouble last year and had nearly been fined for someone not knowing his part, so they were going all out this year, new buckram for the Holy Ghost's coat, new clouds, new wings for the angels, no expense spared.

Selina often had to go with her mother to village plays so this conversation interested her.

'Do you mean that people are fined if they do the play-pageant badly?'

Joan said certainly they were fined; after all, people came expecting a fine show and knew what was what, there was no excuse for slackness.

Selina said no more, but decided when she got back home she would try and introduce a system of fines in the village. Sometimes the local plays were good, but sometimes they were very badly rehearsed, and what a much better idea for competitions to fine people if they did badly, instead of giving them cups if they were good.

Mr Fosse looked at the two boys, and asked what Joan was going to do with them when they grew up. Joan said that they would stick to the stall business, it was a fair living, and if you apprenticed them to a trade it was so long before they earned much. In any case there was time yet, they were only nine and ten, and of course, in Norwich, you mightn't apprentice a boy until he was fourteen. Mr Fosse asked if she was getting them educated. Joan laughed and said not she, they could already do any figuring that was necessary at the stalls and could even read a few words. She had never had schooling, but could read a bit, write a bit and add a bit, and that was all you needed in her business. Mr Fosse asked if she wouldn't like her boys to get on in the world, and to this he got another nudge in the ribs. Times were not what they were, Joan said, it had been possible, and not so long ago at that, to start as an apprentice and rise to be the master, but there was much less of that nowadays, and for her part she thought it best to be contented with your lot; the merchants worked as hard as she did, and though they had more possessions they had a lot of responsibilities too. It must be fine at the real top, great lords had a wonderful time. She had a sister whose husband had been a cook in a big house. What went on there would make your hair curl. Her sister's husband said what was eaten in the big houses had to be seen to be believed. He said that for a party it was nothing to have a great pile of sheep, oxen, pig and the like, and all the game you could think of, and any amount of fish, several swans, and, as to the sweets, they could not be imagined by common folk, subtleties they were called, birds sitting on nests, even figures of the blessed saints, all made in the kitchen. She had sometimes thought of going in for selling foreign spices and such. A traveller had told her that in London there was almost nothing you couldn't buy if you had the money to pay for it. But she doubted if there were enough real high-ups in Norwich for a big regular market, and she did not like dealing with foreigners, you never knew where you were with them. Mr Fosse said surely half of Norwich was foreign, with all these weaving families. Joan gave him another nudge; the worsted-weavers weren't foreign, good Norwich people, she meant strangers from outside, other towns and abroad and that.

While Joan and Mr Fosse talked, the children had been looking round, and they noticed that, as with all fairs, there was a good deal of mess about.

'I expect you have to be careful about drains and things, since the Black Death, don't you?' William asked.

Joan did not seem to have heard of the Black Death. Did William mean that sweating sickness that they had nine years ago? Terrible that had been, herself she did not believe it had come from dirt, as they said, but fussy! Did Mr Fosse know that it was a punishable offence now to throw your slops out of a window? Things were coming to a pretty pass if you couldn't throw your slops where you liked, and if he would believe it the town was paying for carts to pick up the rubbish, and tip it outside. There was a gentleman she had sold eels to that morning who had told her that in London they had special boats for taking dung and that out of the city. A lot of nonsense the whole thing. One comfort, those who worked for the mayor could not have eyes everywhere, so for her part, unless someone was looking, everything went into the street or the ditch as it always had.

A crowd of customers came to the stall and Mr Fosse whispered it was a good moment to get away, he had something very exciting for them to see. It was a shop, and what it sold was completely changing the world; which of them could guess first what it was?

The children tried to remember what they knew about the time, but with so much to look at it was difficult to think.

'Some sort of weapon?' William suggested.

'It wouldn't be that, William Beaumont,' said Elizabeth, 'that isn't a change, they still have those tournaments and all that, don't they, Mr Fosse?'

Mr Fosse said Elizabeth was quite right, tournaments and jousting were still immensely popular, but it was not weapons he was thinking of, had anyone else any ideas?

Grace had.

'Would it be anything to do with t'gutter and that, mister?'

Mr Fosse shook his head.

'It could have been, for in spite of what Joan said, people have got on to the idea that there is a link between outbreaks of plague and dirty insanitary habits.'

'They've taken time to get around to it,' said Selina, 'when you think what the Black Death did to them.'

Mr Fosse looked doubtful.

'In our own time it is not the first street accident that focuses public attention on badly-lit streets, dangerous crossings or whatever it is, but several accidents on the same spot and then, and only then, is something done. It is the same with plague. It is not the history of the Black Death but the small continuous outbreaks and the sweating sickness which has made those in authority think, and make rules, and then they are hindered by ignorant people like Joan.'

Selina stuck to her point.

'They ought to make laws. Then people like Joan have to keep them. After all, it's for everybody's good.'

Mr Fosse looked at the others.

'What do you say? Take the same sort of thing in our own

day. Ought everybody to be ordered to be vaccinated to keep the country free from smallpox? Should all babies by law be inoculated against diptheria?'

'Isn't it odd,' said Elizabeth, 'when it's them, you think: stupid them, they ought to be made to . . . and when it's us, you think: interfering so-and-so's?'

They all laughed. Then Mr Fosse said he thought they were being a bit dense, couldn't one of them think what it was he wanted them to see, something new which affected everybody, no matter what their work, or their way of life?

Robert guessed.

'Oh . . . oh, I know . . . of course, books . . . printing has come.'

It was hardly a book shop as the children knew bookshops. There was no shop window, only a sign hung outside. It was a tiny little place with only a few books for sale. But the man selling the books could easily have belonged to their own day. He had the same way of showing a book, as if just to hold it in two hands was a little rarefied pleasure. He had the same way of stroking the books as if to make sure they knew they were loved; the same way of smelling them, as if their smell was better than the smell of flowers. The bookseller and Mr Fosse were old friends, and as book lovers will, got talking books and forgot anybody else was there. Books were passed from one to the other: a Bible, the *Canterbury Tales*, a selection of religious books in Latin, two books on manners, and a copy of the *Golden Legend* with woodcuts. Mr Fosse, stroking this last, asked the bookseller what was happening to the scribes and illuminators put out of work now printing had come to the world. The bookseller looked quite sad. He said he still had affection for handwritten books, had Mr Fosse ever seen an illuminated copy of *A Book of Hours?* But you couldn't hold back discoveries and inventions, any more than you could hold back the wind. It was beyond imagining what printed books meant to mankind, not only scholars were affected, but people, often the last you would expect, were learning to read. If only the invention of printing were used for good, it could make the world so much finer a place for all. It looked to the children as if Mr Fosse was so busy talking books they were never going to move on, but suddenly he remembered them, waved good-bye to the bookseller and led the way back to the street.

In spite of an effort being made, the streets, by the children's standards, were still dirty. Mess piled outside doors. Wide drains full of murky water with rubbish bobbing up and down in them. Pigs, hens and goats rootling around, and, where doors were open, pushing their way into the houses. Nor was

Joan the only one who thought the proper place to throw slops was the street, for it was painfully evident other people had the same idea. But dirt aside, the town was charming. Lovely graceful houses, some of stone, some of stone and timber, and many of wood and wattle and daub. The general effect was black and white; the black was wood and, from the way it was used, it was clear there were plenty of craftsmen in wood about. One odd thing about the houses was the way so many of them had upper storeys lolling out over the street. The children thought they looked nice, but Mr Fosse said they were not popular with the authorities, for if everybody built their top storeys overhanging the street it would be very unhealthy, with no light and air for anybody.

Mr Fosse stopped outside a very imposing-looking house and, with a little gesture, drew the children close enough to him to whisper.

'The man who lives here is a rich merchant, a very important person. He makes, or employs people to make, worsted, but his money is made by selling abroad. We have not met his type on other journeys for he is new, his sort are on the up of the see-saw. Noblemen may pretend to turn up their noses at him and his like, but it is only pretending, for many of them are merchants themselves on the side, and if they are not they would be glad to be, for they need money if they are going to go on living in the grand style they are used to.'

'What's his name?' William whispered.

'James Dyghton. Now, come on, I am going to knock.'

James Dyghton was a big grey-haired man, dressed in fashionable clothes of quiet colours, but exquisite materials. He looked so grand that the children were very conscious of their shabby unfashionable clothes; but though he looked grand and stand-offish, they found it was only his manner, he was nice when they got to know him better.

The house was very fine. In shape it was something like the knight's house. The bottom floor and the vaults beneath were the business premises. James Dyghton said that on an ordinary day he had weavers and apprentices working and, as well, this was where those who wove at home brought their lengths of worsted. The vaults were his storeroom. He had, of course, agents all over Europe selling for him, but he also made frequent trips abroad himself.

A staircase led up to the main hall. This was still the big room of the house, but there was no longer any need for the family to use it as much, for the idea that it was nice to have private rooms had begun to catch on, for as well as the solar and two other bedrooms there was a room called the winter parlour. Mr Fosse said it must be quite a place to run, and James Dyghton said that no doubt it was, but he was fortunate in his wife, who was a competent woman.

There were so many improvements in living that the children did not know where to look first. All fireplaces were now

against the walls with huge overmantels. They were built in the thickness of the walls so that it would be possible to be very cosy on cold nights. The walls in the hall and the solar and one bedroom were hung with fine tapestries; one bedroom had painted walls and the winter parlour had wooden panels carved to look like folded material. On the solar floor there was a carpet, otherwise rushes were still used. One of the great changes was the windows. They were of greenish glass, and curving outwards so they made nice places to sit. In the windows in the hall there were window-seats, but in the solar and other bedrooms there were chairs, and in the room the children guessed was Mrs James Dyghton's there was an embroidery frame, so it was evidently the place where, in summer time, she sat when she had free time. When James Dyghton began to talk about Mrs James Dyghton it seemed queer she ever had free time. They were looking at the family cradle, which was a sort of solid oak box hung to posts by chains, when James Dyghton said that the cradle was unfortunately empty just now; nine babies had been born in it, but only four were living, the last had died at birth, he hoped he would have better luck next time. When he had visited Italy recently he had been to Padua, where young men from all over Europe were being trained to be doctors; one he had met had come from this part of the country, he hoped he might settle down here as, with better doctoring, some of his children might have lived. He was sure his wife had done all she could, but she had to leave a certain amount of looking after the children to the servants, for she had many other things to do, and she never knew how many she might have to entertain. That was where she was now; distant relatives with a staff of fifteen had come for the fair, and he had no idea when they would be leaving. That meant a lot of work for the woman of the house.

The children felt very sorry for Mrs James Dyghton.

'Aren't there inns?' asked Elizabeth.

James Dyghton said there were, but naturally no one stayed in inns if they had friends and relations. Every house, even the poorest, was full for the fair, they would be ashamed if they were not, it was a pleasant duty entertaining friends. As he took them round his house he pointed out some fine silk embroidered bed hangings, a gay bed coverlet and some chair covers, all of which were embroidered by his wife and the women servants. The tapestries, of course, he bought in France; they were a fine investment. A certain amount of dressmaking was done in the house; all his clothes and his wife's finer clothes were made in the town, but her simpler dresses and the clothes for the girls were cut out and made up in the house.

Elizabeth gave Grace a nudge.

'And no sewing machine. I'll tell my mum about her next time she leads off about needing six pairs of hands.'

Mr Fosse asked whether the children were at school. James Dyghton said certainly his boys had been boarding at a grammar school since they were seven and eight. He had allowed them to come home last Christmas for the twelve-day holiday. They were now thirteen and fourteen, and both he and his wife had been delighted with their progress. They had, of course, fluent Latin, for even amongst themselves they were supposed to talk nothing else, but, judging by his own school days, the Latin spoken amongst the boys was their own invention, and would not be recognized by scholars. They had excellent manners, waiting on him and his wife charmingly. At their school food was still served on the old-fashioned bread trenchers, but when at home the boys used wooden platters as if they had never used anything else. And he had been pleased to notice that when they had gnawed a bone they never threw it on the floor, nor did they ever try and feed the dogs, cats or his wife's monkey at the table. They had splendid training at their school, not only in using weapons but in how to keep them in order. That they worked hard and were obedient was proved by the fact that they were seldom flogged; the elder boy, when he had seen him at Christmas, had not been flogged for three whole weeks.

Robert was appalled, his own school was terrifying, but it sounded positively sissy beside the Dyghton boys' school.

'Don't they . . . I mean the holidays . . . don't they always come home . . . I mean . . .?'

Mr Fosse evidently felt James Dyghton would never understand Robert's stammering.

'It is not the custom, Robert.' He turned back to James Dyghton. 'Shall you send them to a university . . . Oxford or Cambridge?'

James Dyghton said no, thought he would like to. His boys, when they were through with school, would need foreign languages, something you could not do without in his business. He intended his boys to travel all over Europe selling and buying; he had made a lot of money and he intended his boys to keep it, they would learn the worsted market from the bottom up. It was sad to see money amassed by one generation frittered away by the next.

Mr Fosse asked about the girls. What sort of education were they having?

James Dyghton said he left the girls to his wife's care. The eldest was fifteen, and a suitable marriage was being planned. His wife was thinking of sending the younger girls later on into service in a great house. It would, she thought, improve their manners, and they would learn how to run establishments of their own when the time came, for good marriages would be arranged, as he was able to give large dowries. He himself was so much away he had to leave all such family matters to his wife.

James Dyghton had books of which he was very proud and wished to show to Mr Fosse, so he told the children to look round and go where they liked. The children waited until he was out of earshot, then Selina exploded.

'My goodness, his poor wife! All those things to do, and all those babies, and he's going to have some more, he said so.'

'It's the boys. . . . I mean, I think it must be awful being them,' said Robert. 'No holidays.'

'Do stop nattering,' said Elizabeth, 'we haven't all day and I want a real look round.'

There was no doubt James Dyghton was rich, for he had some plates of real gold; they did not look as if they were eaten off, but it was grand just to own gold plates. Except for the wall and bed hangings, even rich men seemed to live pretty simply. There were a few carved chairs, but mostly people seemed to sit on benches and stools. Everybody still kept their clothes in chests, and there were chests full of spare linen, and extra embroidered bed coverings. The beds themselves seemed pretty comfortable, for the children sat on them to see. The drainage seemed to have improved a little, for the house did not smell much, and judging by some basins and jugs, there was water from a cistern for washing.

Fair, or no fair, the cooks were working in the kitchen, there was an enormous clatter going on and a lot of laughter, but as well cries as angry cooks beat the boys and younger cooks for what seemed to the children small faults. Evidently there was going to be a meal, for simply masses of food was being got ready. There was meat of every sort, piles of fish, including porpoises, and many kinds of bird. As well, in an oven built in the thickness of the wall, mountains of bread and cakes were being baked. There seemed far more cooking utensils than they had so far seen, including copper warmers for keeping the food hot. Evidently most food was served chopped up or beaten up, for those cooks who were not hacking something to pieces seemed to be beating it to bits with pestles and mortars. Though many of the cooks handling the food did not look clean, and some of their ways were a bit crude, it was such fun in the kitchen the children would have stayed for hours, but suddenly they felt they were being stared at. They turned round and found a man smiling at them. The man looked about the same age as their fathers, and seemed neither rich nor poor. He was better dressed than they were themselves, but nothing like as grandly as James Dyghton. He behaved as if he knew them, and there was something about him that seemed familiar. Almost at once they could understand what he said. His accent was half-way between Joan's and James Dyghton's, but he used more French words than either of them. He was, he said, a worsted-weaver and wove for James Dyghton. At his home there was his own loom and a second loom, for he employed two apprentices; his own boy would, on his fourteenth birthday, be apprenticed to a master weaver. The children asked if he only had one boy, and he said he was the only living one, there had been another six, but they had all died. He had four daughters living, there had been three others but they too had died; he hoped his wife would soon give him another boy, and they must pray this one would live.

'What did they all die of?' Elizabeth asked.

The man shrugged his shoulders, he did not seem to know, mostly they had died as babies; he seemed to accept that rearing babies was a chancy thing, you were lucky if now and again one lived.

Before the children realized where they were going they were out in the street, and in a poorer part of the town. The worsted-weaver's house was much smaller than James Dyghton's, but still a house and not a peasant's hut. It had a hall, a kitchen, and a small room built on to the upper part of the hall, which bulged out over the street. The wife and the children were at the fair, but there were signs of them everywhere. There was the wife's spindle, and it was clear she made the family clothes, for a partly cut out small dress was on the table. There were toys lying amongst the rushes on the floor, some bricks, a doll made of wood, and a little cart. The worsted-weaver said one of the two apprentices had made them, he often had to beat him for wasting his time whittling with a knife when he should be at his weaving. In a corner was piled the linen thread, and hanks of coloured wools used for worsted making. The weaver said more was sent as needed by packhorse from James Dyghton's vaults. He led them to his loom, and showed them

the length of worsted he was making. He went on weaving while he talked. He said that he had a nice home, as they could see, and in his solar there was a good bed and even plain hangings on the walls; they had a chest and three chairs, and a table, and his wife had all she needed in the kitchen, but of course these things had to be paid for. On a holiday such as to-day he could not afford to take the day off, though of course his apprentices had to have a holiday, and so did his son, though his was being spent acting as he was taking part in a pageant. He would stop work soon and take them to see the pageant. Later he would join some friends at an inn he was fond of, and they would sit outside and watch the bonfires and the merry-making.

Saying he would take them to the play-pageant made the children remember Mr Fosse. William said:

'We have a friend at Mr Dyghton's house.'

The weaver nodded, as if to say he knew, then, as if sure they would be interested, which they were, he told them about himself. He said that his family were what were called Flemings. They had originally come from the Low Countries from a place called Ghent. There were a lot of Flemings in Norwich, but they had been there so long they reckoned themselves English, and were thought of as English by Norwich people, which was not to be wondered at for, going by the churchyard, they had first come here over a hundred and fifty years ago.

'What made them come?' asked Elizabeth.

The weaver said he had not heard, but he supposed it was to better themselves.

Selina watched his clever fingers at work on his loom and was puzzled.

'But have you? I mean, oughtn't you to own a business with people working for you?'

The weaver sighed. That would be fine, and some had succeeded, but not his family, and now it was much harder to get to the top.

'That's what we heard in the market,' said William.

The weaver said they would hear it everywhere, because it was true. At the top there were the great lords, but next came the merchants, men like James Dyghton, new rich they called them, but whatever they were called they were a powerful lot, and often made themselves more powerful by marrying the daughters of lords. There were plenty below them trying to be like them, men who to him seemed rich already. He did not know how to put it, but this new rich lot were very solid, it was nearly impossible for common men like himself to climb out of the rut and join them. Then he looked out of the window at the sun and said it was time they were moving.

The play-pageants were acted, the weaver said, on enormous two-decker carts. The bottom deck was the dressing-room and the top deck the stage. He said they were to see the one his guild was interested in. There were twelve play-pageants, and proper set out places where each cart stopped in turn and the performances given. This one they were to see was about Heaven, his son was playing an angel.

The pageant cart had not arrived, but a large noisy laughing excited crowd was waiting for it. Although the children found the people pressing on them smelly, and terribly rough, they were so gay they could not help liking them and feeling party-ish themselves. Then suddenly there were loud cries, and they and those near them were pushed back to make way for the party of a rich lord. The people around did not seem to resent being pushed back, but the children, especially Selina, were furious.

'What a nerve! We were here first.'

A laugh sounded in Selina's ear, and she found Mr Fosse beside her.

'Don't be cross, Selina. Nobody else is. These grand folk are part of the show, they are staying in Norwich for the occasion, there will probably be polite references to them in the play-pageant, and the people here are getting the same kick out of seeing them that people in our time get from staring at grand people they don't know going to royal balls, or getting married.'

A space was cleared, and the children had for a moment a good view of the grand visitors, and that was when they saw the latest fashions. The clothes were something the same as those worn by the first people they had seen, but twice as

exaggerated, and all the men wore square-toed shoes like the ones the young man had shown off. All the younger men wore their hair to their shoulders. The effect produced, especially by the men, was gay and silly in the extreme.

The great cart lumbered into sight. A howl of pleasure went up from the crowd. Everybody shoved forward and shouted encouragement to the players. The children stood on tiptoe.

It was a good thing the weaver had explained it was Heaven

they were seeing for the children never would have guessed it. As Mr Fosse had told them there would be, Heaven was full of lovely materials, great lengths of glistening gloriously-coloured silks, velvets and damasks. God, all in white, sat on a throne surrounded by His angels. The weaver nudged William, and said the angel third from the right was his boy. The angel third from the right had tow-coloured hair, high cheekbones and blue-grey eyes. William turned to look at the weaver; no wonder his face had seemed familiar.

'What's your name?'

Mr Fosse answered.

'Fish, but he spells it differently—F.Y.S.C.H.E.'

It was rather rude, but William could not help laughing.

'Fancy old John being picked for an angel!'

CHAPTER TWELVE

# *The Wedding*

FROM Norwich they flew by aeroplane to Mr Fosse's house; Mr Fosse said it would be tiresome for John to stay in to-day's Norwich, he would be half at home even if he stayed in an hotel, and he would always be running into people he knew, and on their journey they did not want that, they had no time for to-day's friends. The aeroplane journey passed quickly and pleasantly for the children, though Mr Fosse and the Mummerys may not have enjoyed it as much for it was rather a noisy journey. The children not only made up John's song but sang it till they arrived, each time a little louder than the time before. John helped make up the song, and joined in the singing. The tune was the one belonging to *Sing a Song of Sixpence*.

F.Y.S.C.H.E,
   Was John Fish's name.
His father was a Fleming,
   A weaver of some fame.
John was an appren-tice
   A-learning of his trade,
And in Corpus Christi fair-air week
   An angel fine he made.

Arriving at Mr Fosse's house was like coming home, but they only used it to sleep in, for very early they were in the shooting-brake driving into Devonshire.

'Goodness,' said Elizabeth, when she heard where they were going. 'How posh, a visit to the Selina country!'

By now Selina was getting used to Elizabeth.

'Time you saw it, Miss Hamblett, Devonshire's the loveliest place in the world.'

'And I hope you will think it lovely in June 1610' said Mr Fosse, 'For that is the year we are going to visit.'

As they drove through the Devon lanes the children were inclined to agree with Selina. It was a gorgeous day with a heat haze dancing over everything, but the lanes looked cool with little harts' tongue ferns, and wild strawberries growing on their banks.

'I like those little ferns . . .' said John dreamily, 'do they grow wild everywhere, Selina . . .?'

There was no answer; John looked round and shook his head. Where was he? Where were they? The sounds were wrong. There was no sleepy purr from the car engine. Instead there was the clip-clop of a heavy horse's hoofs, and the rattle-thump-rattle of wooden wheels on a hard bad surface. Then John began to see. He was sitting beside an old man who was driving a wooden farm cart, in which, from the smell, there had been pigs, but now were William, Robert, Grace and Elizabeth. Then he began to feel. The first thing he noticed was that the lane was in atrocious condition. It must be almost impassable in bad weather for water must pour down it, for it was not only a mass of ruts but they bumped over quite large stones. Then he noticed what he was wearing. It was no surprise to find that his clothes were shabby and darned, travelling with Mr Fosse that was to be expected. He had on a coat of chestnut-coloured wool with blue sleeves, held in place at the waist with a leather belt. It was his legs though that reminded him of the period of time he was in, for he had on short very full grey trunks, stuffed with what seemed to be rags, for there was an end of rag coming through a tear. He had on coarse, long, grey, much-darned wool stockings and clumsy leather shoes. He looked at the others: William and Robert were dressed much as he was, but both had their coats open and linen shirts showing. The girls were dressed in frocks cut square and rather low at the neck, with full sleeves, the skirts were wide, made to look wider because the bodices were laced at the back for a tight fit. Elizabeth was wearing green and Grace blue. Elizabeth saw John looking at her.

'If you want to know we've got linen petticoats underneath, we've looked, but our clothes aren't up to much. I'm afraid we're nobodies again.'

The old driver laughed, and John saw it was Mr Fosse, but he looked different for he had a beard. He seemed worse dressed than they were, for his earth-coloured coat fitted very loosely, and was patched, and his stockings were darned and his great clumsy shoes looked as if they had lived out of doors.

'Sorry, Elizabeth, but it had to be. We're simple country folk wearing, as such people usually do, the nearest we can manage to the fashion, as set by those in the big houses, and that is not very fashionable. A hedger and ditcher or cowman of my age could probably step back from our day to this, wearing his usual earth-coloured clothes and not attract much attention.'

Grace looked at her hands, and the hands and faces of the others, which were stained dark purple.

'We're a bit mucky.'

Mr Fosse said if they looked in their baskets they would see they were full of bilberries, in these parts known as worts, which they had been to pick for the cook at the Hall. It was very early, not yet seven o'clock, for the cook liked fruit picked with the dew still on it.

'Still a hall?' said William surprised.

'You will see that though there is still a great main room, the name 'hall' now means the big house, for a hall is a real home, miles away as you will see from the knight's house which, by its drawbridge over a ditch, had a keeping-people-out look, the houses now are built to be admired and to tempt visitors into them.'

As Mr Fosse's voice died away they reached the top of the lane. Below in a valley lay a village. It clustered round a church, and very lovely it looked in the early morning light. The Hall, a great black and white house, lay away from the village. Early though it was, smoke was pouring out of a chimney, so evidently the cook was up and at work. In front of the house were stone steps leading to a terrace and the front door. The children said in a way the Hall reminded them of James Dyghton's house. Mr Fosse said it was the black and white look which made them think it had been built about the same time, but he knew it had only been built about fifty years ago. A grandfather of the present owner had inherited a great deal of money made in much the way James Dyghton had made his, but he had retired from business, bought land from the big landowner in these parts, pulled down the old house, which had been very much like the one the knight had lived in, and built this one.

'Do they do nothing now?' Elizabeth asked.

'Certainly they do things. The new middle people, when they become country gentlemen, make themselves very busy. One of their jobs is to be Justices of the Peace, they share the position of becoming J.P.s with the aristocracy and the near aristocracy.'

'How do they get on with the lords?' William asked.

'Fairly well, I think. The men probably meet for sport, such as bear baiting or cock fighting, and of course on the Bench as Justices, but the aristocracy on the whole are only close friends with each other, they still look down a bit on the new rich, but it is the villagers who are the real snobs, they will take far more from true aristocracy than from the new families.'

'I expect lords and that sort still find it a bit odd that there are other people living like they do,' Robert suggested. 'I—I mean it's not so very long ago there was only a top and a bottom.'

Grace had scrambled up a bank to get a better view.

'It's not the only big house, mister. There's another biggish house o'er yonder.'

William and John joined her. John said:

'That house is nothing like as big, and it's not the same sort of house, it's a farm. Look at all the animals, and the corn and that.'

William pointed beyond the village to other farms.

'There's another, and another, and they're quite big houses.'

Mr Fosse had remained in the lane.

'Farmers are important people. You must have sung songs about the yeomen of England, well, now you are looking at the homes of the yeomen. They are gap-fillers too, yeomen come half-way between the landed gentry and the villagers.'

'The reeve come up in the world,' Elizabeth suggested.

'Or knights gone down,' said William.

Mr Fosse's voice sounded proud.

'Bless them, a fine lot, and England knows it.' Then he became business-like. 'Come along, come along, the cook's waiting for her berries.'

Back doors had come into fashion, Mr Fosse said they were intended for people like themselves, and for beggars asking for alms.

'Lucky,' said Elizabeth, noticing for the first time Selina was not with them, 'that Madame isn't with us, I can't see her fancying the back door.'

Because they had come to the back door they had a good chance to see the outbuildings and what they were used for. There were all the usual outbuildings you would find on a farm: cowsheds, a dairy, a place for chickens, pigsties and all the rest, but as well a fine stable full of horses, and close to it a blacksmith's shop for shoeing them. There was also a slaughter-house where the family could kill their own meat, a carpenter's shop, a pond for storing fish and a laundry with the most enormous coppers for washing the children had ever seen.

Mr Fosse paused by the coppers.

'They have to be large, wait until you see how many people there are in the house. It would surprise you if you knew how much linen is used in a house of this standing, besides the washing is not done as the things get dirty, it is collected together until it reaches gigantic proportions, then there is a big wash day.'

'If me mother was to do that,' said Grace, 'we'd have nowt to wear, no sheets nor nothing.'

'But remember this is the Hall, when you see the homes of the poor you will not find spare clothes or linen, they probably wash what is on their backs and wait for it to dry.'

There were many changes since the children's last visit to a country home; a lovely one was the coming of flower gardens. The gardens at the Hall were really charming, there were lawns, neat little clipped hedges around flower beds, and some trees cut into fancy shapes. The flowers were the sort they had passed in the gardens they had driven through in their own time that morning; roses were the favourites, as they probably would be for ever. Mr Fosse was pleased with the garden.

'With increasing travel, plants for gardens like this one now came from all over the world, and are learning to like living in English gardens. For some time now Englishmen have been great garden lovers.'

The house looked even more imposing close to than it had

from a distance. Mr Fosse said it had been a local effort, a local man had designed it, local workmen had built it and the timbering was the work of local craftsmen. In spite of its size there was a friendly look about the house; it was difficult, the children thought, for a house to look pompous when it might have been drawn in charcoal. It was, too, what the children described as a sensible house, meant to be lived in and made a pet of; the windows looked out over lovely views and those parts of the house made for noise and bustle and dirt were kept

to the back. It was as if the man who had built it had said to himself: 'I've spent a busy life being a merchant and now I've come to live in Devonshire I'll get away from rush and bustle and learn to live with dignity and grace,' for his house was planned for just that.

They had to climb steps to the back door. Mr Fosse said that was because there were cellars under the house. The kitchen was a big room with a butlery, pantry, bakehouse and flour store off it. There was a huge fireplace with a spit that was wound up like a clock. Evidently there was going to be a meal fairly soon, for a large piece of meat was turning on the spit, and there were some good smells coming from the pots standing on iron bars across the fire. Mr Fosse said the family would have their meal at eleven, it was quite a customary time to have luncheon, though of course they did not call it that.

One of the first things that struck the children was the enormous number of servants there seemed to be about. There was a big kitchen staff under a head cook, wearing loose white linen smocks and caps, but the general house uniform for both men and women seemed to be green and blue. The head cook was rushing around, now and again beating his underlings over the head, but the children did not altogether blame him for being cross, for not only was it very early in the morning but there was so much going and coming that, as Elizabeth said, he might as well have cooked in Waterloo Station. As usual, it took the children quite a while before they began to understand what was said, and when they did they found it a bit confusing. It seemed the serving men and maids, who all talked at once with Devon accents, were waiting to take breakfast to the people they served. There was food wanted for the master and mistress of the house, the tutor, the guests, the nursery and the young ladies. The nursery staff were particularly loud in their cries for attention, explaining that the head nurse was in a shocking temper, and would take it out of them if the children's food was late. The food that they were waiting for seemed to the children the most extraordinary breakfast they had ever heard of; it was saffron cakes for the grown-ups and a loaf of bread and a kind of soup with bones in it for the children. Everybody, grown-ups and children, were apparently going to drink ale, for all the servants went to the butlery and came back with foaming jugs.

'If the children get through that lot,' Elizabeth whispered to William, 'I reckon there's going to be trouble in the nursery before the day's out.'

William said 'ssh' in an annoyed way, for he was trying to pick up what everybody was talking about. The first piece of news the children gathered was that this was expected to be quite a day. The eldest son of the house had been away to get married and was returning bringing his bride with him. An elderly woman who was arranging saffron cakes on a silver plate for her mistress said it was to be hoped that the dear boy arrived back early, his mother would not be happy till she had him and his little wife under her roof. There were too many of

these highwaymen about, disgraceful, something ought to be done about them. The head cook said that the trouble was people were so glad to reach home safely, even if they did have to part with jewels and such, that they could not be bothered to raise hue and cry. A grave-faced man coming from the butlery with a jug said what good did it do raising hue and cry? More often than not nothing came of it. One of the younger maids chirped up and said for her part she rather fancied highwaymen. This sentiment seemed to be agreed with by all the younger servants, for a general murmur of something near admiration came from them.

'Are there coppers or anything?' Elizabeth whispered.

Mr Fosse whispered back:

'Or anything describes what there is, very nicely. We have not had time to have a look at the watch before, but it is a system of looking after the public highway, which has been going for a long while. There is a man called the Constable who is in charge of the watch, either in a village or in his particular portion of a town. Householders are called up to serve under him whether they like it or not, and they are not paid for watching.'

Elizabeth had been thinking of highwaymen ever since she had heard the servants talking of them.

'Are they supposed to catch the highwaymen? I bet they don't, those gorgeous men on horses would just flick their fingers at the watch.'

Mr Fosse chuckled.

'I would not wonder if you are right. I do not think that the watch tackle highwaymen, for one thing highwaymen would not be so silly as to come near the watch. The duty of the watch is to stop strangers who cannot give a reasonable account of themselves, and pop them in the stocks till the morning, or, if they run away, to raise hue and cry. You must often have heard the expression hue and cry in our time, and you could have heard it on our journeys, for it is very old. It means pursuing a criminal with horn and voice.'

'What sort of people do the watch have to stop if they aren't highwaymen,' John asked.

'Sometimes poor harmless wretches, often just vagrants, but as well those intending to do wrong, and those who carry daggers and pistols and other weapons of violence, which is an offence. When they do their job properly the watch is a very good thing, it makes people able to sleep reasonably comfortably in their beds, knowing that no strangers are prowling around.'

The house servants had left the kitchen so it was in less of an uproar and the children had a chance to look round at the sort of meal that was being cooked. Apart from the eleven o'clock meal the evening meal, which would be served about six o'clock, was being prepared. For that the favourite dishes of the bridegroom, and some dishes to please the bride, were being got ready. That was what the worts, as the servants called them, were for as there was to be a bilberry tart. The cook said the young master was partial to a nice tart. Evidently meat was a big part of both meals, for apart from the enormous joint turning on the spit there was a great piece of pork, a side of beef and apparently half a sheep to be cooked before the day was over. But meat was not the only dish that was going to be served, for while the children were watching outdoor servants brought food in: great baskets of fish, various game, including partridges and plovers and, as well, chickens and rabbits. The day's bread was carried in from the bakehouse and piled on a side-table, and this gave the children more idea of the size of the household than anything else, for there were enough loaves to fill a baker's shop. Then there was garden stuff: bowls of strawberries and raspberries, herbs and green vegetables. From the dairy came cheeses and butter, and from the hen houses eggs by the dozen. Several barrels of ale and beer were carried in from the brewery to the butlery, and as well large quantities of cider, which was, as Mr Fosse pointed out, to be expected in Devonshire.

John was sure that there was a lot he would like to see in the house, especially the work of carpenters, for there was every sign there were fine craftsmen about. He asked Mr Fosse if he thought anyone would mind if he prowled around a bit, but Mr Fosse in his Fosse-ish way had disappeared, and it was quite a different voice that answered. It was a cheerful, red-faced man who spoke; he was balancing a large platter of saffron buns on one hand and carrying an enormous jug of ale in the other. He was, he said, going to the front of the house on his way to the tutor's room, a nice man the tutor, very friendly and easy to get on with, the children could come with him if they liked, but they mustn't make a noise for the family were having their small meal in the dining-room, which was off the great gallery, and like as not the door through would be open.

The children followed the man down a passage, which led past the back stairs, and the storerooms, wash-houses, larders and cupboards needed for the running of a big house, there they came to an oak door and there the man paused and put his finger to his lips as if to say, 'Quiet now, we're coming to the house proper.' On the other side of the door were the front stairs and a fine carved door standing half open. The servant gave this door a push and the children found themselves looking into the great gallery.

The gallery was a distant relation to the halls they had been in on their journeys in that it was the most important room in the house and a general meeting-place, but otherwise it was as unlike the halls as a chrysalis is unlike a butterfly. The most noticeable change was that it was full of light and, instead of being built like a church, it had a ceiling and, in spite of its great size, looked part of a much-loved home. The ceiling was very grand, patterned all over, with little bits hanging down like pendants. There was an enormous fireplace with a top of coloured marble, carved with a pattern like belts linked together, and there were fat decorated marble pillars holding it up. The walls were wood, the man told them, of oak from the forests on the estate, where they had very fine oak trees. Elizabeth nudged Grace and pointed to the windows which took up much of the wall facing them.

'Look at the curtains, aren't they smashing? If Selina was here she'd go mad over those and would want to show them to her Miss Marion.'

Grace giggled, for Borthwick and Miss Marion were a

never-ending joke between her and Elizabeth. The windows were large, far larger than any windows they had seen so far on their journeys. They were latticed, which meant made up of little bits of glass, held together by a framework or lattice of lead. The glass was now clear, and through it light was streaming, and with the sun on them the curtains certainly were what Elizabeth called smashing. They were ruby red, most elaborately embroidered, and, as they could see from a corner which was turned back, lined with silk. The floor was grand too, for it was made of black and white marble, which after seeing dirty rushes for so long seemed terrific, and as John said, was nearly back to Roman style. Everything in the gallery had a very carved look: there were carved pillars up the sides of the doors, there was carving over the door and on the wall panels. One thing which impressed the children very much was that there was a clock. It was the first clock they had seen on their journeys.

John knew a little about clocks.

'I think clocks have been about before but we haven't seen one because we haven't been much with rich types who have one.'

The man was pleased that they admired the clock; he said the family thought no end of it, it had come from France, so he had heard, and was supposed to tell about the stars and the moon and that, as well as the time.

There was much more furniture than there had been in James Dyghton's house. Plenty of wooden chairs with arms and embroidered seats, substantial sideboards with lots of shiny gold and silver plate and glass on them; in the centre of the room was a great table with stools set round it, and there was a smaller table in the curve of one of the great bow windows. The man said that later, on the tables and the sideboards, dishes would be set out with food for the visitors; those the little bride brought with her who might stay several days, while they were in the house they must feel they could help themselves to a snack whenever they fancied it.

Elizabeth squeezed round the door to get a better view into the gallery, but drew back hurriedly because she heard voices. The man said they were coming from the dining-room, the family were probably in there. The dining-room was a favourite room, in the winter it was warm in the nook round the fire; in the summer it was pleasant to sit in the great bay window, they had a table pulled right into the curve of it, and it got the morning sun and had one of the pleasantest views in the house, for it looked right across the rose garden. Elizabeth pointed to a door on their left which, across the width of the gallery, faced the dining-room door, and asked where that led to. The man said the withdrawing-room, a very handsome room, more formal than the dining-room, the curtains and the chair covers in there were beautiful, of gold and blue silk heavily embroidered; for himself he was scared to go in, for fear of marking anything. It was the kind of room, as far as he was concerned, more meant to be looked at than to be sat in, if they knew what he meant. The children said they knew exactly what he meant, they had all got rooms like that at home. The man said the family used the withdrawing-room for music, especially when solos were sung, for the clavichord was in there but they made general music in the dining-room or here in the gallery. He pointed to two great carved chests and said the house instruments were kept in them and so were the sheets of music. The children guessed the clavichord must be a kind of early piano, but they were foxed by 'house instruments.' John asked what they were. The man seemed surprised at the question. Naturally there were house instruments, woodwinds, viols and so on, everybody who came to the house played something and you couldn't expect them to bring their own instruments with them. It would be as odd to find a visiting lady or gentleman who could not play an instrument as it would be to find one who could not write a verse or sing a madrigal, and if it came to that, there was some nice instrument players and singers amongst the servants.

Grace was the only one not impressed by this music talk.

'Strings and woodwind's right enough, but give me brass, there's nowt to touch brass tha' knows.'

The servant suddenly remembered the tutor, he must not, he said, waste any more time or he would get his ears boxed.

They left the gallery and followed the man up the stairs. At the top there was no passage for they walked straight into a bedroom. It was evidently a man's room, for there were a man's clothes about, and it was probably a guest's room, for the man-servant who was taking a suit out of a cupboard was not wearing the house uniform. Their guide marched on through his master's room, his lady's room and various guest rooms, treating them all as if they were a passage, which to him they probably were. The children would have loved to look round; the girls were especially interested in the room of the lady of the house, where there were the most intriguing collection of jars and bottles on the chest she evidently used as a dressing-table. In every room there were huge four-poster beds with most elaborately embroidered curtains and very carved posts. There were tapestries on all the walls, except one which had a carpet hung on it. There were carved cupboards, chests and stools. In each room there was a basin and jug, and something the children thought must be soap and a towel. On the floors were rushes, but beautifully clean, evidently freshly laid down,

for they still had their nice rush smell. As well in each room there were flowers, mostly roses. A number of servants were working; Elizabeth, who had been near them, whispered:

'Reckon they have flowers around to keep out the smells. These servants don't half pong, and I wouldn't wonder if the people of the house do too.'

William thought Elizabeth was being very Selina-ish.

'It's not so bad as all that. I don't think they wash much, but they're streets ahead of all the others we've met, except the Romans.'

Elizabeth took a deep sniff.

'But still nothing to write home about.'

The tutor's room was small, and a lot of the space was taken up by the bed. There was a charming bay window with a stone-window seat, a stool, a cupboard and two great chests on legs. There was tapestry on the walls and nice clean-smelling fresh rushes on the floor. On the top of one of the chests was washing apparatus, but no sign it had been used that morning. Sitting on the window-ledge was an old Fosse-ish-looking man, wearing a long shabby dark blue woollen coat with a white collar; the coat was open, so they saw that under it he had fairly narrow breeches fastened below the knee. He did not at first notice they had come into the room for all his attention was given to a pot plant. The servant put down the food and drink and when he had gone out the tutor looked up and beckoned the children to come over to him and look at his wonderful plant. The plant did not look very interesting, but to the tutor it was obviously something very special, for with eyes full of pride he said he was sure none of them could guess what it was. The children studied the plant which, now they came to look at it closer, had a familiar look. It was rather straggly with a shrivelled-looking little fruit or berry hanging on it. Suddenly John recognized it, and it was all he could do not to laugh.

'That's a potato, you don't want to grow it in a pot.'

The tutor said he was surprised John knew what it was, for there were still very few about. His was doing nicely, it had borne a flower earlier in the year, and now it had turned into this little fruit. The children thought of the acres and acres of potatoes growing at home.

John said, trying not to sound snubbing: 'It would do better out of doors.'

The tutor said that he had heard that was so, but of course this one little plant was all he had and he could not risk losing it. It had been given to him by a visitor from London. It was a plant from the new world and therefore more than just a plant to him. It was like the key of a door. It was incredible to believe that across the world there was land on which this Virginia potato had once grown, a new world offering new chances and new hope for so many, a place to which the strong and the brave could go and be free to speak as they liked, and pray as they liked, where they could make fine decent God-fearing lives for themselves. He wished so much that he was a young man; had he been nothing would have held him back from sailing from Bristol with John Smith. The tutor turned and gazed out of the window, as if he could see the new world in the garden of his own world. Robert saw the other four were looking puzzled, he whispered:

'He's talking about America—Pocahontas and all those.'

Of course they all knew about Pocahontas, but talking of

John Smith and looking at the potato gave them the funniest feeling. The time they were in was not really so long ago, yet to this man America was as much a dream-place as Mars was to them. The tutor went across to the food the servant had left and helped himself to a saffron bun, and poured ale into a pewter tankard. He said, as he munched and drank, that he was so glad that the weather was nice, Henry was so fond of his home, it was good to bring his bride to it on so golden a day. He wished he could have seen him married, but the wedding was a quiet one because the bride's mother had died recently, so not even Henry's parents had gone to it. He had thought the dear boy might have liked his tutor with him, but he had gone alone except for servants.

The children thought it would have been very odd if a person who was old enough to get married wanted his tutor with him, and evidently the tutor guessed what they were thinking, for he said that Henry had not done lessons with him for many years, as he had been to Eton, but he had given him his early lessons. When he had first come to the house Henry had been a tiny boy, running around with his horn book tied round his neck. He had been very angry at first being held to his books, but he learned to work hard and he had taught him Latin and the other usual subjects.

William asked: 'Did Henry like being at Eton?'

The tutor said he thought he had liked it well enough. He had not cared at first for early rising, for he was fond of his bed, of course at school he had to be up by five for prayers and to clean out his room. He had found it hard, too, to speak nothing but Latin, nor did he like the many floggings which came his way; but Eton had done him a lot of good. It had improved his manners, riding and fencing out of all knowledge. And he had learned to write very pretty verse, and his dancing and his singing had come on nicely.

Elizabeth grinned at Robert.

'Is that what you learn at your posh school?'

Robert, who had been taught that though his school was the greatest in the country, Eton ran it pretty close, felt bound to stand up for Eton.

'F-f-fencing and those sort of things are pretty strenuous.'

The tutor said they certainly were, and the riding training was very hard. As was right every moment of Henry's school days was employed in some way, and that came hard on a boy who enjoyed making his own amusements.

'Are there t'other lads in t'family, mister?' Grace asked.

The tutor said no; there had been five other boys, but they had all died. The family consisted of Henry, three girls in the schoolroom and two in the nursery. There had been other daughters, but they had died. A new baby was expected, if it lived it was hoped it would be another boy. He said 'if it lived' in exactly the same tone as the people in Norwich had talked about babies, so evidently nothing had been done yet to improve their chances of living.

'If there aren't no other lads in t'family, mister,' Grace asked, 'who durster teach?'

The tutor said he taught the elder girls languages, reading, writing, arithmetic, astrology and the scriptures. From Dulverton a master drove out once a week for music and dancing, and another for drawing. Naturally, however, as was right, far more of the girls' time was spent learning housewifely duties than book learning. Their mother, a beautiful needlewoman, saw to it that even little Elizabeth, who was not yet eight, was a good needlewoman. The elder two girls, Mary and Margaret, were great housewives, they did not cook, but they were constantly ordered to watch meals being cooked, and they could make jam and preserves, and knew how to bottle; and they were especially good, as was their mother, in the use of herbs, both those grown in the garden and those picked wild. Mary made crystallized sugar flowers, using violets and rose petals, she was quite famous for them.

'What are the herbs for?' William asked.

The tutor said that many were for beautifying, he must know what ladies were about spots and blemishes, but mostly they were for health. The lady of the house had some wonderful prescriptions which she used not only on her own household but on the whole village. She had a famous remedy for sweating sicknesses and another for fits, and her cures were known to work better than most people's because she was a great one for studying the phases of the moon. As they would know, medicine taken at the right time in relation to the moon had twice the effect of medicine taken at the wrong time. Luckily the tutor looked out of the window again at this, for the children could not help nudging each other and raising their eyebrows.

'What about doctors?' William asked.

The tutor said he thanked God they had not needed a doctor in their household, for he did not think there was a good one nearer than Exeter, and the expense of having him would be enormous.

Elizabeth said:

'But when the babies were ill wasn't a doctor sent for?'

The tutor shook his head, a child ailed and was gone before you could do anything about it. Evidently to him it was a very ordinary matter for a baby to die. There was a tooth-drawer who came now and again, he said, and a man who cut corns, but otherwise most of the curing that was done in the village and the household was done by his lady. He saw the children were looking a bit horrified, so he added, sounding much more like Mr Fosse than the tutor, that it was surprising what common sense and experience, and the sort of mind that recorded things from one illness to the next, could do in a sick room. That many herbs were very good cures for certain illnesses, and though such things as dead spiders and dried bat's blood might be added to a brew, it probably did no harm, for if the patient believed a pinch of bat's blood or a dead spider in their medicine would make them better, it probably did help, for faith in the cure was a large part of doctoring.

The children felt glad they did not live at a date when doctors were not easily got hold of. They thought of the ambulance men, the hospitals and the nurses and doctors of their own time; they might not need them, but it was nice to know they were there if you did. The lady of the house might be clever with herbs, but it would be pretty frightening to be really ill and have to depend on her, and perhaps a few herbs and a dead spider to get you well.

There were children's voices in the passage. Little children evidently did not change much, for a small shrill voice was asking someone called Nan why it couldn't take its best doll into the garden, and was being told, in a fat, cosy Mrs Mummery-ish voice, that want would have to be her master. The tutor said that was the head nurse sending the younger children to play in the garden.

Elizabeth asked where the elder girls were. The tutor said that they would be with their parents. They joined them for family prayers, and afterwards usually read a chapter of the Bible with their mother before the day's work. To-day, as there were guests, relations come to look over the bride, there would be no ordinary lessons, though of course they would do tasks for their mother. As they could imagine, Mary and Margaret were very excited at the thought of a new little sister.

The tutor had carried his ale to the window, and had his back to them, so behind it the children made puzzled faces, and signs to each other to be the one to ask.

Elizabeth took on the job.

'How d'you know it's going to be a girl, you said you hoped it would be a boy?'

The tutor swung round, his blue eyes danced with laughter. He was not talking of the new baby, they were not expecting that until Christmas, he was talking of the bride.

Elizabeth spoke scornfully.

'If they think the bride's going to play with them they've got another think coming. Brides don't.'

The tutor's voice blew like a cool breeze over Elizabeth's scorn.

This bride, he said, was less than a year older than Mary, and the girls should have a lot to talk about, for Mary was to be married in the spring.

'How old do they do lessons then?' William asked, 'for you said Mary was in the schoolroom?'

The tutor saw they were puzzled and spoke in a slow, explaining voice. Mary, he said, was twelve. He paused while the children took in that if Mary was twelve the bride must be thirteen. It was, he said, a very suitable marriage that had been arranged. Henry was going to the Inns of Court to learn

something about the law to finish his education, and the girl was to finish hers in his home. The marriage had been planned for a long while. Although this branch of the family were no longer directly connected with business themselves, they still had interests in it. The grandfather of the present master of the house had made his money as a merchant trading overseas, but mostly in Europe, for in his day the known world was much smaller and a big trade in Europe was enough, but every day the world was growing larger.

As the tutor said the words 'growing larger,' so great was his feeling of living in a world of marvels, that in a little way the children began to feel with him. New lands known about, people going to them, trading with them, bringing back things from them, settling down in them, it must feel as if the world was growing under their eyes, and would go on growing. The tutor felt their sympathy for he went on in the sure voice of a person who knows he is being interesting. The bride's family had not only trading interests in Europe but with the Levant and Turkey, and with a place called Goa in the Indies, and were thinking of new trade with East India, and if the colony grew with the new world itself, they would trade with Virginia.

The children looked at the potato in its pot, and saw it not as a potato but as the little miracle it was to the tutor. Then they remembered the wedding.

'So Henry's to wed for nowt but brass, mister?' Grace said in a shocked voice.

The tutor said that arranged marriages were usual, it was a good plan for young people could not be expected to know who they wanted as companions for life, and a boy's parents were the right judges of which girl's dower would best serve his ends.

While the tutor talked he opened one of the chests. It was

full of books. They looked very dull books, but he picked out two and showed them to Grace. They were, he said, novels, she would enjoy reading them when she was older, for they were about romantic love which, from her tone, he gathered she believed in.

William was impressed by the number of books the tutor owned, for he had thought they were still scarce.

'They are mostly for teaching I suppose. I mean Latin, French, history and things like that?'

The tutor answered in a serious voice, but his eyes were twinkling. They must not give him away, for his employers believed that when he was reading in his room it was something deep, and often it was, but as well he had one or two of his favourite books, which were murder stories.

'Thrillers!' said Elizabeth. 'Fancy you having them!'

The tutor said that as well as murder books he had murder pamphlets, and not only murders, for there was a glorious one he was very fond of which was about a lion who ate his keeper.

'Do they have a library in the house?' William asked.

The tutor said of course both the master and the mistress were great readers, each had a chest of books. The master was very fond too of broadsheets and ballads, he had them bought for him in London, and it was a big day when a packet of them arrived. Many of them were bloodcurdling descriptions of real events. The master had to keep a sharp eye on them, for there were plenty wanting to read them. It was said that the moment a packet arrived the house carpenter found a job that needed doing in his master's room, and he had read every ballad before he admitted the job was done.

Robert, surprised, asked:

'D-do all the servants read now?'

The tutor took a flat shabby hat from his cupboard and led the way into the passage. By no means, he said, but more could than anyone would suppose, and these ballads and pamphlets had a lot to do with it. One who could read helped another, and they figured the words out between them, and they were so eager to find out all the gory details they found learning to read a pleasure.

'Where's ter barn to, mister?' Grace asked.

The tutor said he had to go to the church, they could come too if they liked.

William was thinking of the packages of pamphlets.

'How do packages get here from places like London?'

The tutor thought that an odd question, for he laughed and said what should be difficult about it? If it was only a package it would be probably brought on horseback, but if there were great parcels they would come by cart. The master had an agent in London who bought goods for him, and it was he who arranged the forwarding of whatever he had bought.

They were half-way down the front stairs when they heard singing. It was unaccompanied part singing. Elizabeth skipped up to the tutor, and put her hand through his arm.

'Could we see who's singing, it won't take a minute?'

The tutor nodded, and quietly pushed open the great door into the gallery. The master of the house, the mistress, the three girls and six guests—three men and three women—were all singing. The children looked upon part singing as a serious occupation, you were grouped according to the part you were singing, and you never for a moment took your eyes off the hand that was conducting you. Singing in 1610, or at least the way this family sung, was not a bit like that. They sang, as people in the children's world sang, for fun, or in their baths, doing other things at the same time.

The master of the house was leaning against the mantelpiece watching his men guests who, in a casual sort of way, were throwing dice, using one of the chests as a table. Mary and Margaret were playing with a little thin brown puppy and Elizabeth was bouncing a ball. The mistress of the house was sitting on one of the window-seats at her embroidery frame, and the lady guests were sorting and admiring her embroidery silks. They were a rich, colourful-looking group. The men had very stiff-looking clothes. Padded tunics pleated below the waist, of rich stuff worn over an under-tunic of a different colour. Full breeches to below their knees, fine plain white muslin collars and turned-back cuffs. The women and the children, including little Elizabeth, wore even stiffer and starchier-looking clothes than the men. Very tight-boned bodices, laced all down the front to finish in as narrow a waist as their shapes made possible, for two of them were quite fat. The bodices finished in big

pleats which would have fallen to about their hips, only the frill were balanced on great round frames. From the frame the over-skirt fell to the ground, but it was cut away in front to show the under-dress. They had wired lace collars which stood up behind their heads. Perhaps it was because of the size of their skirts, but what the children noticed most was their tiny feet, wearing pretty little shoes, trimmed with bows and flowers.

The song came to an end, and one of the dice players asked the master of the house if he knew a tune, and he whistled it. The master went across to a chest and took out a wind instrument, and tried to pick out the air the other was whistling. The lady laid down her embroidery, and told Margaret to look at the new sheets of music that had come from London, she believed that the song was in the packet. Margaret apparently read pages of music as the children would read headlines in a newspaper; she found the song, sorted the sheets and handed them round. There were not enough for all, but they shared and after a little humming, sang the song as if they had known it all their lives. The children could have stayed listening and watching for ages, but the tutor closed the door and said they must go.

They crossed part of the gardens to reach the village. Under a tree an under-nurse was sitting with the youngest child on her knee, and two other under-nurses sat beside her sewing. The little girl who had wanted to take her doll to the garden was playing by herself. Although she had on what were evidently garden clothes, she still looked very stiffly dressed compared to little girls of their own day, but games did not seem to have changed. As the children passed her they saw her hand a leaf with a flower petal on it to an imaginary guest, and say in a party voice that she did hope they liked quince pie.

The life in the Hall had impressed the children. To Robert, used to a father who shouted, it gave a feeling of gentleness and dignity. To Elizabeth, used to a small noisy home, it was a glimpse of a new way of living. It was the beautiful things in the house, and that they were not merely for show but to be used and enjoyed that meant most to John. William had a funny feeling that he knew how it felt to live like that, and yet nothing could be further from the busy shabby vicarage. Grace, saving up descriptions to take back to her home, was sure she had collected one that morning that she would not forget; she could almost hear her mother's thoughtful: 'Must have been right nice folk, tha' knows.'

Because they had been so impressed by the Hall the village came as a nasty shock. It had looked so pretty with its church, its enclosed grassy common, its shops and its inn, but the way they came to it took them past some of its poorest homes, and they were very poor homes indeed, some of them little better than the huts on the knight's manor. The houses, if you could call them that, were built of wood or wattle and daub, they had only one room and that had a mud floor. The tired-looking women of the house, dressed much like themselves only worse, were doing the housework, some were washing and the children remembered what Mr Fosse had said about only having what was on their backs, for the garments they wrung out and hung up to dry were just rags. Some were cooking; there was only a small window so, though it was without glass, the smoke did not get out and hung like a fog and mixed its smell with other smells, and very revolting the collected smells were. Small children were playing outside and so were cats, dogs, goats, hens and pigs, and all wandered in and out of the houses when they felt like it. In many of the homes there were babies lying on the straw-filled mattresses, which were the only beds. The one improvement was that each house had a quite decent garden, in which evidently they grew much of the family food. Children of four and five were often working in the gardens, and their harassed mothers looked out every now and then to see they were not slacking, and shouted at them to get along with it or they would get into trouble when their father came home.

Elizabeth turned on the poor tutor as if he was responsible for how the people lived.

'Those up at the Hall ought to be ashamed of themselves letting people live like this.'

The tutor could not see what Elizabeth was complaining about. He said these houses were nothing to do with the Hall, except that the people who lived in them had not been able to pay for the four acres of land they had to have before they might build, and so the master had agreed to these houses being put up on his waste land, which was very good of him.

'Good!' said Grace. 'Where I come fra t'pigsties look better nor that, mister.'

The tutor had walked on, and did not seem to know Grace had spoken. William said:

'Come on, all of you. It's no good cursing at him. It's not his fault.'

'It—it's everybody's fault,' Robert stammered. 'People oughtn't to allow it.'

The tutor heard that and gave a very Fosse-ish chuckle. Elizabeth called out as if he had spoken to her.

'We may have some beasts of houses in our time, but we do think them awful, you don't even do that.'

They turned a corner and came to the village proper, and here in some ways it was charming, as it had looked from the distance. There were lots of nice houses, most of two storeys, with large latticed windows. These were the homes, the tutor said, of tradesmen and craftsmen: the carpenter, the shoemaker, the tailor, the baker, and so on. One of the richest men in the village was the miller, he lived outside in a house by his windmill. The 1610 people still had slovenly ways. The main village street was very dirty and twice they just missed having slops thrown over them from an upstairs window.

The church was in the centre of the village. It was not new, it must have been built by Saxons, the children thought, for, although it was of stone instead of wood, it looked rather like the church near the thane's Hall, but it must have been rebuilt, for it had big windows. The children expected to find the best of everything in the church, but this church was very plain inside. The windows did not look like church windows, for they had white glass like the houses. The altar was just a wooden table with no embroidered cloth on it or anything like that. The tutor had come to look at the Bible, which was chained to a reading stand. He said his master had thought a page had become loose, and had sent him to see. The children, waiting while he looked, noticed the Bible was printed in English now instead of Latin. John asked the tutor about this and he said that only papists used Latin Bibles.

Behind his back the children made remembering faces at each other. Of course parish churches were not Roman Catholic any more, there had been that Reformation they were always hearing about.

'There must have been lovely things belonging to the church,' William said, 'what happened to them? Were they taken away?'

The tutor was vague, for it was all hearsay, but he thought not. He had heard there had been rich furnishings at one time, but when they could no longer be used he believed they had been sold.

'What happens . . . I mean, there must be some Roman Catholics left. Where do they go to church?'

The tutor said, in a voice which showed that it was not respectable to be a Roman Catholic, that Catholics, Puritans and other such, did not go to church at all, and not going to church was an offence for which they came before the justices and were fined.

Outside the church they met a man who was a friend of the tutor's, and it did not take the children long to realize he must be one of the yeoman farmers Mr Fosse thought so well of. He wore rougher, thicker clothes than they had seen at the Hall, and he talked like a farmer in a broad Devon accent, and he smelt like a farmer. He greeted the tutor with a great friendly roar, and asked what time they were expecting the bride and groom. His wife had been on at him all day to find out, and he would make a wager she would find her way down to the village by the time the coach was due.

The tutor asked how young James was getting on at Blundell's.

The farmer said very well so far as he could gather, it was a fine school, and he was glad his boy was one of the first to go there. It was the right school for his boy, he would pick up no fancy ways, but come out ready to get down to farming. James was to be married next year, they had just settled everything: he thought Margaret would make a good wife.

Elizabeth said:

'What, Margaret from the Hall?'

The farmer howled with laughter, and said no indeed, James's Margaret was the daughter of a small farmer, but one who was up and coming, and had no sons to leave his land to. He could not see Mistress Margaret from the Hall as a farmer's wife, nor would he approve of such a match. He was a farmer, and proud of it, and had no wish to look outside farming families for wives for his sons.

A boy came by, and as he passed he grinned at the tutor and gave his front hair the pull that was a sort of taking off of a cap. The farmer asked who the boy was. The tutor said he was a groom at the Hall, but a remarkable boy of unusual intelligence; he got very little free time, but when he had any he came to him to be taught not only to read and to write but to hear about the new world.

The farmer looked disgusted. That was the sort of foolishness which was ruining the country. If you gave every poor toad—he pronounced it to-ad—education where were the farm labourers and all the other workers to come from? What he liked to see was a whole family getting down to work, from the father to the little four-year-olds, whom he used as bird-scarers. Between the whole lot the poor to-ads only earned enough to keep their bodies and souls together, there was nothing like a bit of a pinch to make sure they all worked, and when they had finished a day on his farm they had no time for books or any such nonsense.

The tutor said there were exceptions, and this boy was one, but he did not convince the farmer. He said filling the poor to-ad's head with nonsense would bring him before his master on the bench. That sort turned out trouble-makers.

The children were just going to tell the farmer he was very mean when there was the sound of horses and wheels, and into the main street came quite a procession. First a boy

on horseback followed by several servants. Then a clumsy coach drawn by four horses. Then ten carts piled high with luggage.

The farmer gave a groan, and said it was the bride, and his wife not there. He would never hear the end of it.

The cavalcade came sweeping along and at once windows were opened and heads hung out. From nowhere people sprang up and called out to each other the bride was coming. As the procession came up to them the boy, who was Henry, waved and shouted to the tutor, asking wasn't he surprised to see him? They had come no end of a rate, nothing had passed them on the road.

The coach had no windows, but the door was banged open and a girl's face peered out. It looked greenish. The village people made sympathetic sounds, no wonder the poor little thing was sick, the motion was terrible in these coaches it was said, and you got black and blue with the bumping. The bride paid no attention to the villagers, who might not have been there for all she cared. Her eyes flashing, she turned on Henry like an angry kitten, telling him just what she thought of the journey.

William turned to the tutor.

'What's Henry's name? Is it Edgecombe?'

Elizabeth answered.

'Of course it's Edgecombe. My goodness, I'm sorry for Henry married to Selina!'

CHAPTER THIRTEEN

# *London Town*

THE children had a holiday at Mr Fosse's house. He said he thought that a bit of running about and doing nothing would do them good and get them in fine form for their last two journeys.

'You visited Devonshire with very little help from me, but from now on you will have less help. I want you to be accustomed to finding your own way back, so that for ever you will know how to take a journey whenever you feel in the mood for one. I am afraid our last two journeys may be a bit of a scramble, the nearer the journeys become to our own time, the more difficult it is to choose what to look at. When we were on the hillside above Bath life was so simple we could look at everything we were able to see, but where we are going next there will be so much going on that unless you think hard you will get in a muddle and come back confused.'

Elizabeth gave Mr Fosse's hand an affectionate little pat.

'As we've only two journeys left there's nothing to be awfully secret about, so would you mind telling me if its Robert or me we see next?'

'Where are we going?' William asked. 'That's what's more interesting.'

Mr Fosse walked to the window and looked out.

'I don't mind telling you where you're going. It will be to London, in the very early years of the eighteenth century, 1712 to be exact.'

Elizabeth looked across the table at Robert.

'Then I bet it's me, and I don't mind telling you straight off it'll be very low life. There's nothing grand about my family.'

Robert was getting to feel less of a fool every day, and

the less he felt a fool the less he stammered. He grinned at Elizabeth.

'My lot weren't any great shakes to start with, but I bet London's you, for I think our thread started in Lancashire.'

Grace gave Robert an approving look.

'They're fine folk in Lancashire, tha' knows.'

Mr Fosse's reed-in-the-wind voice blew across the table.

'I particularly want you to explore while you're here. I want you to look over my property very carefully. We shall come back here when we have finished our journey and I am going to ask you a question which has to do with my land. The best answer given to that question will win that prize I told you about.'

Selina did wish that Mr Fosse had a more orderly mind. She never had thought not knowing what the prize was for satisfactory.

'I do think we should know what sort of thing to look at on your property.'

Elizabeth dug her elbow into John, who was sitting next to her.

'Hark at the child-bride. Poor Henry!' Then she turned to Mr Fosse. 'All the same, Selina's right. I do wish we knew more about that prize. It's an awful thing going in for a competition when you don't know what sort of competition you've gone in for.'

Mr Fosse swung round from the window.

'My dears, put the competition out of your heads. You can only do what you can do. I can promise you one thing: it is a perfectly fair question. None of you has a greater likelihood of winning the prize than the other.'

Before starting to explore Mr Fosse's property the children learned Selina's song. They lay on the front lawn and William sang the words he had made up for it. They went to the tune of *Hush-a-bye Baby*.

S'lina at thirteen in a great coach
The roads are so bad we fear she will lurch
And when she gets there so coach-sick and sore,
She'll be mar-ried to Hen-ry for ev-er more.

When they had all learnt the song Selina said:

'I saw yesterday what Mr Fosse meant. It isn't the sort

of people that you are when you start that matters, but the sort of people you go on being. When he talked about the colour of the thread and all that, I thought mine was going to be simply gorgeous looking, all blues and golds and scarlets, but I see now it's just ordinary coloured.'

William thought Selina was missing the point.

'I think your sort of thread has been awfully useful. I mean, there was Henry's father, who was going to be your father-in-law, from what you told us he's still a J.P., I mean your father is. And there've been Edgecombes in Parliament, haven't there?'

Elizabeth thought back to the family at the Hall.

'And though your mother doesn't go round giving everyone herbs, like the tutor said the one who was going to be your mother-in-law did, from what you've said she never stops doing good to people. I mean, you told me yourself she's on committees every day, and she's president of the women's something-or-other, and always opening bazaars and boring things like that.'

Selina nodded.

'She is. In fact, I don't think the Edgecombes have changed much, only somehow I thought we were grander.' She tried to find the words to explain. 'It's been a surprise to me that being important doesn't matter as much as being strong, not tailing off and going down.' She looked at John, and remembered Norwich. 'You were craftsmen, you may have stopped being craftsmen and your father may have to sell vegetables, but from what you've told us he's never stopped being proud of doing things with his fingers, and you've got a place in Norwich Technical to learn to be a craftsman. I mean, that's the sort of thread you were, and the sort of thread you are.'

Robert looked at Grace.

'I suppose you've come down a bit.'

Grace put out her tongue at him.

'Don't you believe it, lad. You won't find tougher thread in all the pattern than you'll find in us Thwaites. You take me dad. Been down the mines since he was a lad, trouble with his chest he has, but has that got him down? Not it. There's six on us, and many a time brass is tight, but we get by, and you couldn't find a finer home than what ours is. Nothing fancy mind you, but we owe nowt to nobody, and always keeps our heads high, and I reckon if them Vikings was to see us now they'd find nowt to grouse about.'

'I should think, if there's been any slipping, we've slipped most,' said William. 'I mean, you've seen how it is, knights and those types could go up or could go down. There was a part of my family that went up, but my lot have never done anything much, and now we're all so poor we couldn't be poorer. We've never done anything really, I mean been Members of Parliament or famous soldiers. We've just lived in the same places we've always lived, and no one has ever seemed to want to shine.'

John suddenly knew something.

'I reckon you're the one who could fit in best though, if you found yourself back where you joined the pattern.'

Elizabeth was chewing a grass. She spat it out.

'I feel it in my bones I was picked for this journey so that you can see how once you get to the bottom you always stop there.'

They laughed at that. William said:

'But you're not stopping there, you always say you won't.'

Elizabeth rolled on to her back.

'Quite right, William Beaumont! But we are going backwards on these journeys. Seeing me be somebody we'd have to go on a journey into to-morrow's time.'

Selina got up.

'Well, I'm going to explore in to-day's time.'

* * *

A week later they were back in Brown's Hotel in Dover Street, London. Their first day the children spent sightseeing, as Mr Fosse said he wanted them to carry some sort of picture of twentieth-century London into eighteenth-century London. Early the next morning they started on their journey.

They were finishing breakfast when Alfred brought a message. 'Mr Fosse says he wants to see you all. He seems excited like.'

Elizabeth swallowed her last mouthfuls of bread and honey. 'Take a deep breath, dears, you're going slumming to see how the Hambletts lived.'

Mr Fosse did look as if it was an important day. He was in his sitting-room. He had an old map of London on a table. He told them to have a good look at it, and they would see that quite a lot of the London that they had seen yesterday would be there in the London into which they were going to walk. But before they went into the eighteenth century he wanted them to be prepared a little for what they were going to see.

'You know you can never go by the behaviour of a big town, for the way of life of a country as a whole, and it is particularly important you should remember this in the London you are visiting in the spring of 1712. You will see goings on which will be a great surprise to you, so do not forget, when you are feeling surprised, that a large part of England at the beginning of the eighteenth century would be just as surprised as you are, for what happens in London is not the way they behave back home. London is not just a great city and an immense business centre, nor just the social centre because the Court is here, nor merely the centre of government, it is, for all who can manage it, the place to come to, to have a good time. Now, when you walk into the eighteenth century, try and remember this as you look around. You will find the streets crowded, for one-tenth of the whole population of England and Wales is by now living in London, and though the population of England and Wales is only about five and a half millions, whereas to-day it is somewhere in the neighbourhood of forty-three millions, as you can see by this map, the London you are going to visit is tiny compared with the London we are in at this moment, therefore the tenth of the population who live in it, and visit it, make it crowded.'

'I suppose,' said William, 'there are less people in it since the plague, aren't there? That killed off an awful lot of people, didn't it?'

'Yes, the big outbreak of plague has thinned the ranks, but there has always been plague, and it has always thinned the ranks. The outbreak of plague that you mean, William, was the one which came before the great fire, and the great fire happened years before the time we are going to visit. That outbreak of plague has always been remembered because it was the final flare up of the plague, there has never been another outbreak of that type since. But London has not allowed her business to be interrupted by plague, as indeed London has never allowed her business to be interrupted by anything. All England is at this time drained for labour for London, and, as you will see, the river is swarming with shipping, and much of it brings in poor immigrants only too anxious to work in London. So by one means and another the population has kept fairly steady.'

'I feel it in my bones,' said Elizabeth, 'us Hambletts are poor immigrants.'

Mr Fosse rumpled Elizabeth's hair.

'I am not going to tell you anything about yourself, however much you try and get round me.' Then he looked again at his map. 'The 1712 London is like a magnet, she draws people to her and often the sort who only come for what they can get out of people's pockets. Cheapjacks with stalls or selling novelties from trays round their necks, thieves and pickpockets, and, above all, beggars. All the beggars you will see, and you will see a lot of them, will not necessarily belong to London, but begging is their profession, so they come where the money is. Of course, as well, you will see real Londoners, families who lived in London and who then, as now, though living the lives of ordinary city people, look upon that part of London in which they live as their village, going outside it only to work, except, of course, on special occasions like Lord Mayor's Show days and for Royal doings. They are a special kind of people, city bred, with sharp wits, who take no share in the goings-on which, by visitors from abroad and England as a whole, are looked upon as the daily life of London. Here we have two of to-day's Londoners, Elizabeth, a true Londoner, and Robert, spending part of his time in a London flat; but I feel certain that some of the places you saw to-day were as new to them as to the rest of you.'

Grace laughed.

'Tha's right, mister, tha' knows. Neither one nor t'other had ever seen changing of the guard.'

Mr Fosse said he was not at all surprised, he thought lots of Londoners were like that, in fact most of them. Then he pointed to the map.

'Listen carefully because I am going to teach you a magic that you can use for ever. It does not want handkerchiefs, it does not want anything except your imaginations. Now look hard at this map. Here is the Thames, that's London Bridge, only one bridge you notice. There's St Martin's, but still in the fields, and there's Covent Garden. You went there this morning to see the fruit and vegetables arriving. They are selling fruit and vegetables in Covent Garden where you are going to now. You will have noticed that in all magic sound comes first. Look at the map, decide the exact spot on which to step. Then listen.'

The children stared at the map.

To-day's sounds faded. The traffic outside, the noise of the lift doors shutting. A radio playing. Then, in their place, came an ever-growing roar of voices. Mr Fosse's spoke in a whisper, which they heard through the clamour.

'Can you hear horses' hoofs?' As he spoke they could: clop went the horses' hoofs, rattle went the carts, bumping over cobblestones. Rumble went coaches. Again came Mr Fosse's voice and this time it was as if it gave them a push, and sent them forward into space. 'Bells. Street cries. Did you ever hear such a noise. Now step forward into the map.'

Thinking of it afterwards, the children remembered eighteenth-century London as the noisiest place in the world. Never were there such a lot of bells ringing. Every bell in London seemed ringing that morning. As well all London seemed to have something to sell and shouted or sang about their wares. They were walking up a cobbled street, and other people were hurrying by, for there was the clickerty-clack of smart shoes, and the slipperty-slop of down-at-heel ones. Then a coach rattled by, they could hear the coachman swearing at his horses and using his whip. Then suddenly came smells. They were near Covent Garden Market, for there was the smell of cabbage stalks trodden under foot, of root vegetables and of flowers. Then they began to see.

They were walking away from the market. The girls found

themselves wearing plain woollen frocks, almost to their ankles; they had caps on their heads and they wore aprons. The boys had on coats and breeches in dark wool, and so did Mr Fosse. They were as usual, as Elizabeth would have pointed out, the most plainly-dressed people about, only Elizabeth was not with them. In spite of it being early morning, a great many people seemed to be up, and not at all always the sort of people you would expect to be up early. There were smartly-dressed ladies, with great hooped skirts and very low-cut bodices, with their hair hidden by little lace or linen caps. With them were what by their aprons seemed to be their maids, who, though more plainly dressed, looked as much like their mistresses as possible. Evidently the ladies and their maids had been to the market for fruit and vegetables, for nearly all the maids carried baskets, and the ladies sometimes flowers. Although they had been to the market and had done their shopping they seemed in no hurry to get home, but walked up the road looking around in an eager way to see if any friends were about.

Near the market there was a parking place for what the children recognized at once as sedan chairs. They were carried by men in dreadful frowsty-looking old clothes, and hats, which must once have been black, but were now mostly green with age. The sedan chairmen seemed very like taxicab men in the way they behaved; they shouted to each other the gossip of the day, and had quick cockney jokes for anything that caught their eye, for there were roars of the equivalent of 'enjoyed your trip, mate' when an unfortunate painter

and his ladder fell over. They had, too, the same way of keeping their money under all their clothes, for when a gentleman got out of a sedan chair and paid his fare the sedan chairman pulled back his top coat, unbuttoned his greasy waistcoat and fumbled in his very dirty shirt before he found change.

The 1712 gentlemen were, the children thought, very dressy. They had what they took for long hair, but Mr Fosse said were wigs. He said, if they could look through the walls of the houses, they would see gentlemen without a hair on their heads, sitting in very expensive dressing-gowns waiting for the wig man to finish curling their hair before they could go out. They wore lovely brocade coats with masses of buttonholes, fine handsome turned-back cuffs, white lace at their wrists and necks, long waistcoats, with again rows of buttonholes, breeches to the knee and, of all gorgeous things to wear, many of them had red heels on their shoes. On their heads they mostly had huge turned-up black hats, bound with gold braid.

It was lucky the children saw some well-dressed men before they saw the ones lounging around the market, for whatever they may have looked like when they went out, they were looking a terrible mess when they saw them, for they had obviously been up all night. Their wigs wanted curling, their faces wanted shaving, the lace at their necks was torn and dirty, and at their wrists it had sometimes been dragged off, their hats were on one side and some of them looked as though what they had eaten and drunk in the night had not agreed with them, for they were a very funny colour. But mostly they were in grand spirits, for they were full of plans for the day. They would go to a coffee house, then, after they had been home to tidy up, they would meet again for what they called an 'ordinary,' which Mr Fosse said would be their three o'clock meal, probably in the same coffee house. What they did the rest of the day seemed to depend on what their ladies fancied, but it seemed there was a great deal to choose from, for they talked about all sorts of places of amusement, including Vauxhall Gardens, Hoxley in the Hole, Ranelagh and Her Majesty's Bear Garden. But the most popular entertainment for that day, and not only the men were going but the ladies too, was to see a hanging. The children thought wanting to see a hanging was disgusting.

It was not only fashionable people and those with things to sell who hung round Covent Garden Market. There were beggars, diseased and misshapen men, women and children, pulling themselves along on their hands, because their legs would not work, fumbling their way with sticks because they were blind, or shuffling along bent double because they could not stand upright. The effect of all these beggars the children thought most depressing, but they did not worry the people of the time; some threw them money, but most of them passed them by as though they were bits of scenery. Nearly all the beggars, whatever was the matter with them, seemed to be able to make cries of some sort, and dismal pleadings for money made a sort of background noise to the

already very noisy morning. But it was not until they left Covent Garden and walked into Long Acre that the children knew just how noisy a street could be.

Everybody who could sell anything seemed to be selling or trying to sell it in Long Acre that morning. There were the usual morning tradesmen, such as milk girls and bread-sellers, but as well bellows' menders, shoe-blacks, gingerbread sellers and men who wanted to grind knives and scissors. Then came a mixed cry. A man's harsh voice and a little boy's shrill one. Up the road came two black figures, one large and fierce-looking and one very, very small. Mr Fosse said they were chimney sweeps, and the little boy had to go up the chimneys. The children knew about chimney sweeps, but they had never thought of the boys used being quite so small, this one did not look more than six. Mr Fosse said he was afraid that they could not judge a child's age by its size at this time, for when you were made to work hard when you were young, and were given very little food, you did not grow much.

Walking down a main road at the beginning of the eighteenth century was, the children thought, a most dangerous occupation. Nobody seemed to care in the least whether you were hurt or not. Coaches dashed by without the driver bothering to look if anyone was under his horses feet. Sedan chairmen pushed their way through crowds, caring about nothing except at the end of the journey earning a fare from the person they were carrying. Then the roads were in a shocking state. There were great holes, which were full of water and mess, if you stepped out into the middle of the road it was quite easy to get splashed all over, or, worse still, hit by the whip of a passing driver. Workmen seemed to behave very casually, men ran by with the tools of their trades, not minding who they knocked down. There were coal carts coming up from the river, and the drivers of these were careless with their coal, which fell off, adding coal dust to the other dirt in the road. If passers-by walked too close to the houses the danger was worse; the awful habit of throwing slops from the top windows had not finished, and there was the chance of a workman without a word of apology dropping a bucket of paint or water on to them. Then the custom had started of making holes in front of houses for coal to be put in, and some of these were left partly open, and it was quite easy to drop into a cellar. To make conditions worse the only answer to being annoyed with your neighbours seemed to be to fight them. The children saw two fights in Long Acre, one between a couple of workmen and a much worse one between two women; both fights attracted the usual crowds, which made it more difficult to get along.

In spite of having to look where they were going, the children managed to notice a great deal. There were street lights, lamps in iron brackets. Every shop had a sign hung over it; they had seen these shop signs before in Norwich, but there had been nothing like so many of them. On lots of the houses there were badges or crests which Mr Fosse said he was glad they had a chance to see, because they were the signs of fire insurance companies. They were the beginning of two things: the great insurance companies, which would bring an immense amount of money to London, and indeed to the whole country, and the beginning of a fire service, for each insurance company ran a fire service to protect their property. They would probably think the fire service very funny compared to their own, but the people they were with now thought them one of the great sights of the town.

They left Long Acre and turned down St Martin's Lane, and there they saw the most extraordinary sight. Two sedan chairs swaying along as fast as the legs of the chairmen could take them. The passengers in the sedan chairs were two young men who hung out of the windows urging the leading carrier on by shouting at him. The crowd took sides, some yelling for the sedan chair in which the passenger had a pink coat, and some for the passenger who wore green. Mr Fosse said this was a race for a wager. That there was almost nothing that young men of the type riding in the sedan chairs would not bet on, and if it came to that the entire population were fond of a wager.

John said:

'I suppose they need something like that because they haven't got football pools.'

Mr Fosse chuckled.

'They do not have football pools, of course, but there are few other forms of gambling missing; every sort of game of chance is played, and they sell lottery tickets in the streets, and half the population are willing to risk their all in some wildcat scheme. You will see for yourselves presently the fortunes of a family changing because of gambling.'

'Are the sort of merchant people like I was marrying going in for gambling?' Selina asked.

'On the whole no. I think it is more often those members of the old aristocracy, who have nothing to do with business, who are finding it hard to live up to the style of rich merchants and so try get-rich-quick methods to make up their falling fortunes. It is a great time for people who have money, for they can snap up the properties of those who need money. The clever ones amongst the great landowners are building on their London properties. When you get back to our time, if you look at a map of London, you will see how much of it belongs, or has belonged, to a few great families, for you will find their names in some form in the names of the streets and squares which they built.'

Mr Fosse led the children through alleys and passages to bring them into Castle Street. There he stopped in front of a house, and looked up at it as the tutor had looked at the potato; and just as the tutor saw the potato as more than a potato, so Mr Fosse showed by his voice that he thought the building he was gazing at was more than just a building.

'Look at the second floor. Behind those windows is the first public library. It is very hard for us, who can borrow a book whenever we like, to imagine a world in which such things as libraries are unknown, and, of course, except for the few, this building does not mean much at this moment. But what an idea lies behind those windows! I feel a light should shine from them.'

'What sort of people use the library?' William asked. 'I mean, can anybody?'

'Judging by the diaries kept by a man called Evelyn it is mostly scholarly young men, the sort of young men who coach the sons of great families, or perhaps are private chaplains in great houses. That sort will not have money to buy books, but the brains to read and profit by them.'

'I should think,' said Selina, 'that lots of people would want to borrow books; I mean, when we were in Devonshire even the servants were beginning to read, and I suppose there are more schools now.'

Mr Fosse nodded.

'Certainly there are. Besides the great public schools there are any number of grammar schools, and they are wonderfully cheap educations. In our day parents spend fantastic sums sending their children to paying schools, but at this time it only costs about twenty pounds a year. Of course, twenty pounds a year is worth a lot more now than it means to us, but it is still a very small sum to pay for a year's education, especially as, for the twenty pounds, the boy boards as well as getting his clothes and his schooling.'

'Do they have the same sort of education now as they've been having all along? I mean, Latin and all that?' John asked.

'There is some talk that too classical an education is a mistake, and a bigger variety of subjects might be an idea, including in some schools learning such useful things as how to keep accounts. There is too a feeling, though I do not think it is more than a feeling, that you do not get the best out of boys by beating them all the time.'

'How about the girls?' asked Selina. 'Do we go to school?'

Mr Fosse had moved on again. He talked as he went.

'I think girls have a rough deal compared with their brothers; they are still being educated more with a view to their early marriages, and being able to run a house than that they should have trained minds. There has been a gradual slipping back in the training of girls since the sixteenth century, when girls —Lady Jane Grey was an outstanding example—were magnificently educated. All the same, judging by the letters written now, women are managing to get educated, for many of them are wonderful correspondents.'

They were in a less built-up part of the town, and this gave the children a chance to think about what they had seen, and they found they had noticed several things. One was how many rich people there seemed to be about, driving in their coaches or carried in their chairs. How well-to-do and pleased with life the tradespeople looked. How gay, if rough, London seemed to be. Then they thought about the houses. There were still old timbered houses left, but all the new houses were more or less like town houses in their own time. They were brick, or stone, sometimes several storeys high, with big-paned windows. The children were particularly interested in the windows, because they were the first they had seen on their journeys which would push up and down.

Selina thought out loud.

'I suppose they didn't change the houses again. I mean, those that aren't bombed down, or haven't fallen down, are the same houses people like us live in.'

'The nicest ones people like us live in,' John said. 'I think the houses here are much better than anything we build, I think the proportions are better.'

William turned to Mr Fosse.

'I suppose there's been an awful lot of building since the Great Fire?'

Selina picked up her skirts so that she could get along faster.

'Not here, the fire didn't come this way, did it?'

William remembered.

'No, of course it was in the City. I suppose all this is going to be built up soon, isn't it, Mr Fosse?'

There was no answer, and looking round the children found Mr Fosse had done one of his vanishing acts.

'Don't upset yourself about him, lad,' Grace said. 'He knows his own business best. I reckon somebody will turn up to put us on t'right road.'

Grace had hardly finished speaking before the 'somebody' turned up. He was a very disreputable boy of about their own age. Dirty, with matted hair and torn clothes, and so thin his bones stuck out and gave him a knobbly look. But he was very gay and talkative. At first the children understood

nothing he said, but by degrees his words twisted in the air until they reached their ears in a shape they could follow. When talking of him afterwards they called the boy Cock-sparrer, for that is what the boy called them. He lived, he said, outside the gates; he worked on the riverside, his father had been a docker but he had been killed in a fight. There were six at home, and his mother had a job to find victuals for them. All but the youngest, Annie, who was only three, earned a bit.

Selina sounded disbelieving.

'How old are they?'

Cock-sparrer said he was thirteen, Joan twelve, Lizzie ten, Charlie-boy was eight, but he wasn't at home any more as his mother had sold him to a sweep, and Zaccy was four. There had been a lot more who had died, he didn't know how many, nor did his mother remember.

Selina, holding up her frock, skipped along to keep up with Cock-sparrer.

'But what do little children like that do?'

Cock-sparrer winked and looked as if he was full of secrets. There were plenty of ways to earn a bit if you were smart and kept your ears open. Round where he lived there were many had to lie low in the daytime, and needed messages and so on taken by someone who wouldn't attract notice. Sometimes they wanted what they had stolen taken to those who would buy. Zaccy was the boy for that, face like an angel he had, no one would suspect him.

Selina was appalled.

'But if Zaccy carries stolen stuff how will he know it's wrong to steal?'

Cock-sparrer grinned at Selina, and asked who said it was wrong to steal?

William thought that a stupid thing to say.

'Well, it is. I mean, it's one of the Commandments and all that.'

'Don't you go to church or chapel?' John asked.

It took time to understand, because having seen the Church come into people's lives, the children could not quite believe Cock-sparrer at first, but in the end they had to because it was obvious he was speaking the truth. He knew nothing about Christianity. He had no idea what people went to church for, had never been inside a church.

'Don't you go to any sort of school?' William asked.

Cock-sparrer said there was a free school started, so he had heard, but it wouldn't be for those from where he lived. No one ever came there, it was too rough.

'Would tha' like to learn, lad?' Grace asked.

Cock-sparrer seemed shy of putting his private thoughts into words, he only liked talking about things which were common property and something to get a good laugh out of, but Grace had asked a sensible question and clearly expected a sensible reply. Slowly, like a chink of sunlight through a crack in a shutter, Cock-sparrer's innermost dream shone out. Working on the river bank, though living less well than the wharfside rats, he had watched and been interested in all that went on. He had seen what went out in the ships. Masses of merchandise all making money for someone. The money that came into the City! Often he hung around the coffee houses and heard the talk, and he had a lot of friends amongst thieves, and they had told him how people lived and the money they had. Gold plates to eat off, silk on their beds, and more clothes than they could wear. There was unskilled work to be had in the storehouses of those rich merchants, and in the shops, but you got nowhere in work of that sort, there were always skilled men over you. He was taking them to see where he lived, and they would see no one would choose a boy coming from where he came, to give a chance to, and there was no reason why they should. He had his health and strength, and as soon as his mother and the little-uns, as he described his brothers and sisters, could manage without him he was hopping it. He would find a ship going to America, and when he got there he would slip off. There were fine chances in America, he had heard, for all who weren't afraid of hard work.

Looking at Cock-sparrer, skipping along, dirty, smelly, a nobody in eighteenth-century London, the children felt certain they were seeing the first thread of a new pattern. They had heard of the pattern when the tutor had talked of his potato. Now they were looking at a thread that would be part of it. Cock-sparrer's thread would be tough all right, and it would stay a gay colour. It was no good saying anything to him about it, for he would not understand, but they could see the sort of descendants he might have: successful outspoken Americans of their own day. Though it seemed odd, looking at Cock-sparrer, it was likely that his pattern might be really important.

Robert said:

'If . . . I mean, if you don't know anything about the Bible . . . or what's right and wrong . . . I mean, why do you have to wait for your mother and your brothers and sisters to be all right before you go?'

Cock-sparrer glared at Robert. Did he want a fight? What sort did Robert think he was? Didn't have to go into one of those churches, did you, to act right by your mother and the little-uns?

Cock-sparrer calmed down as soon as Robert apologized and led the way down a narrow alley and they came out on the river bank.

Yesterday, when they were sightseeing, the children had hung over Westminster Bridge. They had watched a pleasure boat going to Hampton Court, and two water buses going Greenwich way; they had seen what Alfred had said was a river-police boat, and watched several barges go under the bridge, pulled by a tug. It had been the sort of traffic to be seen on the Thames any summer's day.

The Thames Cock-sparrer led them to looked very different. There was no bridge to lean over, they just stood on the bank. On the opposite bank there was a great house, which Cock-sparrer said was Lambeth Palace, and next to it a church, but otherwise there were scarcely any buildings, just gardens and flat marshy country. But it was not seeing that so much of the London they knew was not yet built that surprised the children, they had expected that, it was the use made of the Thames. The Thames in 1712 was like a busy street. There were dozens of colliers; Cock-sparrer said they came from the north, he had often run messages for the men and found the way they spoke hard to understand. They did a wonderful trade though, cost a lot of money coal did, people like his family never used it, of course, they depended on wood they picked up or stole for any cooking that was done, they could seldom manage a fire just to warm themselves. Not only coal was travelling by water, but all types of merchandise, and as well it seemed the usual way for people to travel, for there were countless small craft, some privately owned, some hired, and some working as if they were buses, picking up passengers and taking them up, down and across the river. There were so many sails in sight the children could not count them, and, as for the small rowing boats, they were as thick as midges on a hot afternoon in June. One thing that amused the children was the rudeness of the boatmen; they could not understand half they said, but what they did understand was rude enough, shouting insults at each other seemed a sort of boatman's hobby. Cock-sparrer did not of course understand why the children thought it odd to see the river so full of shipping, but he said it stood to reason everybody sent their goods by water if there was water to carry it, for the roads were not only very rough, but the highwaymen made them dangerous, and then of course there was the question of expense; water travel was cheaper than road, there were places, so the coalmen said, that never saw coal, because they had no water for it to travel by, and the roads were too bad to carry it.

Just off the river was the part of London in which Cock-sparrer lived. He led them to a street near his home, and there without a word left them.

The children were not in Cock-sparrer's part of London long, but they never forgot it. The rotten old houses falling to bits, full of bugs and rats. The dreadful streets, the terrible sights. Drunken men and women, undersized miserable little naked or ragged children. The faces of some of the people were terrifying, savage and brutal. They saw a street fight, which began between two men, but soon all the street seemed to join in, using any weapon they could find, slamming at each other with old furniture, slashing with broken crockery, blood streamed, the noise was terrible; one person at least was killed but nobody seemed to care about the fight, for no one tried to stop it. Mr Fosse's voice sighed through the uproar.

'Come along, come along, we have not all day to stand about here.'

The children were glad to go, and they were so shocked and upset by what they had seen that they were past Westminster Abbey and walking into St James's Park before anybody spoke. Then William, looking round at the busy, cheerful, noisy, happy, prosperous town, burst out:

'Why isn't something done? Why don't the watch interfere?'

Mr Fosse knew how they felt.

'The London you have just left is a dangerous part to interfere with; you had to see it, but you know now it is only a small part of the whole.' He stopped and beckoned to a girl and a boy. 'Come here, you two, and talk to us.'

The boy and girl were a brother and sister, their names were Moll and Robin. They had a country look about them, and when the children began to understand what they said they found they were from Worcestershire. As they spoke of their home it was clear that both, for all they were proud to be in London, were a little homesick. They came from the village where the young Lord Amphlett, whom they served, owned a country house. They were children of a carpenter, who came from a line of carpenters. Their father had a thriving village trade. They had a nice home, for their father owned his house, which had been built by his grandfather. Robin could read and write a little, but he had not been to school regularly, for his father had meant him to be a carpenter, and had taught him his trade, and there was good sport in the country to fill his time, always fish to take and snaring; wonderful game there was to be snared in his parts. Moll, it seemed, had spent her time at home at housework and spinning. She had fun as well. There were the Gingerbread Fairs, and Plough Monday, and she liked going to the woods; once she had almost seen a fairy, but she was scared of the witch that lived at the end of the wood. Her father said there was a time when a witch was ducked in the pond. Their witch, at her home, cast spells; it was said that once she had turned a child into a toad.

The children looked at Mr Fosse, to see if Moll was

pretending to believe in fairies and witches, but he shook his head and spoke to Robin, asking why he had left the country if life was so good there.

Like many country people, Robin's thoughts took time to come out in words. He said it was a fine life, plenty to eat, plenty to drink, but Mr Fosse knew how it was, those who had been to London talked about it, and the wonders to be seen, and the great times everybody had, until you felt you had to go there. Moll agreed with Robin; from most homes down their way some of the family had left for London, so why not them? Their father had not wanted them to leave, but he hadn't held them back; he had two other sons, both better carpenters than Robin, so here they were.

'Do you like it now you are here?' Selina asked.

Both found it hard to answer that. London was as wonderful as they had heard, they had been everywhere with their master and mistress, and seen things they could not have imagined, but lately they had been less happy.

'Why?' William asked. 'Are you homesick?'

Robin and Moll looked at each other and slowly the story came out. Young Lord Amphlett, only he wasn't Lord Amphlett then, was a wild one, had a marriage arranged for him by his father to the daughter of a London merchant, a very rich young lady, but not of course of their lord's world. Five years ago Lord Amphlett, the young man's father, had died, and he had come into the property in Worcester and the title, but the property wasn't worth much, for there was a mortgage on the house. It had been hoped that the young lord would pay off the mortgage out of his rich wife's money, but that wasn't his idea at all. He was all for having a good time, spent his wife's money like water. Two years back he had a disappointment. They wouldn't understand politics, but the young lord was a Whig, and he had thought he was going to get a fine job in the Government, but the Tories came in and that was the end of that. He had seemed to go mad ever since, gambled on everything; it was said amongst the servants that he had lost the country house on the gaming tables, and it was known his father-in-law had lost patience and would give him no more money, and this last week things had come to a head: there had been no wages. That was why they were out early, they had been to see about new situations for themselves. They were going back now to get their things.

'What'll happen to Lord and Lady Amphlett?' Selina asked.

Moll and Robin exchanged looks and both shrugged their shoulders. The young lord got on very badly with his lady. In spite of her bringing him all that money he looked down on her and made jokes about his father-in-law's business. It could be her ladyship would take the children and go to live with her parents, but they doubted it, for she had taken

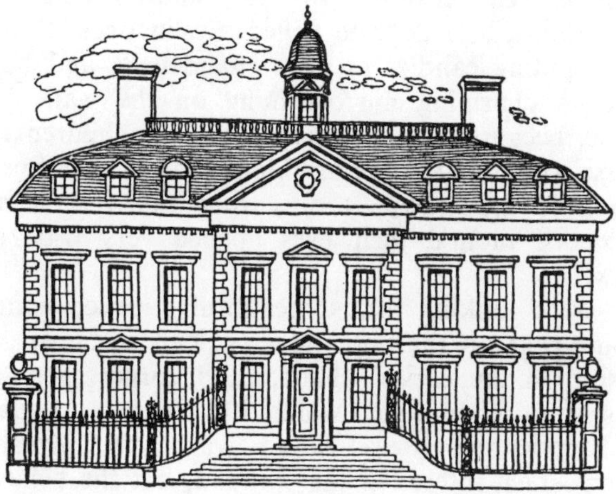

to the life of the town. Most likely they would live in a cheaper style somewhere.

'How many bairns have they?' Grace asked.

Moll said there were eight, all girls, there had been some boys born so she had heard, but they had not lived. It would come hard on the children if things were as bad as kitchen gossip said, for the eldest girl was only thirteen.

They came to Jermyn Street, and stopped outside the Amphlett's house. It was a house of a style of which lots were still standing in the London of the children's day. It was built of brick with a handsome front door reached by a flight of steps, and good windows except at the top, where they were small and half under the roof. Robin and Moll were whispering with some other servants up the road, and as the door was ajar Mr Fosse said he thought they had better walk in.

It seemed awfully rude walking into Lord Amphlett's house, but as soon as the children were inside they could see it was the only way to get in, for there were no servants about, and none came running though a bell was being rung for them. Inside the walls were panelled, with niches here and there in which blue and white china was standing. On the left of the hall was what looked like a library, for it was full of books, and on the right was a little breakfast-room. Both rooms and the stairs were carpeted and both were full of elegantly carved furniture. In the windows were charming heavy curtains, and delicate frilled muslin ones. Both rooms had for lighting candles in glass chandeliers, and both were reflected in charming mirrors hung on the walls. Walking on tiptoe, because of still feeling rude, the children followed Mr Fosse to the first floor; on the landing they stopped. They were outside the drawing-room, from which came screams. They peeped in and their eyes opened very wide at what they saw.

They were looking into a beautiful panelled room, with handsome rugs on the floor, great golden curtains, gold and green silk on the carved chairs. In a corner there stood a piano sort of instrument, which Mr Fosse said afterwards was a harpsichord. It was not, however, the furnishings of the room which interested the children, but the behaviour of the people in it. Sprawled in a high-backed chair, kicking and screaming, was Lady Amphlett, at least they found out later that was who she was. She was only partly dressed; she wore a wrap over her hooped petticoat, and, though she had on a smart cap, it had fallen on one side and showed her hair, which looked as if it had been screwed up all anyhow. She had fine shoes, but no stockings, and she did not look as if she had washed that morning, for both her legs and her neck could have done with a scrub. Watching her with a sneering expression was Lord Amphlett, looking just as Mr Fosse said smart gentlemen looked before they went out in the mornings. He wore a magnificent dressing-gown of stiff brocade, but his head was absolutely bald. The children thought however nice men might look in wigs it could not make up for

having to look so awful when they had not got them on. He too looked as if he could do with a good wash. Standing over Lady Amphlett, alternately fanning her and trying to catch one of her hands to pat it, was a lady who turned out to be a visiting friend.

As the children got used to the screams they began to find out what the trouble was. It was the sort of trouble that Robin and Moll had said might be coming. Lord Amphlett could not pay his debts, the bailiffs, or what Lady Amphlett called the bum-bailiffs, were in; they were taking away everything in the house to sell to pay the people who were owed money. Between Lady Amphlett's screams the children could hear the bailiffs upstairs throwing open cupboards and drawers and moving furniture. Every time they made an extra noise Lady Amphlett screamed louder and moaned about this gown and that petticoat, her bed, her jewellery and the shame of being turned naked into the streets. This was what his lordship's gambling had brought them to, and if he did not care about her did he not care about his children? Lord Amphlett did not seem to care about anything except that no servant answered his bell, which he kept picking up and ringing furiously.

The children missed what happened next, for two of the bailiff's men came down the stairs carrying a carpet. Seeing the bailiff's men made the children nudge each other and smile, for they were old friends, they had seen them in pantomime, where they were called broker's men. The two bailiffs' men passing the door, could easily have been acting in *Cinderella* as the brokers' men in Baron Hard-up's castle.

Seeing the bailiff's men actually pass by her door was too much for Lady Amphlett, who gave a loud moan, fell back, shut her eyes and seemed to have fainted. The friend fanned more violently than ever, but obviously thought the whole fuss funny. She smiled at Lord Amphlett and asked where he planned to go. Lord Amphlett stopped ringing his bell and said he was not such a fool as Lady Amphlett thought. He had some property in the country, in Chelsea, it was not much of a house but it must do. He had secretly moved some valuables there, and they would lie low until he made back all he had lost. Fortunately Chelsea was no distance and he could easily get to the gaming tables by boat. Lady Amphlett, who seemed to be able to hear through her faint, opened her eyes at that, but the children missed what she said, for there was a clatter on the stairs, and down came some of the little girls.

The Amphlett children were pretty, but like their parents, they could have done with a wash. They were dressed rather like their mother, though much less stiffly. The younger ones were crying for their nurses, who had evidently left with the other servants, and the older ones grumbling they had not had anything to eat. At the sound of her children's voices Lady Amphlett rushed out of the drawing-room and knelt

at the foot of the stairs, trying to hug them all to her at once. Tears poured down her cheeks. She told them they were ruined, there would be no more nurses, and probably very little to eat; their father was taking them to live in a hovel in the village of Chelsea. Lady Amphlett would have gone on crying and talking but she was interrupted.

Down the stairs swept the eldest girl. She pushed through her little sisters. She was dressed properly. She had a great hooped skirt of white, with a flowered blue and white underskirt. Under a stiff lace cap she showed fair ringlets.

She had blue eyes which, at that moment, were blazing with anger. What, she wanted to know, was this caterwauling about? Her mother should be ashamed of herself to show so little control before the children and the bailiffs. What was the matter with Chelsea? For herself, she thought it would be rather fun. Her father might be suffering misfortune, but that was not the end of him, his luck might turn. One thing was certain, tears would not help. They must make the best of things as they were until they could live in a manner more suited to their position.

The girl's words had some effect on her mother, but far more on the children.

'My word,' said John, 'as soon as we heard her coming we might have guessed she would be Elizabeth.'

CHAPTER FOURTEEN

# *The Mill*

THEY were back in the sitting-room in Brown's Hotel. Motor traffic hummed in the street outside. A radio blared. The change was so sudden the children blinked. Then John saw Elizabeth.

'Look who's here. Who'd have thought you were a peer's daughter.'

Elizabeth was only half back.

'Was I? I thought . . . but the name was Amphlett, wasn't it?'

Mr Fosse was putting away the map.

'That is right, but names got mispronounced and mis-spelt. The Amphletts went down and down in the world. The title died out. Elizabeth married a distant cousin of the same name, and it is her descendants who, under the name of Hamblett, now live in Pimlico.'

Elizabeth was quite back now.

'My word, we haven't half slipped.'

Selina knew she had understood something.

'But the thread that had faded until it hardly showed is coming back with Elizabeth. That's what you think, isn't it Mr Fosse?'

Mr Fosse looked purr-ish.

'That would not surprise me.' Then he got down to plans. 'To-morrow we shall fly north.'

'To Lancashire to meet Robert's folks,' said Grace.

'That's it. To have a look at Robert's part of the pattern. From there we fly to my home. And that will be our last stop on our journey.'

There was a marvellous lunch waiting for the children. Mrs Mummery thought nothing of it because she had not cooked it herself, but the children thought it superb.

Elizabeth, forgetting manners, spoke with her mouth full.

'Angel Mrs Mummery, did you know that we had nearly finished our journey? Will you miss us? I'll miss you and Alfred awfully.'

Mrs Mummery gave her fat chuckle.

'I was saying to Alfred only yesterday you had become like me own family, but there's no good-byes to be said. We shall meet again, shouldn't wonder.'

'D'oust mean we shall be asked again?' Grace asked.

Mrs Mummery patted Grace's shoulder.

'Never mind what I mean me dear, you'll see what you will see, and it'll all come out in the wash.'

In the afternoon Alfred took the children to the Zoo, and in the evening both Alfred and Mrs Mummery went with them to the first house at the Palladium. In between the Zoo and the Palladium, they made up Elizabeth's song.

The song was difficult, and it was really Elizabeth herself who found the tune for it.

'How about *Now the Day is Over?* It's got a sad sound, which it ought to have seeing what happened to the Amphletts.'

All the time they were tidying to go to the theatre, in the hire car which took them to the theatre, and in the hire car coming back from the theatre, the children sang, more and more dismally, Elizabeth's song.

Lord Amphlett was a pee-eer
Who gambled all away,
The name got changed to Hamblett,
Elizabeth's of our day.

The Mummerys bore the singing very well considering, though Alfred did say that hearing that tune too often did something to his stomach.

* * *

They did not stay in Lancashire, for Mr Fosse said he thought they could visit the year 1810 very easily, from a helicopter. Before they started their journey backwards they had a look at the Lancashire of their own day. Busy Liverpool, with the Mersey crowded with shipping from all over the world. Manchester with its great buildings, and streets full of hurrying people. Then they flew inland. Everywhere it was the same, houses crowded together, and masses of workers filling the streets. The children looked at the towns, the villages, and the little hamlets, and what so many of the people were busy about became clear, for as bees cluster round a beehive, so the people of Lancashire clustered round mills. The mills were not very new looking, and had great chimneys, out of which poured black smoke. Mr Fosse told their pilot to fly low and he would show them where they were going. He had maps for them, so they could walk into 1810 without trouble, but they might like to have a look at the place to-day.

The place Mr Fosse wanted the children to look at was not far from Bolton. Not exactly a village, a straggly collection of dirty streets and dark cramped-looking houses round a mill. Besides the usual buildings such as chapels, schools, cinemas, and shops, almost on top of the mill, was one very big house. From the helicopter the village looked a rather sad little place where nobody would want to live. But as they flew lower the children saw the people who lived in it, and they did not look sad at all, in fact they looked very cheerful. They were on their way to work, and they clattered up the dirty streets talking and laughing, as if they thought the place they lived in was the nicest place in the country. The children of the place ran up the streets to school, and older children went off by train to grammar and technical schools. Women sometimes with shopping bags on their arms, came to their doors and had a few minutes gossip with their neighbours.

Mr Fosse told the pilot to stooge round for a bit. Then he told the children a story.

'This is our last journey, and it is going to be a little different from the others. You already know that you are going to look at Robert's thread, so this time I am going to tell you something about it before you start. The grandfather of Robert Ackroyd, whom we shall meet in 1810, was a weaver. He lived in a little stone cottage, able to keep himself and his wife and children, not very well, but they got by. Then changes came. First machinery run by water power. Then steam power was invented. Thousands of people watched this power put into use in the mills and did not see what it would mean; but the father of the Robert of 1810, George his name was, saw and understood, and so became a rich man. First he made money using water power, and later invented a piece of machinery which had to do with steam power. This last brought him enough money to build his own mill. The mill he built is that one we have been looking at, and he built the great house next to it to live in, and he built the houses those people we saw came out of, and nasty cheap houses they were and are. I am sorry to say this of your ancestor, Robert, but George Ackroyd was not a kind man, very successful, but ruthless, he did not care what sort of houses people lived in, or how they lived provided he got rich. Of course people like George, born in labourer's cottages, were the newest sort of new rich, and men in the government thought about them, and knew they would be very important, so a politician you may have heard of, called Pitt, decided that men like George had better vote for his party, which was called Tory. To be sure he had George on his side, he made him a baron, so he became the first Lord Ackroyd of Colne.'

'So that's why you're Honourable, Robert,' Elizabeth said.

Robert, who did not at all like what he had heard of his ancestor George, looked red and said nothing.

'It's not your fault, Robert,' said Selina.

Mr Fosse passed maps to the children. They were postcard size, and showed the streets, the mill and the big house. It was easy to see which road they were to go along as there was only one that led straight into the main street. Although the maps were small, the children found the magic they had been taught worked wonderfully. They stared at the road on the map until it became blurred, and as it blurred sounds began.

First came the clatter of wooden shoes on stones. Then the creak of opening doors, and as the doors opened, smells. The dreadful smell of poverty, of overcrowding, of unwashed bodies, and stuffy unwashed clothes, and the smell of long-forgotten meals. Then came feeling, the children found they were cold, and as they began to feel cold they noticed it was very early morning and a nasty chilly day.

The girls were dressed in dark dresses to the feet, with bonnets on their heads, the boys had long trousers, and short coats. Mr Fosse was not there, but another man was. It was difficult to see him in the dim light, but he told them he was a clergyman, and led the children up the street and knocked on the door of a poor little house. There were shuffling steps, and mutters, and the door opened.

The children longed not to have to go into that house. The door was opened by the father of the family who lived in the front room. He was wearing very patched and worn breeches, darned stockings, and a deplorable old coat, his hair needed cutting and washing, but the most noticeable thing about him was the hang-dog beaten look on his face. He opened the door wider, and when he saw the parson, with a jerk of his head, invited them all in.

The family were having a meal of bread, with a scraping of fat on it, and water. Not that any of them knew or cared that they were eating, nor did they know or care that anyone had come into the room. The mother, a terribly thin, grey-faced woman, who looked any age, because she had lost most of her teeth, was leaning half asleep over a broken table, putting pieces of bread mechanically into her mouth. She wore a dress which had once been green, stained and torn, a shapeless bonnet, and a very old cape. There were six children, the eldest a boy who might have been twelve, and the youngest a baby lying on some rags on the floor. The five children did something the children had never seen before, they ate in their sleep. Their eyes were tight shut, their grey, dirty, pinched faces unconscious, but somehow the food went into their mouths and was chewed. Their clothes were indescribable, so dirty and so patched, and it was obvious they never came off. The mother became conscious that eyes were on her children's clothes, she said, not apologizing, but explaining, that after fourteen hours in the mill she could only just

get the bairns home, and they were far too tired to take off even their top clothes, but fell down as soon as they got inside the door. And it was all she could do to get them on their feet and a bit of bread into them before they left for the mill each morning.

The children were glad for Robert's sake he was not with them. William asked in a whisper what kind of work the children did. The parson answered. He pointed to a five-year-old boy and a six-year-old girl, and another boy of eight. Those three, he said, were what they called scavengers, the mills were full of dust and fluff, and children like these were employed to crawl under the machinery and clean the floor. Only small children such as these could be used for that work, as the machines were low, and only little children could get under them. The two older children, a boy and a girl, were what was known as piecers, they looked after several machines. Both these two had over eighty spindles in their charge, and it was their job to go from machine to machine, looking out for a broken thread on one of their spindles and mending it. The mother seeing horrified expressions on the faces of the children, said again not apologetically, but simply stating a fact, that the little ones earned a shilling a week, and the older ones one and six, it was either work in the mill, or die of starvation.

John thought back to Norwich and the worsted weaver. It was true that the weaver had said he could not take a holiday, but he had had a nice home. John knew about machinery, but it seemed extraordinary from weaving being a respectable profession, where the workers belonged to guilds, that you could come to this dreadful family with little children of five and six being made to work. He looked at the father.

'Don't you get paid enough to keep them?'

For one second there was a gleam that once might have been pride in the father's eyes. Twenty years ago he could have earned enough to get by, but not now. Wherever there was a mill, people collected, often they came from far away places like Ireland, round this mill alone there were twice the number of people that were needed. Wages had dropped and dropped, even a year ago he could get sixteen shillings a week, but now he was lucky if he got ten. The mother added it was said they would be lucky if they could earn five and sixpence by this time next year.

'D'ouster work thissen?' Grace asked.

The woman nodded. There was an old woman who saw to the baby, and cleaned a bit now and then; the children looked round, it was obviously the only room the family had, the walls were plaster, black with soot and smoke, the plaster of the ceiling was coming away, and hung down in unattractive blobs with cobwebs clinging to them. There was a bed of a sort in one corner, with quite unspeakable blankets on it, and some piles of rags on the floor where the children evidently slept, and on these too, were dreadful blankets. There was the broken table, a bench of sorts, a stool and some boxes, in the grate was a cooking pot and a kettle, on a box beside the fireplace stood a broken jug, and on a wooden platter a small hard piece of what might have been rabbit. The whole effect was indescribably depressing, for not only was there nothing of beauty anywhere but none of the family had the strength to care. A shrill whistle came from the mill, and seemed to reach some part of the little workers' minds, for at once each staggered to its feet, dragged round itself a cloak, or in the case of the boys a coat, and with blind faces but as if some magnet drew them, struggled out into the street. It was only then the children noticed bent legs, and that in height the eldest boy was not so tall as a boy of eight of their own day. The father and mother in the same queer hopeless trance-like way, and without a word, followed their children to the mill.

With horrified faces the five turned round to face the parson, but he stopped their saying anything by speaking first. The man was right, there were too many workers, and far too little work, the mill owners could pay what they liked, they knew their workers faced near starvation. If they could have got children to do the work they would employ only children, for why pay nine or ten shillings to a man or a woman when a child could do the same work for one and six? Fortunately the children were not capable of doing any more than they were doing. When you had worked fourteen hours a day in a mill since you were five, your brains were not as sharp as they might be. If these little workers lived to grow up, they would be able to handle the machines, but of course many of them would not live to grow up. The mill was an insanitary building, the dust and fluff bred diseases, it was necessary to keep the mill hot, and that bred diseases too. There was a great wastage amongst the children, but usually when he had to take a funeral of a child, he could not feel sad, for he knew for the child it was a blessed relief to have left so suffering a world.

The parson said he was going to show them one other unfortunate child before they went up to the mill-owner's house. But before they saw anything else to shock them, he would like them to remember that there were men and women all over the country who were fighting day and night for reforms of all sorts. There were doctors, there was a fine man called Percival in Manchester, for one, who had not minced his words when they had had an outbreak of illness twenty years ago or so; in this mill the children had died like flies. There were a great many people working to regulate conditions in the mills, and he thought, with God's help, the reforms would come, and that he would live to see them.

'What about schools?' John asked. 'Don't children go to school at all?'

The parson said not this sort of child. Apprentice boys who would have been a charge on the parish, but had been bought by mill owners and were housed by them had to have a little education. In many parts of the country there were schools for poor children from just such terrible homes as these. A great deal of money could not be spent on education of course, but a very good plan had been thought of. Those boys and girls who had learned to read and write, were put on to teach the other children, some of the London schools he had heard, were very large, but there was only one master, all the teaching was done by the older pupils. In Lancashire what they had been calling British Schools had been opened. He thought himself they were a bad thing, for there was no church teaching, all children were accepted, no matter what their faith, they could be heathens if they liked. It was true that they read the Bible, but schools should be church schools for church children. Anything else undermined religion. Something better was now being started, only last year a society was formed for national schools, which promoted the education of the poor in the principles of the established church.

William could not see how any parson could worry himself about what was taught in the schools, when he knew that children like the ones they had just seen were no better than slaves. He looked so disapproving the parson felt it, his voice sounded very like Mr Fosse's. He patted William's shoulder. It was no good beating about the bush, the coming of machinery had produced ghastly conditions; but it was not fair to the times to think that nobody cared. They must keep on remembering those people who saw what was evil, and were working for a better world.

From upstairs came screams. The parson said that he was afraid those screams were coming from the other child he wanted them to see. He led the way into the passage and up a horrible dirty little staircase to the next floor. The screams came from a back room. The parson spoke in a whisper. He said they were going to call on a sweep and his boy apprentice. Twenty-two years before an Act had been passed improving the conditions of chimney boys. One rule was that they had to be eight before a sweep employed them, but unfortunately when the Act was passed, no arrangements were made to see the sweeps obeyed the Act, so it might just as well not have been passed. Then six years ago a society was formed to do away with climbing boys altogether, but none of these things really affected the conditions of the climbing boy as they would see.

The sweep's room was an even nastier room than the family's downstairs. There was no furniture, a bundle of rags for the sweep to sleep on, and bags of soot for the boy. There was a dirty blanket on the sweep's bed, and an unspeakable old coat which must have belonged to the sweep, on the boy's sacks of soot. By the fire there was a stool, which seemed to act as a larder, for on it was a plate with a hunk of unpleasant-looking meat, and half a loaf of bread, and two or three bottles of gin. The sweep and his climbing boy were in front of the fire. The boy a miserable, delicate little thing, was howling and his tears made little white channels down his dirty face. The sweep nodded at the parson, but paid no attention to the children. He said he was hardening his boy up, he was a new boy, not yet seven, that he had bought in Leeds. He would have starved if he had not taken him. The boy had his coat off, and his little elbows were turned to the fire. The sweep now swung him round and took a handful of brine from a jar and rubbed it into the child's elbows and on to his knees. The children then saw what the screams were about. Both elbows and knees were raw, all the skin was rubbed off. The sweep paid no attention to the child's howls of pain, but turned him round again and forced his elbows to the heat of the flame. He shook his head at the parson, and said it was terrible what these boys had to suffer, but as the parson would know, they climbed with their elbows and knees, and their lives depended on their elbows and knees being tough. Naturally a new boy like this lost the skin on his elbows and knees as he climbed, and came home streaming with blood, but every day he toughened the skin with brine well heated in. There was nothing he said, to touch rubbing brine in, and though the boy would not believe him, the day would soon be coming when his elbows and knees would be as hard as a piece of leather and he would not feel a thing.

Selina clutched William.

'I can't stand this, I'm going outside.'

None of the others were sorry for an excuse to leave, and all five ran down into the street, and up the road and leant against a wall.

'Goodness,' gasped Selina, 'how awful!'

'Knees and elbows like leather,' said Grace. 'I'd give him "like leather" if I could lay hands on that sweep.'

'If only it wasn't true,' said William, 'if only it was all made up and never happened.'

John kicked a stone into the river.

'Well, we know it did happen. I say, what's happened to the parson?'

They looked round and there was no parson, but instead a girl of about fourteen stood in front of them. She had a neat blue woollen dress, and a very clean long white apron. A blue bonnet, and a warm blue cloak. On her arm was a basket with fish in it. She smiled at the children and said were they coming to the master's place? She was a maid there, and would be pleased to show them the way. She said her name was Alice. Her mother had been in service with a great lord, and she and her sisters had been put to service as soon as they could be of use in a house. She hoped, when she got home next Mothering Sunday, to see whether her mother would let her change her place. This Lord Ackroyd was not really a lord, if the children knew what she meant, he was one of these new rich, which was a very different thing to real gentry. Of course they had everything very nice in the house, nothing but the best, but he didn't know how to treat them. You never found that with real gentry, always free with their good mornings, and sometimes would speak a word or two, it made all the difference if you were treated as a human being, no one liked being considered of less importance than a chair or a table.

In spite of rather looking down on Lord and Lady Ackroyd, Lord Ackroyd because he was new rich, and Lady Ackroyd because she was a poor spiritless thing, Alice bragged about the household. The Ackroyds, according to her, had more servants working for them, than any other mill owner in these parts, and spent money like water, something new every day. Sometimes it was a new horse, another time a new coach or carriage, then sometimes it was porcelain figures. The clothes he bought for her ladyship! Always on at her he was to be getting the newest things, and to be sure to wear them, where the other mill owners' wives could see them. They would never guess what his newest extravagance was going to be. Alice had no idea what it would look like, nor had anyone else. It was called gaslight, and it was said that it lit the whole house, every corner of it, as bright as though the sun were out. His lordship had been down to London where it was used in shops, and as they would have heard, it was going to be used as an experiment in two streets. No one in these parts had seen it

except his lordship, and no one thought of using it. When they had it, they would be the talk of Lancashire.

Selina asked how many Ackroyd children there were, and learnt there were four girls, who did lessons with the governess, Miss James, the elder son Robert, who was at school, and two little boys in the nursery. The young ladies were being brought up as though they were princesses. They must learn the newest things: all the young ladies could play four instruments, and

a gentleman came to teach them to dance, and another to teach them to sing, but the trouble was there wasn't enough for them to do. She often felt quite sorry for them, you couldn't learn French, writing, reading, and geography all day; it was sad to see them looking for things to do to fill up the time. They embroidered slippers for their father at Christmas, made pretty things for their mother's dressing-table, worked in wax, and made little rugs, and painted on glass, to tell the truth, they made so many things that really there was nowhere to put them down when they were finished. Sometimes she was glad she was not a young lady, for it was more fun to be kept busy. If they would believe it, the young ladies did not know how to cook, their mother had thought they should at least learn how to make pastry, but his lordship wouldn't hear of it, he said he had not piled up money so that his daughters should be cooks.

Enthralled at hearing about Robert's family, the children had not noticed where they were going. Suddenly they found themselves outside the great gates of Lord Ackroyd's house.

The house was reached by a most imposing drive. It could quite easily have been a short drive, but it twisted round and round to make it seem longer. On each side of it were shrubs, very dismal and sooty-looking. Everything was terribly neat, and that was no wonder for on the drive alone the children saw four gardeners working. The house was built of brick and stone combined, it looked dirty, which it probably was, for it was so close to the mill, that a hum went on the whole time as the machines turned. It had a lovely front door, with big columns on either side, over the door there was a little urn. There were nice big windows. The children thought they were going in at the front door, but Alice, horrified, with a jerk of her thumb directed them round to the back. Before the children went to the back door, they peeped round the side of the house at the front garden. It was a most neat garden, and had been very carefully made. There were not many flowers, but a lot of ornaments. There was a great piece of water cut out of the middle of the lawn to look like a lake, and at the end of a twisting path across the lawn there was a sort of summer-house, which was built to look like a ruin. Although it was not a big garden it was made to look bigger than it was by neat little twisting paths, which led behind bushes and then came out again as if they were new paths. It did not look the sort of garden any child would dream of playing in, so it was no surprise to the children that there was no boat on the artificial lake, or dolls' clothes in the summer-house, or a ball on the lawn.

The house was an extraordinary shape. Considering how big it was, and how many servants the Ackroyds had, the kitchen part was terribly small, dark, and inconvenient. It was pushed right away at the back, so that there were long

passages up which the food had to be carried to the dining-room, so it was certain that all the food was cold before it reached the table. The children did not spend long in the kitchen, which looked very like an old-fashioned kitchen of their own time, the only difference being that there seemed to be some sort of spit in front of the fire. The servants, the children decided, put up with a lot, for they had nowhere to sit and amuse themselves, and they slept far too many to a room in miserable little attics. Alice did not seem to find anything to complain of, so they did not tell her what they thought. She said there was always fun to be had when there was a house full of maid-servants and men-servants, and they had to leave it at that. Selina, looking at Alice, thought what a marvellous present for her mother it would be if she could take Alice with her to her own day, her mother was always saying how difficult it was to get good servants, and an Alice who seemed to be quite happy to work from morning till night for very little wages, to have a bed in an overcrowded attic, and who pitied the young ladies because they had not enough to do, must be what her mother meant by 'a treasure.'

Alice rushed off to do some work when they got into the house, and it was the governess who showed the children round. Of all the people they had met on their journey, the governess seemed the dreariest. She kept telling the children her parents had once had money, how she had been brought up, waited on hand and foot, but unwise speculation on papa's part had reduced their circumstances. She was a sad-looking lady, wearing a buff-ish-coloured dress, and she had buff-ish-coloured hair, and a buff-ish-coloured face. She said it had been so fortunate that she had received a good education, for it made it possible for her to be a governess, which after all was the only way a lady in reduced circumstances could live. Would they like to see the drawing-room? She thought they might look in as Lady Achroyd was out.

They stood in the doorway and looked at the drawing-room. It seemed that Miss James found it as overpowering as the children did, because she seemed to grow buffer than ever as she looked at it. The general effect was strong peacock blue. The curtains were not only peacock blue, but had peacock blue bobbles along the sides and bottom of them. The wall-paper had a peacock blue design on a lighter background. On the walls were what the children supposed might be the young ladies' efforts, for there were paintings on glass, as well as prints and two Chinese-looking pictures. There was a good deal of glass, two big mirrors on the walls, and two great glass chandeliers. The furniture was partly of bamboo, but some of it was of other wood painted gold. The governess pointed out a recent purchase, which was a sort of settee with a high back and fussy legs. All the same it was a comfortable-looking room, for there were deep chairs and thick carpets, and though it was stuffy, for it didn't smell as though the window was ever opened, that was probably a good thing, for it kept out the smoke from the mill. The dining-room had a wallpaper of olive green and olive green curtains. On the side-board was a little mahogany chest for tea, and a copper tea kettle, as well as some large pewter dishes.

'Do you and the girls have meals here?' Selina asked.

Miss James said that sometimes they came down for their dinner, but more often they ate upstairs. It was, she added, a great privilege to eat with the family, but she did not sound as if she thought it was a privilege, and said almost at once that she was very fortunate to earn fifteen pounds a year. It looked rather as if she had to remember the fifteen pounds each time she went into the dining-room. The children did not care for the colouring in any of the rooms, but they could see there was a good deal of comfort. Good feather mattresses on the beds, thick carpets and curtains. A sort of general expensive look. Selina noticed that somebody embroidered nicely. Miss James said that Lady Ackroyd was a very good embroideress, and the girls worked many hours a day at their needles. There were a few books in every room, except the dining-room, but they did not look as if they were ever read, they were laid about more as if they were ornaments.

In the schoolroom the four girls were sitting round the schoolroom table working. They looked so very good, their backs straight, their heads neatly bent over their books, that the children thought they would be awful bores to know. But when Miss James turned away for a moment, one of the girls picked up her lesson book to show them that underneath it were some funny little cut-out figures, with heads that came off and would fit on to any of the bodies, suitable or unsuitable. As they showed the figures to the children they giggled. Miss James, horrified, turned round, but before she could say anything the door opened, and in came Lady Ackroyd.

Lady Ackroyd was dressed in what the children supposed to be the height of fashion. She wore a huge bonnet, and a high-waisted silk dress of flowered material over a darker underskirt. Round her shoulders was a beautiful silk cloak. At that moment Lady Ackroyd was not thinking of her appearance. She sat down in a chair, looking as if she might faint.

Robert, she said, who as Miss James would know, had been in poor health for some time, and was as she also knew, in constant trouble, and received daily whippings, had suddenly after a whipping, collapsed, and was unconscious for quite a while. Now the school had decided he was not a suitable pupil, and his father had driven over to fetch him home. As Miss James could imagine his lordship was terribly angry, she did not know how he would endure having the boy sitting next to him in the coach. If there was one thing his lordship hated more than another, it was a weakling. She did hope that Robert would say nothing to incense his papa, but she was very troubled. Robert should have been a girl, where weakness was an advantage. How was a boy, who could not take a daily whipping, to manage a great mill?

The girls, who were clearly on Robert's side, suddenly exchanged frightened looks, and one of them called, 'Mama, I think I hear the carriage, and papa's voice.'

Lady Ackroyd, looking green with fright, opened the schoolroom door. Everybody, including the children, went outside and hung over the stairs, where they could see the front door.

The front door was open, and nervous menservants hurried in with Robert's boxes. Then came shuffling feet, and into the hall came an older servant carrying Robert. Lord Ackroyd followed the servant. He spoke in a roar and glared at his son. Things had come to a pretty pass when a boy could not take a whipping, but had to be carried into his house, as if he were a newborn baby. Perhaps Robert would like a nurse got in for him. Did he realize he was thirteen, an age when his father had been able to fight any boy in his school and knock him senseless. He would get a tutor for him. For two or three weeks he could work at home, until another school was found. But when he said work at home, he meant work. Did Robert understand?

The Robert of 1810, though the clothes were different, looked extraordinarily like the Robert of their own day. The same green anxious eyes peered out from under a lot of sandy hair, he even had a stammer.

'Yes . . . oh, yes. Indeed I understand, papa.'

CHAPTER FIFTEEN

# *The Prize*

FOR their last supper Mrs Mummery had excelled herself. She had remembered all the things they most liked to eat, and was determined they should eat them.

'Come on, me dears, don't pick at your food, you've got a tiring day to-morrow, don't forget you're going on a journey.'

That made the children laugh, seeing all the journeys they had taken lately, and what long ones some of them had been. Elizabeth said:

'Angel Mrs Mummery, you do know, don't you, we think the supper simply gorgeous, but we're all kind of fussed about this prize.'

Selina put down her knife and fork.

'D'you know a bit what it's going to be?'

Mrs Mummery made a don't-ask-me face.

William's eyes, behind his tortoiseshell glasses, twinkled with laughter:

'But you're not going to tell us?'

Mrs Mummery looked shocked.

'No, indeed, dears, Mr Fosse would be most upset.'

'But Mr Fosse would never know,' said Robert.

Mrs Mummery spoke in a whisper:

'I wouldn't be too sure of that. Mr Fosse has never been one to have to be in the room to know what's been said. Now eat up, do, while I get the sweets. Though I says it as didn't ought, the meringues I've made'll melt in your mouths.'

After supper the children were called into the library. Mr Fosse, looking like a prize-giving, was sitting at his desk under the window. On one side of him sat Alfred, and on the other Mrs Mummery. Both Alfred and Mrs Mummery looked like people listening to a sermon, hoping not to interrupt it by an unexpected sneeze or dropping their prayer books. On the table were the snacks: tiny iced cakes, crystallized fruits, and sweets on silver trays, just as they had looked on their first evening. The drink was on another table, a beautiful decanter full of amber-coloured nectar, round it were placed nine glasses.

The party started by the children singing all their songs, starting with Robert's song which was sung to the tune of *Pop Goes the Weasel.*

Ackroyd's mills have made things hum,
For weavers t'isn't funny,
But you can't blame our Robert's dad,
For machinery made his money.

They finished up with *Aquae Sulis*. When the singing was over Mr Fosse said:

'I am going to ask a question. Mummery and Mrs Mummery and myself will judge which of you gives the best answer to it. Here is the question . . . If all that I own belonged to you, house, land, and money, how would you use it to strengthen our pattern?'

The children gaped at him. What a puzzling question.

'Durst'er mean, Mister . . .?' Grace began.

Mr Fosse held up a hand.

'I'm not going to say any more. I have asked a nice, clear question. Each one of you, if you search your mind, has an answer to it.'

'If you don't mind my saying so . . .' Elizabeth broke in.

Mr Fosse, his blue eyes shining, looking very prancy, shook his head.

'Not another word. Mummery, let them draw a number to see who speaks first.'

The numbers were in a hat.

Robert drew one, Grace two, John three, Selina four, William five, and Elizabeth six. Robert felt awful being the first to have to speak. He felt perfectly certain he would put any ideas he had badly with the other five and the Mummerys listening. Mr Fosse said:

'Bring a chair up, Robert, and don't hurry.'

Robert pulled up a chair. He leant forward so he could rest his arms on the desk.

'I think . . . I mean I'm sure I would try and get people back to the country. I mean . . . ever since Elizabeth came into the pattern, people have been going to the towns. I know that it isn't much good them all thinking of farming here, but there are other countries like Australia and Canada. I think lots of people are living in towns that don't want to, who would be happier in the country.'

Mr Fosse said:

'How are you going to choose your people?'

Robert had not thought of that.

'I don't know, I suppose advertise and all that. They would live in the house and work the land. I should think probably your land could be made to pay, even if it didn't make anything it might keep them.'

Mr Fosse turned to the Mummerys.

'Well, that is Robert's idea. He wants an agricultural college here. Not at all a bad suggestion. Now, Grace, what have you got to suggest?'

There was a lamp on Mr Fosse's desk, in its light Grace's red hair shone, it reminded the children of Viking Grace.

'I reckon that there's many would like trips like we've taken, and not only bairns, me dad would like to hear about Vikings and all that. I'd fettle this place for holidays like. I'd have people telling them what went on, and they could see the huts like the one we lived in in '43. And there'd be films and that. I think there's too many don't know their part of t'pattern, nor how things happened.'

Mr Fosse nodded.

'A very good idea. You understand Mummery and Mrs Mummery? Grace would like a kind of holiday camp here, for people to get to know their own history.'

John had no doubt at all what he would do.

'I know you can't hold back inventions, machinery had to come, but when we were craftsmen we had something. Men made everything with their hands and were proud of what they did. I'd make this a place where people could come and see the sort of stuff that used to be made, and learn to make it themselves, instead of buying factory stuff. Fine furniture, pottery, metal work, all of it. I reckon there's many would feel quite different if they could look round at fine stuff they'd made themselves.'

Mr Fosse smiled.

'That's clear, I think, and the kind of answer I expected from you, John. Selina?'

Selina knew what she would like.

'I'd have people here. I'd show them the things we've seen, and I'd want them to copy some of the things. I mean sing-songs and play instruments, like they did in my day, and weave and embroider and, though we didn't see any of it, I'd like them to do the sort of dancing they did. There must be thousands of people who would love to come and stay here and stop being present-day people, sort of live without telephones and things. I expect they could learn to weave their own clothes.'

Mr Fosse smiled.

'You'd like to return to so-called "Merry England." '

William, looking very worried, took his place by the desk.

'I don't know exactly what I'd do, but I think I'd make it a place for holidays, especially for boys, though perhaps girls too, though not so many of them. They would learn about chivalry. I know you can't have it all, I mean half of it's out of date, but the sort of things that they learnt in my day were awfully good. It sounds idiotic, but all that being kind to the weak, and good manners was fine, and the service in the church at the end must have been grand. But I haven't really worked it out. I've only said the beginning of what I mean.'

Mr Fosse nodded. Then he turned to the Mummerys.

'You know that these children have visited those years where they joined the pattern. The chivalry William is talking about belonged to Norman times. A boy was sent to a great house or monastery to learn how to conduct himself, to honour women, how to fight in a just cause, and at the end of it all there was a very beautiful service, at which the young man received his spurs and his sword, and dedicated himself to God's service. William thinks that this house and land could be used for a modernized form of that training.'

Alfred nodded gravely.

'And very nice too, wouldn't you say so, Mrs M.?'

Mrs Mummery looked fondly at William.

'I should think games would be nicer than learning to fight, dear, but the church service sounds beautiful.'

Elizabeth, who had found it hard to listen to the others and not argue, bounced up like a cork flying out of a bottle.

'I wouldn't do any of the things the others say they'd do. I can see what Robert means about farming, but if he thinks half of us living in towns want to live in the country, he's wrong, we'd hate it. Anyway, there are so many people in England now, they couldn't grow enough for them to eat, however many farmers there were. So if you don't mind my saying so, Robert, I think that's a silly idea. I don't mind Grace's idea so much, but I can't see this place a kind of holiday camp with history thrown in, it wouldn't work. I knew you would say everybody could come here to learn crafts, John, but people who want to do that go to evening classes, so why waste this place? I like you much more than I thought I would like you Selina, but if you don't mind my saying so, your idea seems to me frightful. Goodness, can't you see them, all that awful folk-dancing in clothes they wove themselves. I think William's idea is the best, Mr Fosse, though it's a bit whimsy-whamsy for me, but I think he ought to get the prize. There's hundreds in Pimlico could do with learning a bit of chivalry.'

Mrs Mummery said in her fat cosy voice which, even if she tried, could not sound cross:

'I don't think Mr Fosse asked you to be judge of who should take the prize, Elizabeth. What he asked was what you would do with the place if you had it.'

Elizabeth sat down in the chair by the desk. She leant forward, her eyes sparkling.

'Sorry. That's the worst of having drawn number six, I got all worked up about what the others were saying. But I know what I would do.' She leant across the desk and patted Mr Fosse's arm. 'You remember Cock-sparrer, Mr Fosse, dear? Of course, there's nowhere in England as bad now as where he lived then. Everybody has chances if they like to take them, and everybody can go to a doctor and all that, but I think there are still lots like him about. In a way, I'm like him myself. So what I would do is to make this house into a boarding school, a little like the posh schools Robert and William go to, but different. I mean those that went to it would learn other things, like looking after animals and, as there's plenty of land, growing things. I've been thinking, what we haven't got, as much as they used to have, is being pleased with ourselves. I mean such a lot of people just go on like my mum and dad do, they never hope to be different to what they are, never want to really. All through our journey I've been wondering why some people stop at the bottom, and some come up. My school would find people like Cock-sparrer, and girls too, who have got something. The sort of person who could become a spiv, or a crook, if nobody did anything, but who might be simply marvellous if they had a chance in a place like this.'

Mr Fosse said quietly:

'And what is your school to teach them, Elizabeth?'

'Partly, I suppose, William's chivalry, but mostly that they are free, none of that slave stuff we saw, and to be proud of themselves. Not to crawl around, for they are as good as anybody else, and not to be put upon.'

Mr Fosse leant back in his chair.

'Thank you, Elizabeth.' He turned to the Mummerys. 'Elizabeth would turn this house into a school where children would learn to be proud of their birthright, to think for themselves, not to be put upon; to remember they are free men, made in the likeness of God. That is it, isn't it, Elizabeth?'

Elizabeth grinned.

'Sort of, but you make it sound grander.'

Mr Fosse looked at Alfred.

'Which is the best scheme?'

Alfred cleared his throat.

'I've got my ideas, but what do you say, Mrs M.?'

Mrs Mummery shook her head.

'It's difficult for us, Mr Fosse, knowing what we know. Living here, as we do, it's hard to see this house used in any of the ways the children would use it. But what must be, must be. Taking things all round, I think young Elizabeth has got the best idea.'

Alfred nodded.

'That's my feeling, Mr Fosse. I think there's something in what they've all said, but we can't put the clock back, and maybe Elizabeth is the only one who doesn't want to do that, though mind you, for myself, I wouldn't mind seeing Robert in charge, farming would keep the place looking nice. Taking it all round though, I think I agree with you Mrs M., I'd give the prize to Elizabeth.'

Mr Fosse, with one of his cat-like springs, jumped up and went to the window.

'Pour out the nectar, Mummery. Mrs Mummery, hand round the snacks, we shall all feel easier with a glass in one hand and food in the other.' Alfred and Mrs Mummery handed round the food and drink. Mr Fosse went on talking, but not to anyone, unless it was to his garden. 'On the whole I am inclined to agree with the Mummerys—I can see that school of Elizabeth's. Children of spirit who could so easily miss their chances, collecting here, learning to be free men and women, sure of themselves and their destiny, and when they leave bringing new colour to our pattern.' He turned to the children. 'You want to know about the prize. I may live only a few years more, or if it comes to that I may die to-night. When I die the prize-winner, Elizabeth, will find she is my heir.' He beckoned to Elizabeth and laid a hand on her shoulder. 'I should like it very much if, when that day comes, you do not try to manage everything alone. I should like to see you call in William, Grace, Selina, John and Robert to help you. Mummery and Mrs Mummery will be here to see to the running of your house, but to bring your school to life six heads will be better than one. You will find that I have laid down no rules, all I shall ask in my will is that you use my gift to strengthen the pattern.' He lifted his glass. 'Shall we drink a toast to that?'

Elizabeth was so surprised that for once she was silent. She was made more surprised by what Selina said.

'I can see Elizabeth here. I never expected to think this, but I should think she's the best one of us to have it, though I think it's a good idea we should all help.'

Mr Fosse lifted his glass to the light. The amber-coloured nectar glowed as if there was a flame in it.

'Let's drink to that. To the hope that you six will remain friends. That from our journey together something fine may come. Before we started I said I hoped we might find a treasure that many have lost, and through the finding of it be granted understanding of our past, courage in our present, and faith in our future. I think we have seen that treasure in the pride Elizabeth spoke of, but I would add "fearlessness." I thought that the best of those we met were a proud and fearless lot, more so than many of us are to-day. Many of the services which are ours to-day are splendid, but perhaps, unless we are careful, too much care from the state will make us a dull lot. So my toast is to the good future of my house and land, in a proud and fearless England.'

Mrs Mummery was quite overcome by this. She gave an enormous sniff as she gulped some nectar.

'I don't like to think of you not being here, Mr Fosse, but what must be, must be.'

Alfred shook his head in a solemn way.

'That's right, Mrs M. But seeing changes must come I shall enjoy watching what goes on when young Elizabeth here, with the others to help her, takes over.' Alfred looked into his glass as if it could show him the future. Then he said, as if what he had seen had surprised him. 'Maybe I'm not the only one who would like to know what will happen then.'